Billions for Defense

For

**Kenneth, Amy, David, Carol,
Maria, Gary, Steven, and Kian**

Billions for Defense:

Government Financing by the
Defense Plant Corporation during
World War II

GERALD T. WHITE

The University of Alabama Press
University, Alabama

Library of Congress Cataloging in Publication Data

White, Gerald Taylor, 1913-
  Billions for defense.

  Bibliography: p.
  Includes index.
  1. Defense Plant Corporation.   I.   Title.
HG3729.U5W5   353.008′25   79-10931
ISBN 0-8173-0018-X

Contents

Tables, Maps, and Charts

Preface

The Defense Plant Corporation was a significant innovative agency of the emergency government during World War II. DPC was a subsidiary of the depression-created Reconstruction Finance Corporation, which, in turn, had its origins in the War Finance Corporation of World War I. Despite its importance, DPC's role until the present has been little studied. It invested nearly $7 billion, mainly in commercial-type, government-titled industrial facilities to speed the flow of war goods. During the defense period, it was the subject of much controversy both within and outside government, but after Pearl Harbor its value was fully recognized. The bulk of its investment was in the aircraft and closely related industries. Large investments were also made in the steel and chemical industries and in pipeline transportation. A new industry, synthetic rubber, was brought from infancy to maturity. DPC brought government capital and private initiative into fruitful union, eliminating risk to the contractor with respect to the cost of the facilities and providing the contractor with the necessary production capacity to fulfill its supply contracts.

Except for an article I published in 1949, the work of the Defense Plant Corporation has been little recognized.* Indeed, when I was carrying on my research three years earlier for the War Records Section of the Bureau of the Budget, DPC's peacetime successor, the Office of Defense Plants, had yet to run its course. Although Congress had decreed in the Surplus Property Act of 1944 that government property not needed by government departments or agencies would be sold, the bulk of DPC's vast array of plants and equipment in 1946–1947 was still government-titled.

It seems to me that the time has come for a full-dress study of DPC lest it be lost to view to an even greater extent than is true at this moment. It never had the visibility of an agency like the Office of Price Administration, touching directly the lives of millions of people, nor the dramatic character of the Office of Scientific Research and Development designing an awesome weaponry. But DPC supplied the capital for a substantial increment to the nation's industrial plant, most of which continued in use postwar.

DPC seems deserving of study for two reasons. Conceivably, in the

---

*"Financing Industrial Expansion for War: The Origin of the Defense Plant Corporation Leases," *Journal of Economic History* 9 (Nov. 1949):156–83.

event of another military emergency in which private capital was timid and the nation's danger great, government capital might again be called on for use after the pattern DPC pioneered in World War II. If this should be the case, policy makers would be helped to have on the record a study of the earlier experience. A number of the World War II emergency agencies like the War Production Board, it can be noted, drew heavily on the experience of World War I.

The second reason relates to times of peace, not war. Historians today recognize that the innovations of wartime have a significance that runs beyond the circumstances of their origins. Innovations can become a part of the general reservoir of ideas susceptible to adaptation and adoption in the attempt to find at least partial solutions to the problems and crises of peacetime. Thus the heavy reliance of the New Deal on the adaptation of World War I precedents, to take one outstanding example, is today widely acknowledged. Could the DPC experience be useful in helping the nation meet some of the problems of peacetime—say, the energy crisis? I believe it could.

This study of DPC falls into three parts. The first four chapters deal with developments relating to the establishment and the evolution of DPC prior to Pearl Harbor. During this period, there was a deep conflict between liberal New Dealers and conservative leaders in business and government over the scope and shape of DPC operations that abated only with the outbreak of war. The next four chapters are concerned with the conduct and extent of DPC operations, including the disposal of its plants and equipment following the war. In the final two chapters I attempt to assess the effectiveness of DPC and to speculate concerning the utility of the means it used to help deal with some of the problems of peacetime.

My debts in the preparation of this manuscript have been substantial. The American Philosophical Society has made two grants to facilitate my research. The staff of the National Archives, and especially John Taylor, have been of great help to me. Lewis Froman and Sheen Kassouf of the University of California, Irvine, and Albert Lepawsky of the University of California, Berkeley, have very kindly permitted me to draw on their expertise through their careful readings of the manuscript. And Natalie Korp has handled the typing chores with her usual skill and efficiency. I am deeply grateful to each of them.

Irvine, California   GERALD T. WHITE
April 1979

Billions for Defense

1

The Problem of Industrial Expansion

When war burst out in Europe in September 1939, the United States was forced to look to its defense for a second time in this century. As in World War I, it had to start from far back. The military establishment created for that first war had been dissipated soon after victory. War industry, too, had long since been either dismantled or converted to the production of civilian goods.

The need for speed in expansion of the nation's war plant was sharply underlined in May 1940 when the stalemate in western Europe was broken with dramatic suddenness. During April and May, the neutral nations of Denmark, Norway, Holland, and Belgium were rapidly overrun. By late June, France had fallen. In the west, Britain fought alone against the Nazi onslaught.

In recognition of the ominous quality of the times, President Franklin D. Roosevelt appeared before Congress on May 16, 1940, to point up the necessities of national defense. He found the navy strong, the army gaining strength, but both services sadly deficient in air power. Although production of military aircraft was growing, Roosevelt properly considered the rate of increase far from sufficient. "Our immediate problem," he declared, "is to superimpose on this production capacity a greatly increased production capacity. I should like to see this Nation geared up to the ability to turn out at least 50,000 planes a year." The president asked Congress for funds to purchase essential equipment for a large and better proportioned army, to modernize and replace old army and navy equipment, "to increase production facilities for everything needed for the Army and Navy for national defense," and to put all factories with army and navy supply contracts on a twenty-four-hour-day basis.[1]

How was this great expansion in the production of war equipment and supplies to be achieved? By what means could the steady and integrated flow of raw materials and parts so essential for the manufacture of aircraft, small arms, artillery, tanks, ships, and munitions be provided? The task, obviously, was immense. Toward the end of 1939, the army of the United States, including its trained reserves and air force, stood sixteenth in size among the world's armies, sandwiched between Spain and Bulgaria. The aviation industry, of which so much was expected, in

1939 ranked thirty-sixth among American industries in the number of its wage earners (just below candy and other confectionery items), and forty-fourth in the value of its products. The following year the industry managed to turn out slightly more than three thousand combat and large transport aircraft, of which twenty-three hundred had been ordered by foreign governments. President Dwight D. Eisenhower's comment in his farewell address in 1961 that until World War II "the United States had no armament industry" was close to the truth.[2]

Planning for industrial mobilization had been going on in the office of the assistant secretary of war since 1920, but the successive plans and modifications would prove of little help. They were predicated on a war less demanding than World War I, and they gave too little attention to the changing patterns of warfare, notably the use of air power. Thus the planners were little concerned with the financing of additional plant and equipment. From fiscal 1917 through 1919, private capital had handled 90 percent of the cost of such facilities. Undoubtedly, the planners believed the supply of private capital would again be adequate. As late as Army Day, April 6, 1940, Assistant Secretary of War Louis Johnson told an audience of veterans, "With the striking exception of aviation, there is no munitions industry in this country." But he made no mention of a need for new plant and equipment; rather, he spoke of converting existing plants from the production of civilian to war goods. The planners were also fallible in failing to reckon with the possibility that munitions and supplies might again be needed to aid our allies.[3]

Some headway could be made by converting existing civilian plants to war production. Extending the workday to round-the-clock operation would help, as would bringing back into production depression-idled plants. But, clearly, much new construction over a considerable period of time, requiring financing from either private or public sources, would be necessary to meet the goals set by the president. A *New York Times* correspondent reported after a presidential press conference on May 17, 1940:

> Refusing any prediction of how quickly his goal of 50,000 fighting planes might be attained, the President said he hoped to be able to supply the answer in two or three weeks. Meanwhile, the government was holding constant conferences with representatives of industry with a view of expansion and expedition of present facilities.
>
> Neither could the President explain by what means his aerial expansion program might be realized, but he visualized a situation in which private capital would be cooperating to the fullest with government authorities and in which the lag caused by reluctant capital would be filled by loans advanced through the Reconstruction Finance Corporation.[4]

Nine days later, on May 26, 1940, the president stated in a radio address to the nation:

I know that private business cannot be expected to make all the capital investment required for expansion of plants and factories and personnel which this program calls for at once. It would be unfair to expect industrial corporations to do this, when there is a chance that a change in international affairs may stop future orders.

Therefore, the Government of the United States stands ready to advance the necessary money to help provide for the enlargement of factories, the establishment of new plants, the development of new sources of supply for the hundreds of raw materials required, the development of quick mass transportation of supplies. The details of this are now being worked out in Washington, day and night.[5]

The problem of providing materiel for a greatly enlarged defense force was politically as well as economically complex. For example, the nation was badly split over foreign policy. Isolationists generally supported national defense efforts but were bitterly opposed to any actions they believed could contribute to American involvement in a war away from its shores. A potentially still greater source of trouble was the deep distrust between the business community and the New Deal administration. For years, much of business had lived in fear of the New Deal as a threat to free enterprise. The business community could be expected to examine the defense program with great care for any taint of socialism and to seek a large degree of control in its development. The business community could also be expected to guard against the creation of productive capacity in mature industries that could prove a hazard to profitable operation when the emergency was over, and, since the necessity for the defense effort in many minds was uncertain, to favor production for the civilian market over military needs.[6]

For many business firms, World War I was a sour memory. Because the national government was poorly prepared to conduct that war, much of its conduct was far from businesslike. Many supply contracts were issued in good faith but not in strict conformity with the letter of the law. Many contained no cancellation clause, for, as one colonel later stated, "We thought it would be a four-year war." Difficulties and delays had been the common lot of many firms awaiting payment. Some believed their claims had been settled penuriously. According to Colonel Leonard P. Ayres of the First National Bank of Cleveland, these unpleasant memories contributed to the apathy, if not hostility, with which a good many Ohio manufacturers greeted the defense program in 1940.[7]

For their part, New Dealers were distinctly hostile to the influencing or controlling of public policy by business. Many New Dealers, as well as isolationists, had taken deeply to heart some of the Nye committee's more sensational findings of shameless profiteering during World War I. New Dealers noted numerous questionable practices, including prices in supply contracts sufficiently high that a contractor could pay off his investment in plant and equipment with government funds and thus receive the facilities virtually as a gift. They also feared that business would try to use the exigencies of defense to undermine the social and economic reforms achieved during the depression years. The linkage of the military with business in drawing up plans for industrial mobilization helps explain why President Roosevelt shunted aside nearly twenty years of planning in the fall of 1939. Instead of implementing the report by the big-business-studded War Resources Board, appointed at his request by the assistant secretary of war, Roosevelt merely received the plan and locked it up.[8]

Thus the summer and fall of 1940 did not witness the orderly implementation and development of a plan, however inadequate, based on the experience of World War I and matured over many years of military-business collaboration, but, rather, muddling through a more disorderly set of improvisations. This procedure had the virtue of muting the outcries of both isolationist and antibusiness elements that surely would have resounded if the plans of the War Resources Board had been adopted. It also permitted the development of some new and fruitful options.

Financing the necessary huge expansion in defense industries was one important area of innovation and conflict. The Council of National Defense and its Advisory Commission (NDAC), revived by the president under legislation existing since 1916, was the emergency agency primarily concerned with this problem. The Reconstruction Finance Corporation (RFC), the Department of the Treasury, and the War and Navy Departments were other government agencies that were also inevitably deeply involved. They sought to devise means to stimulate private investment and, where necessary, to provide for the use of government funds. As a result, by the end of 1940 mechanisms had been established through which new plants and facilities were created during the war years at an ultimate cost of approximately $25 billion. This was more than one-half the dollar value of the nation's manufacturing plant at the beginning of 1940.[9]

Roosevelt appointed the Advisory Commission to the Council of National Defense at the end of May. A heterogeneous aggregation of talent, it consisted of seven commissioners, each heading a division. Edward Stettinius, Jr., in charge of the Industrial Materials Division, had served as chairman of the ill-fated War Resources Board and was chairman of the United States Steel Corporation. William S. Knudsen, commissioner of industrial production, was president of General Motors. Ralph Budd, transportation commissioner and president of the Chicago, Burlington and Quincy Railroad, had long experience as a railroad executive. Leon Henderson, in charge of price stabilization, was a well-known New Deal economist and bureaucrat. Sidney Hillman, commissioner of the Employment Division and president of the Amalgamated Clothing Workers, provided representation for organized labor. Chester C. Davis, agriculture commissioner, had served as administrator of the Agricultural Adjustment Administration and was president of the Federal Reserve Bank of St. Louis. Harriet Elliott, head of the Consumer Division, was a dean and political scientist from the University of North Carolina. Representatives of business dominated the first three of these divisions; representatives of the New Deal were more in evidence and powerful in the latter four, particularly the Price Stabilization and Employment divisions.

Industrial Production, obviously, was the key division concerned with expanding industrial capacity. Its commissioner, William S. Knudsen, exemplified the fulfillment of the American dream. Arriving in New York as a twenty-year-old Danish immigrant, he had risen through the shops—shipyard, rail, and auto—to his position of industrial leadership. Knudsen had a legendary reputation for getting things done. John D. Biggers, president of Libby-Owens-Ford, was his right hand. Knudsen's counsel was Frederick M. Eaton, an able young graduate of Harvard Law School and a member of the Wall Street firm that served as counsel to General Motors.[10]

There is no question that these men brought a business bias to Washington along with their concern for defense. Within a month, Eaton appeared before a Senate committee to argue against a 7 percent limitation on profits deriving from ship and airplane contracts. He prophesied that manufacturers would be "less eager to cooperate" in achieving the necessary production and their "attitude might become one of hesitance and resistance" if profits were too tightly limited. The evident big-business ties of Knudsen and his associates had caused the ardent New Dealer Harold Ickes to react with dismay at the news of Knudsen's appointment.[11] To others, surely, like the business-minded Jesse Jones, these appointments brought assurance that the defense effort would be in good hands.

On July 10 the NDAC formally set up a committee to deal with the problem of plant financing. John Biggers was its chairman. Donald Nelson and Leon Henderson were the two other most significant members of the five-man committee. Nelson, recruited from his post as executive vice-president of Sears, Roebuck and Company, was coordinator of national defense purchases. He was an exceptionally able and public-spirited businessman. Nelson has called his colleague, Leon Henderson, "perhaps our most vigorous expansionist." Henderson, who was totally committed to the need for more production, had been a New Dealer from the beginning. He had served as director of research and planning for the National Recovery Administration, as executive secretary of the Temporary National Economic Committee investigating monopoly, and, most recently, as a commissioner of the Securities and Exchange Commission. Like Knudsen, he enjoyed the esteem of Bernard Baruch. David Ginsburg, who had come directly from Harvard Law School to the Securities and Exchange Commission in 1935, was his chief legal aide.[12]

The committee could readily recognize that arsenal-type facilities of limited or no peacetime value would usually have to be financed by the government, as in World War I. Plants for the production of essential military supplies like guns, shells, explosive powders, and other ordnance fell largely into this category. The plants could be operated for the duration of the emergency by the government directly or, much more likely, by private firms for a management fee. Thereafter, each plant would revert to the government department or agency that had advanced the funds for its construction. Recommendations for approval of the construction of these facilities were referred by each of the armed services to the commissioners of the NDAC meeting as a whole. This cumbersome procedure was soon superseded by the simpler process of seeking approval through Donald Nelson's office, though tighter controls were installed later on, especially after Pearl Harbor. The basic planning, in any case, had already been carried out by the initiating department or agency.[13]

The pattern of direct government financing usually called for the sponsoring government department or agency to commission a private firm to construct and operate the desired war plant. That firm provided the skilled staff to draw up plans and joined with the government department or agency in supervising construction. In return, it received a nominal fee. The costs of construction were paid from congressional appropriations. The profits to the firm came from the supply contracts it negotiated and filled through its operation of the plant. Some plants were huge. The largest, the Sunflower Ordnance Works in Kansas, cost over $180 million. Several others came to more than $100 million. Ultimately, about $5.4 billion in defense and war plant was constructed by the War Department, $2.9 billion by the Navy Department, and $600 million by the Maritime Commission. These plants, particularly the early ones, were well constructed. The armed services were determined that many of them be kept in being for national defense following the emergency instead of being scrapped as after World War I.[14]

The NDAC committee on plant financing, encouraged by industrialists and bankers, wished to open up opportunities for private investment in commercial-type defense facilities. Industrialists were anxious that as much of the defense program as possible be carried on within the profit system, and bankers were clamoring for the opportunity to participate. Robert M. Hanes, president of the American Bankers Association, claimed that "private business and independent banking are now as capable of executing the government's program for defense as they were in 1917 and 1918 for its program of offense."[15] Moreover, congressional appropriations for government construction of defense facilities were far from adequate. The total provided in three supplemental appropriation bills during the last six months of 1940 amounted to no more than $750 million.[16]

Tax amortization seemed to offer one practical financing alternative. It had been used by the United States during World War I as a relief measure. The Revenue Act of 1918, signed late in February 1919, had permitted owners of facilities built or acquired for war production to seek tax relief by writing off the cost of the facilities to the extent to which they possessed no postwar value. The terms of this act were later amended to allow war contractors to seek relief as late as six years after the armistice. Ultimately, tax amortization provided some relief to owners of about one-eighth of the nearly $5.5 billion in private capital invested in new plant and equipment for war production during World War I.[17]

The NDAC committee envisaged tax amortization not as a retroactive relief measure but as a means of inducing private investment. In the words of John Biggers, "We feel it is to the national interest to utilize a maximum of private capital and to minimize the call upon Government credit." The committee sought to let contractors know in advance the allowable rates of accelerated depreciation as a protection against loss for facilities that might have limited or no value when the defense emergency was over. The more they considered tax amortization, the more they also became conscious of the desirability of keeping down prices of defense supplies and of preventing unwarranted gains to defense contractors. In the one case, members of the NDAC wished to protect the economy from the effects of inflation. In the other, they were interested in preserving an equality of competition among private firms.[18]

After prolonged discussion within the administration and extensive debate in Congress, a tax amortization provision was enacted early in October in the Second Revenue Act of 1940. It provided for accelerated depreciation to the full value of all qualified defense facilities (including the cost of the land on which they stood) that were completed after June 10, 1940. Under this provision, the private investor could write off annually 20 percent or more of the cost of the facilities, depending on the length of the emergency, in contrast to the standard depreciation rates of 5 percent for buildings and 10 percent for equipment allowed by the Bureau of Internal Revenue. The date for the completion of facilities eligible for the amortization privilege was later pushed back to December 31, 1939. At the time the bill was under consideration, Biggers argued that at current tax rates, the savings in taxes to private firms through tax amortization would be no greater than the interest charge to the government if the government had borrowed funds to finance the facilities. Although tax savings by private firms at the expense of government revenues obviously became greater as tax rates were pushed upward, these gains were held justified in that, to the extent the amortization privilege was used, private capital was being induced to share the burden of war plant financing.[19]

To protect the government, the Second Revenue Act of 1940 contained a statement of requirements that had to be met by the petitioning firm before it could qualify for tax amortization. Accelerated depreciation was possible only if the firm requesting amortization had received a certificate of necessity signed independently by NDAC and by the War or Navy Department. This certificate was granted only in instances when, on the basis of data submitted by the firm, both the Advisory Commission and one of the armed services considered the new construction essential to the production of increased supplies for defense.

The act also provided that in order to be eligible for tax amortization the firm could not include depreciation as a factor in the price charged for its product on any time interval shorter than the life of the plant and equipment. Thus, while the firm could write off the cost of the facilities for tax purposes over a five-year period (or less, depending upon the period of the emergency), in determining a price for its product it could figure in only normal depreciation as a cost factor.[20] As witness to this fact, the firm was required to obtain a certificate of nonreimbursement from the NDAC and from the War or Navy Department. If, however, the price for supplies included charges for depreciation greater than the normal rate, the firm had to obtain a certificate of government protection from the same sources. This certificate stated that the government's financial interest in the facilities, acquired through payments greater than normal depreciation, was recognized and protected. Copies of the necessity and nonreimbursement or government protection certificates were filed with the commissioner of internal revenue.

During the early months of the defense period, tax amortization proved less of an incentive than its sponsors had hoped. The lapse of four months between the first discussions and the enactment of tax amortization influenced contractors who were considering expanding their facilities to wait until the precise terms were known. Moreover, after tax amortization became law, the process of granting necessity certificates and, especially, certificates of nonreimbursement or government protection was fraught with delay. Partly the delay was caused by a fear among the more liberal NDAC staff members that tax amortization might be abused to permit the enrichment of business firms at public expense. They were aware, for example, that the legitimacy of fully one-third of the relief through tax amortization following World War I had been subsequently challenged by a Senate committee. They wanted to open no new opportunities. In some cases, delay was also caused by the influence of business representatives within the NDAC. Obsessed by the depression psychology of a "mature" economy, they feared that tax amortization could lead to excess capacity and diminished profits later on if the capacity of some industries were expanded to provide more production during the defense period. Because of these delays, in October 1941, Congress withdrew the power of the NDAC to issue all three certificates. Henceforth, the War and Navy Departments, with their bias for action, were made the sole issuing agencies.[21]

After Pearl Harbor, the procedure was simplified further. In February 1942, Congress reduced the requirement for qualifying for tax amortization solely to the possession of a certificate of necessity. The armed services, anxious for more production, readily granted the certificates. Thereafter, it became the responsibility of the negotiating or contracting officer to determine (if he could) whether charges for depreciation greater than actual wear and tear were being included in the price of the product. As a result, the door was opened to widespread legal profiteering, for savings from amortization were not subject to renegotiation and recapture as excess profits. The issuance of certificates of necessity was not again brought under firm control until authority to issue them was transferred to the War Production Board (WPB) at the end of 1943. By that time the pressure for more production was easing.[22]

Overall, tax amortization was utilized to cover nearly $6.5 billion in plant and equipment. This was more than one-fourth of the total investment in new facilities during the defense and war years. Investment under the tax amortization privilege was particularly heavy in aircraft and related industries—aviation gasoline, light metals, machinery and electrical equipment, and machine tools. In addition, more than one billion dollars in railroad investments were covered and substantial sums in other industries, including steel, chemicals, and shipyards. Some of these investments were large. Eighty-nine big companies received necessity certificates for slightly more than half of the total amount. U.S. Steel was the largest recipient ($301 million), followed by Alcoa, Bethlehem Steel, and five railroads, each of which was certified for tax amortization on investments in excess of $100 million. But most certificates covered relatively modest outlays, indicating either the construction of small plants or the extension of existing facilities. Certificates of necessity issued by the War Department, the major certifying agency, were for projects of an average cost of less than $300,000. Tax amortization, moreover, accounted for a larger portion of the industrial expansion completed in the defense period than later on. Of approximately $1.75 billion in defense facilities completed by December 31, 1941, 57 percent had been privately financed. On the same date, only 18 percent of commitments totaling $7.4 billion were being similarly financed. Private financing was thus relatively more important during the defense period; the vast demands and greater risks of war itself required government funds in increasing measure.[23]

While the NDAC was exploring various means of financing, beginning in June 1940, its industrial commissioner, William Knudsen, was turning inevitably to the Reconstruction Finance Corporation as an immediate source of capital. The RFC seemed to offer the only sure means for a prompt launching of the vast and urgent expansion of the aircraft industry. Knudsen was recommending loans to aircraft companies that would be repaid from supply contracts with the armed services and could permit the companies to wind up with RFC-financed plants as windfall gains.

Meanwhile, within the RFC, some young lawyers had also been anticipating an RFC role. Passionately convinced of the urgency of the defense program, they were prime movers in drafting legislation, passed at the end of June 1940, that widened the opportunities for RFC's participation. As government attorneys, they were concerned with protecting the government's interest in any defense facilities government capital might create. They viewed skeptically the loan provisions being pushed by Knudsen. As a counter, they proposed that government facilities be leased to the contractor, with an option permitting the contractor to purchase the facilities at the conclusion of the emergency. This lease proposal, which could result in the government retaining title to commercial-type (as opposed to arsenal-type) facilities, was vigorously resisted within government. It led to a sharp conflict with the NDAC, which was developing another means of plant financing, the Emergency Plant Facilities Contract, using private capital. The fashioning and use of the lease provides a valuable example of the impact an alert and dedicated staff may have on the decision-making process.[24]

Nearly one-third of the $25 billion invested in plant during World War II was supplied either by the RFC directly or, to a far greater extent, through its defense-related subsidiaries. Of the latter, the Defense Plant Corporation, which pioneered the lease mechanism, was by far the most important. Its twenty-three hundred investments in plant and equipment totaled about $6.982 billion. The average of approximately $3 million was more than ten times the average investment under tax amortization. DPC's investments were primarily in commercial-type facilities—the aviation industry in all of its ramifications, including enlarged production of aluminum, magnesium, and aviation gasoline; synthetic rubber; steel; chemicals; ordnance; and shipbuilding. In addition, DPC's capital profoundly stimulated the machine tool industry. The War Department, in particular, sought DPC intervention, as did the Navy Department to a lesser extent; so did a number of other agencies, including the War Production Board, Maritime Commission, and Department of Agriculture.[25] Ultimately, DPC was responsible for adding more than 10 percent to the nation's wartime productive capacity.

2

The Bases for RFC Involvement

The RFC's experience and heritage made it an especially appropriate agency to finance an emergency expansion of the nation's industrial plant. It had been created by Congress in the dark days of January 1932 at a time when financial institutions, industry, commerce, and agriculture were reeling from the force of the depression. Its purpose was to supply private banks, insurance companies, mortgage companies, agricultural institutions, and railroads with financial assistance to withstand depression and thereby to speed the process of recovery. The RFC had been capitalized at $500 million, all of which was subscribed by the secretary of the treasury for a ten-year term.[1]

Its activities undoubtedly diminished the intensity of the depression. Largely through RFC, the nation's financial structure was maintained, though severely shaken, and its rail transportation network kept in operation. During the period when depression was most severe, RFC provided financial assistance to more than seventy-three hundred ailing and closed banks to the extent of approximately $3 billion.[2] Aid in substantial but smaller amounts was also afforded insurance companies, building and loan associations, and mortgage loan companies. Railroads, too, received RFC's attention. With the approval of the Interstate Commerce Commission, $732 million had been disbursed in loans to various railroads by the end of June 1940. Approximately $1.8 billion was supplied to national, state, and local governments to meet the problem of human suffering during the years 1933–1935, when the depression was at its worst. Prior to 1940, an additional $1.45 billion was lent by RFC both to buttress the agricultural credit structure and to make direct loans to farmers through the Commodity Credit Corporation.

The addition of section 5d to the RFC Act in June 1934 permitted the corporation to supplement the activities of commercial banks in providing business loans.[3] Thereafter, RFC made loans to business firms that, for one reason or another, had been denied credit by private banks. If RFC considered the loan application to be sound, it made the loan. These loans were chiefly for amounts of less than $10,000 and to small businesses. Banks were invited to participate with RFC in these loans. RFC disbursements in business loans totaled $228 million through June 1940.

Self-liquidating construction loans were another means by which the government sought to combat depression and advance recovery. Several great projects of the 1930s were RFC-financed. These included the San Francisco–Oakland Bay Bridge, costing $73 million; a 210-mile aqueduct, costing $208.5 million, to carry water from the Colorado River to southern California; a $22 million power line from Boulder Dam to Los Angeles; and numerous lesser projects. In addition, RFC made loans to the Rural Electrification Administration, disbursing a total of $48 million during the corporation's first seven years.

These RFC activities were directed and administered by an RFC board comprised of five members. It was both a policy-making and a managerial body. Subordinate to the board were a series of offices, including secretary, treasurer, and counsel, and the following divisions: Examining; Railroad; Self-Liquidating; Drainage, Levee and Irrigation; Statistical and Economic; Auditing; and Agency. The names of these offices and divisions suggest the nature of their functions. The Agency Division centralized and supervised the thirty-one RFC loan agencies that represented RFC at some thirty-eight locations across the nation.

Not all powers given to RFC subsequent to the original act were administered by RFC directly. Although RFC exercised authority directly with respect to business loans, self-liquidating loans, and loans to the Rural Electrification Administration, it channeled certain other powers through subsidiary corporations. In June 1940, these were the Electric Home and Farm Authority, the RFC Mortgage Company, the Federal National Mortgage Association, and the Disaster Loan Corporation.

Each of these corporations had been created to perform a specific function. The Electric Home and Farm Authority was organized in August 1935 to assist in financing the sale and distribution of electrical equipment to homes and farms in areas where satisfactory financing was not available. At the time of its transfer to the Department of Commerce in February 1942, the Electric Home and Farm Authority had facilitated the purchase of nearly $50 million in electrical equipment in thirty-nine states.

Two other subsidiaries were created to supply more funds for mortgages. In March 1935, on authorization of Congress, RFC established the RFC Mortgage Company to make the market for mortgages on income-producing properties and on older homes more liquid. A companion RFC subsidiary, the Federal National Mortgage Association—"Fannie Mae"—was organized in February 1938 to provide an additional market for mortgages insured by the Federal Housing Administration.

The final RFC subsidiary organized in the predefense period was the Disaster Loan Corporation. Created in February 1937 following a disastrous Ohio River flood, it was originally intended to last only a year, but its life was subsequently extended. The Disaster Loan Corporation functioned usefully in authorizing rehabilitation loans to numerous victims of castastrophes.

These subsidiaries were distinct legal entities with their own officers and organizational patterns, but were served by RFC personnel from the established RFC offices and divisions. Their expenses were paid from RFC funds. Their field functions were taken care of, not by separate field offices, but by the RFC loan agencies. The subsidiaries were not so much separate organizations, as bodies with special powers and a separate legal status. They suggested one way by which special defense and war powers, if granted to RFC, could also be handled.

But the RFC was more than a financial institution. It was an organization of men brought together at a time when the federal government was the nation's great "growth" industry. The RFC was a remarkable aggregation of talent running a spectrum from conservative to passionate partisans of the New Deal.

While Jesse Jones was in the federal government, there was no question as to the seat of power within RFC. In 1932, President Herbert Hoover had appointed him to the original board, and in 1933, Roosevelt made him its chairman. Jones was a rugged product of Texas capitalism. He had made his fortune in lumber, banking, and office buildings and owned a Houston newspaper. Self-made, assured, proud of his "horse-trading" abilities, he towered above the national financial landscape like a government-created J. P. Morgan. He was easy, approachable, a good listener. He made RFC a highly efficient organization. Not a reformer, his goal was to help the society work better within conventional limits. He was inordinately proud of the RFC and its lending record, which he sought to protect and improve. His banker mentality made him abhor risk and loss. Authoritarian and paternalistic, he was known to the RFC staff as "Mr. Jones" or as "Uncle Jesse."[4] He expected loyalty and rewarded loyalty.

RFC was his fief. His close ties to members of the Texas congressional delegation and his awesome reputation among congressmen as a self-made man and a legendary poker player made him all but invulnerable politically. Twice he escaped jousts with Roosevelt unscathed. In the early summer of 1939, Roosevelt, suspecting with good reason Jones's New Deal loyalties, sought to break his hold on the RFC by appointing him to the newly created higher-echelon post of federal loan administrator. But Jones was more than a match for his wily adversary. He accepted the new title and retained his old office in the RFC headquarters, where he continued to keep a close eye on RFC affairs. The next year, Roosevelt sought again to break RFC loose by appointing Jones secretary of commerce. Once more the powerful Texan circumvented Roosevelt. He persuaded his congressional friends to pass legislation enabling him to continue to serve as federal loan administrator while secretary of commerce.[5]

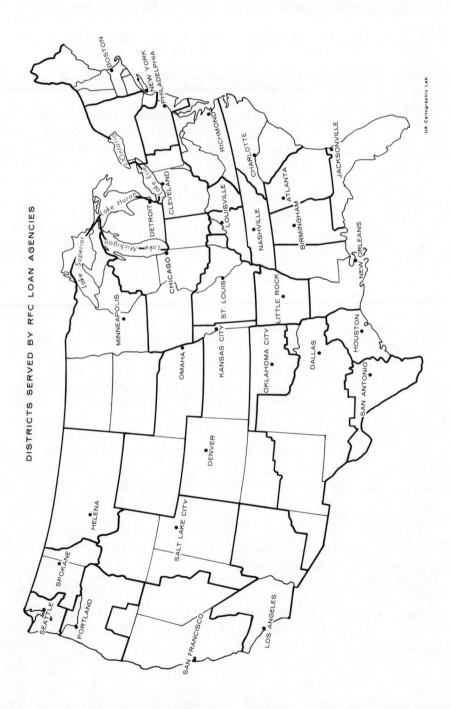

DISTRICTS SERVED BY RFC LOAN AGENCIES

Emil Schram, successor to Jones as RFC chairman in 1939, came closer to being an independent force than any other member of RFC's board. A former farmer and specialist in public drainage and levees, he had come to the RFC in 1933 as chief of its Drainage, Levee and Irrigation Division. In 1936, he was made a director. Schram was open to a wider range of ideas than Jones and offered both an ear and some protection to the more maverick members of RFC's staff until he resigned in June 1941 to become chairman of the New York Stock Exchange.[6]

Members of RFC's Examining Division—former bankers like Sam Husbands or Howard Klossner—were cut closest to Jones's cloth. Husbands and Klossner were able operating men who later became representatives of Jones on the RFC board. In checking out loans, they repeatedly proved their ability to protect RFC's balance sheet through careful scrutiny of business details. Within RFC, they were disciples of the status quo. They tended to lack imagination and generated few ideas for enlarging the sphere of RFC's functioning and influence.[7]

Its legal staff probably gave RFC its greatest distinction. For several years, Stanley F. Reed and Jerome Frank were RFC counsel, and the ebullient Thomas Corcoran long maintained a tangential tie. In addition to these better known counsel were such able lawyers as the suave Claude Hamilton, RFC's general counsel from Alabama; Clifford Durr, a fellow Alabamian and former Rhodes Scholar; the youthful Hans Klagsbrunn, a brilliant graduate of the Yale Law School; Schuyler W. Livingston, a Harvard Law School graduate who had served with the Wall Street firm of White and Case; and others. RFC had made good use of its market position in recruiting lawyers just out of law school or from the diminished rosters of corporate law firms. The exhilarating atmosphere of the New Deal encouraged these men to view government and society as their clients in contrast to an earlier day when they might have found satisfying careers in corporate law.[8]

Clifford J. Durr and Hans Klagsbrunn deserve special notice, for in the summer and fall of 1940 they were jointly responsible for shaping what later became RFC's giant Defense Plant Corporation program. Durr, a scion of a distinguished antebellum cotton family, had been a corporation lawyer with the Alabama Power Company in Birmingham. In 1933, he joined RFC where, during the banking crisis, he had served as chief of the legal section concerned with the recapitalization of banks. Later he became a top legal aide in railroad reorganization, chief of the Litigation Section and, in 1936, assistant general counsel. While working in these capacities, he came to know Hans Klagsbrunn well. Born in Vienna of Jewish heritage, Klagsbrunn had come to the United States as a child. He attended Yale as an undergraduate and later its law school, where he ranked first in his class. After additional legal study at Harvard and a brief teaching assignment at the University of Chicago Law School, in 1933 he had become a member of RFC's legal staff. In the spring of 1940, Durr and Klagsbrunn had been on loan from RFC with Oscar Cox of the Treasury Department and others to help devise means for financing industrial facilities in support of the British war effort. The two men were passionately concerned over the threat of Nazism to humane values.[9]

On several occasions during the spring of 1940, Durr, Klagsbrunn, and other RFC lawyers individually and jointly considered informally the problem of how the nation might meet its production needs in a war they felt sure was coming. This problem took on greater urgency following Roosevelt's "50,000 planes" speech to Congress in mid-May. "Klagsbrunn asked how I thought the matter should be handled," Durr recalled, "and I stated that in my opinion the bulk of the money would have to be put up by the Government—and that if the Government put up the money it should own the plants. I also expressed the thought that in view of the speed required it would not be practical for the Government to try to operate many of these plants itself, but that existing organizations should be used so that these plants should be leased to private manufacturers or else private manufacturers employed to operate them on a management basis." These ideas, and others, Klagsbrunn shared.[10]

Klagsbrunn had an opportunity to open the way for their implementation when Claude Hamilton asked him to assist in drafting a bill authorizing RFC to make loans and purchase stock in corporations for national defense purposes, either directly or through subsidiaries. This action was in conformity with suggestions made by the president. On his own initiative, Klagsbrunn went further, adding provisions authorizing the purchase of strategic and critical materials and also authorizing the construction, expansion, and equipment of industrial plants.[11]

Both Durr and Klagsbrunn were uncertain how Jones would react to these latter provisions. Financing the construction of a large expansion in the aircraft industry, for example, would be a risky undertaking with possible adverse effects on RFC's balance sheet. Through Claude Hamilton, they sought to persuade Jones that the additional powers would be merely a "shotgun in the corner" to encourage others to take up the burden of defense financing. Jones was convinced and agreed to support this enlargement of RFC's powers.[12]

As introduced late in May, the bill stated in a key paragraph:

> The Corporation is authorized to create or to organize a corporation or corporations with such powers as it may deem necessary to aid the Government of the United States in the national defense program, when requested by the Federal Loan Administrator with the approval of the President, and to subscribe to the non-assessable stock thereof, and to make loans to any such corporation or to any other corporation to assist in such program. Such loans may be made for the purpose of acquiring and carrying strategic and critical materials and other raw materials, for plant construction, expansion

and equipment, and for working capital, and may be made on such terms and conditions and with such maturities as the Corporation may determine.[13]

Jesse Jones told the members of the Senate Banking and Currency Committee that the additional authority was necessary in order to ensure "machinery" adequate to permit the nation to meet its defense needs. "I am not presenting a plan," he stated, "but presenting the machinery to get ready to do something." This machinery, he suggested, would be used only as necessary, and in cooperation with the NDAC. In response to questions as to whether the RFC was planning to use the requested powers to enter into manufacture of aircraft, Jones replied that the government had "no plans at this time to go into the manufacture of airplanes," but it might have to assist. He suggested the possible evolution of a system in which RFC "might build a plant, own it, and let a private corporation operate it." Jones further stated, in reply to a question by Senator Prentiss Brown, that the new amendment was being offered at the request of the president.[14]

This request for such wide powers sparked opposition in both Houses of Congress. Senator Robert A. Taft, its most vigorous critic, conceded the need for additional legislation so that RFC could be used effectively for defense purposes. He denounced the new amendment, however, as "the most outrageous legislative proposal that has been made to the Congress since I have been here."[15] His complaint was based on powers so sweeping, he said, that the "Government could go into just any business it chooses" in competition with private enterprise. Largely as the result of Taft's criticism, the bill was rephrased to make its language more precise and its grant of power less inclusive.[16] Similar limitations were included in the House version of the measure with the intent of keeping RFC from entering into competition with private enterprise in the manufacture of items other than "arms, ammunition, and implements of war."[17]

The measure, which was signed by the president on June 25, 1940, consisted of two major parts.[18] The first part made explicit the power of RFC to lend money for national defense purposes. Until this time, RFC had been able to make business loans solely on the basis of the soundness of the loan. A new purpose—national defense—was now added as a determining factor. This provision proved to be of lesser consequence in meeting the problem of war plant financing because most loans granted under it were primarily for working capital. Nevertheless, a few large loans amounting to more than $365 million were made for plant construction and for purchase of equipment during the defense and war years.[19] The first clause gave RFC power:

To make loans to, or, when requested by the Federal Loan Administrator with the approval of the President, purchase the capital stock of any corporation (a) for the purpose of producing, acquiring, and carrying strategic and critical materials as defined by the President, and (b) for plant construction, expansion, and equipment, and working capital, to be used by the corporation in the manufacture of equipment and supplies necessary to the national defense, on such terms and conditions and with such maturities as the Corporation may determine.

The second and more important clause authorized RFC to create corporations at the request of the federal loan administrator and with the approval of the president. These corporations were empowered

(a) to produce, acquire, and carry strategic and critical materials as defined by the President, (b) to purchase and lease land, to purchase, lease, build, and expand plants, and to purchase, and produce equipment, supplies, and machinery for the manufacture of arms, ammunition, and implements of war, (c) to lease such plants to private corporations to engage in such manufacture, and (d) if the President finds that it is necessary for a Government agency to engage in such manufacture, to engage in such manufacture itself.

The act authorized RFC to purchase the capital stock of and to make loans to such subsidiaries.

Under this second clause, RFC organized four major defense subsidiaries during the summer of 1940. Two of these, the Rubber Reserve Company and the Metals Reserve Corporation, were created on June 28. The Defense Plant Corporation, which was the third, was organized on August 22, 1940; the last, Defense Supplies Corporation, came into being a week later. As the names indicate, each of these corporations was created to exercise the defense powers granted RFC in a particular phase of defense activity. Thus, the Defense Plant Corporation was created as an instrument by which RFC could help in meeting the problem of bringing about the great expansion in the nation's industrial plant required for the defense effort. Although the other subsidiaries were not primarily concerned with the problem of plant, they also facilitated plant expansion in some degree in their particular lines of activity.

Each of the subsidiaries had a director of RFC as its president. The board of directors of each was appointed by the RFC board from among its own members and from other RFC officials. Consequently, the RFC board became a higher integrating agency for the subsidiaries. It could discuss the activities and problems of all of the defense subsidiaries at a single RFC board meeting.[20]

3

From Stormy Start to Smooth Sailing

Even while the amendment clarifying and liberalizing RFC's defense powers was before Congress, Knudsen was trying to enlist RFC's aid in financing the most crucial of expansions—that of the aircraft industry. At the time, few could imagine the full extent of the expansion (4,000 percent over the next three years!), but obviously it would be large. In June 1940, for example, there were only three American manufacturers of high horsepower aircraft engines and only thirteen significant airframe plants. Of the engine manufacturers, Wright Aeronautical, a subsidiary of Curtiss-Wright Corporation, was the largest, followed by Pratt and Whitney, a subsidiary of United Aircraft Corporation. The Allison Division of General Motors, which produced a liquid-cooled engine, was a poor third. In addition, discussions were going on concerning the manufacture under license for American aircraft of the British liquid-cooled Rolls Royce engine. If the president's goal of fifty thousand military aircraft was to be achieved, the industry would require massive infusions of capital. The sheer size of the expansion made virtually certain that much of the financing would have to come from government sources.[1]

After discussion with various government officials in the Treasury Department and elsewhere, Knudsen recommended that the RFC set up a subsidiary, the Defense Finance Corporation, to centralize its defense loans. He proposed that RFC lend capital for fixed investment at 3 percent per annum. These loans would be a charge solely against the plant thus created and were to be paid from an agreed-upon portion of the sales price to the government of each unit manufactured. If the emergency should end before a loan was fully paid off, the manufacturer could either turn the plant back to the RFC or, after a joint appraisal, negotiate with the RFC concerning payment of the remainder. If a loan for an RFC-financed extension of an existing plant had not been fully repaid, RFC would be required either to sell the extension to the manufacturer or demolish it. Knudsen also initially proposed that the Defense Finance Corporation lend funds at no interest for working capital. In a later version, a 2 percent interest rate was specified.[2]

This recommendation was intended to supply government capital to power the defense program and at the same time relieve the fears of conservatives both in business circles and within the RFC. Many businessmen feared that government-titled commercial-type facilities might be operated by the government in peacetime and threaten private enterprise. Some War Department contracts written during the defense period pledged the government not to "use the plant or any part thereof for business or commercial purposes" within twenty years of the completion of the plant. An associated fear was that government title might result in industrial capacity in excess of peacetime needs, leading to cutthroat competition after the emergency.[3] Within RFC there were those who feared the effect of defense plant financing on RFC's hard-won reputation as a sound lending agency.[4] A special-purpose subsidiary like the proposed Defense Finance Corporation might allay these fears by segregating RFC's defense loans from its more conventional and sound financing activities. Knudsen and his associates were also keenly aware of and sympathetic to the desires of the banking community to participate profitably and with minimal risk in defense financing. These questions were the more powerfully debated because private financing, in the main, had been adequate for the industrial expansion required in World War I. RFC's resources could provide a stopgap until the NDAC was further along in formulating its own plans for drawing on private capital.

Within this framework, beginning in mid-June, RFC received from Knudsen several progressively larger requests for loans to Wright to build an aircraft engine plant and for working capital. The first of these requests touched off a vigorous debate over defense financing that would rage for several months.

On June 20, Knudsen asked RFC to assist the NDAC and the War Department in increasing the production of airplane motors by granting a loan to Wright. The proposed War Department contract called for production of 12,100 motors, with an option for an additional order of the same size. "We can conclude the arrangements," Knudsen wrote, "providing the RFC can furnish the money for a new fully equipped plant in which to manufacture the motors, the magnitude of the undertaking being too great to handle with their own capital."[5]

Since Knudsen's request was for a loan, RFC action took that form. After a discussion with M. B. Gordon, vice-president of the Wright Aeronautical Corporation, RFC agreed to lend a subsidiary of Wright an amount not to exceed $33.5 million for plant construction. In contrast to the terms suggested by Knudsen in his plan for a new RFC plant-financing subsidiary, the interest on the loan was specified at 4 percent per year and a definite maturity established of eight years. The principal was to be amortized at the rate of $800 per motor. As sole security, RFC was to receive a first mortgage on the plant and equipment. In addition, RFC offered to lend Wright up to $22 million for working capital. The interest rate on the working capital, while not specified, was not to be more than 4 percent per year.[6]

To some of RFC's staff, the terms of the Wright loan seemed outrageous. Clifford Durr, RFC's counsel for defense financing, and others among his associates considered the proposal clearly adverse to the government's interest. The borrower, Durr wrote Jones, after investing no money and incurring no risk, would receive title to a plant paid for by the government in the sales price per engine. He argued that the government's interest should be protected through any one of three alternatives: (1) government ownership with private operation of the plant under a management-fee contract; (2) government ownership with private operation under a lease; or (3) direct government operation. In each case the government would retain title to the new plants.

Any of the three alternatives, Durr maintained, would have "a number of advantages for the national defense program and for the national economy as a whole." Construction of government-owned plants would eliminate the possibility of large profits through windfalls, avoid serious tax and depreciation problems involved in private construction of defense plants, and ensure selection of locations for the plants solely on the basis of strategic and military considerations. Moreover, government construction would be advantageous not only for the defense period but for the future. Durr argued that government retention of title would result in "standby productive capacity" in peacetime, which could be maintained by government "much as it maintains its battleships and forts." These plants could be kept up-to-date by using them to supply the peacetime needs of the armed services. They would also be available to provide the increased production required in a future emergency. Consequently, the economy would be subjected to a lesser strain because a large part of the facilities needed for defense production would already exist. This would not be the case if, as a result of windfalls to contractors, the future operation and maintenance of government-financed plants was subject to the will of private owners.[7]

Jones was apparently sufficiently impressed by Durr's arguments that he discussed with Knudsen the possibility of a lease arrangement as an alternative if Knudsen and Wright should care to follow that route. At the time, neither was willing to consider government ownership. This was merely the first round.[8]

Despite the favorable nature of RFC's proposal, Wright took no action. Wright was troubled by tax and depreciation problems and uncertainty as to the effect of the amended Vinson-Trammel profit limitation law on its potential profits. As of June 28, 1940, under pressure from those who would "take the profits out of war," the Vinson-Trammel Act was altered so as to restrict profits in the manufacture of military aircraft to not more than 8 percent. Previously, the law had permitted a profit of 12 percent. A final problem was that the coordinating of army and navy needs for aircraft engines required that Wright have facilities considerably larger than those originally planned.[9]

Jones sought to solve these problems by making Wright a new offer. RFC proposed purchasing two hundred acres in Hamilton County, Ohio, near Cincinnati, as a site for the projected Wright plant and leasing the site to a Wright subsidiary for five years. In addition, RFC would include options in the contract permitting the renewal of the lease for a second period of five years and the ultimate purchase of the plant site by Wright "at a price to be agreed upon." RFC offered to lend the Wright subsidiary up to $37 million for a plant and an additional $35 million to Wright, its subsidiaries, and responsible cooperating companies for working capital. Another $20 million was to be made available to "responsible cooperating companies . . . for the purchase of machinery and equipment and other facilities to produce necessary parts for the construction of the motors."

All loans were to bear interest at 4 percent per year and were to be amortized in five years "with a schedule of payment consistent with the delivery of the motors, or otherwise mutually satisfactory." Loans for plant and equipment were to be secured by a first mortgage on the new plant and equipment for which the loans were used, while the working capital loans were to be made "upon the credit of the Wright Aeronautical Corporation or, if agreeable to the RFC, upon the credit of the cooperating company." Jones also stated, "If for any reason you should not get contracts with the United States Government for this number of motors, or if, after getting orders for the motors, all or part of the orders should be cancelled, the RFC will expect you to immediately cancel all commitments for plant expansion, equipment, materials, et cetera, not necessary to complete definite and uncancelled orders, and repay to the RFC any of said borrowed funds not expended or committed."[10]

When the plan was presented to the RFC board for approval on August 7, 1940, it provided for the creation by RFC of a subsidiary, Defense Corporation, to purchase the plant site for lease to a Wright subsidiary. The Wright subsidiary was to lease the land from Defense Corporation for eight years at a rental of 4 percent per year of the cost of the site.[11] Thereby, under an established Treasury Department ruling, the Wright subsidiary would be able to depreciate the plant for tax purposes over an eight-year period, since it did not own the land. The proposed contract, however, also included an option permitting Wright, at the conclusion of the lease, to purchase the plant site from the Defense Corporation at the original price paid by the RFC subsidiary. The effect of this arrangement would be to permit Wright to gain the plant tax free.

According to the plan, $800 per motor would be charged the Wright subsidiary to repay the RFC loan for plant and equipment. This charge was considered sufficient to permit full amortization of the loan in eight years. Durr later wrote, "One problem still remained—how to eliminate the $800 per engine in determining the profit limitations under the Vinson-Trammel Act. This was solved with equal simplicity. The parent company would sign the supplies contract and manufacture the engines. The $800 would be paid over to the subsidiary as rent, thus offsetting the additional income with an equal expense item."[12] This arrangement was approved by the RFC board.

Although Durr, in his capacity as assistant general counsel, prepared the resolution concerning the prospective Wright loan for presentation to the RFC board, he refused to initial the resolution indicating his approval. Instead, he wrote a memorandum indicating the reasons why he felt he could not. The memorandum stated:

> Notwithstanding the fact that the Parent Company will not be hazarding its credit for using its own property, it will receive net profits on the engines sold to the Government at the full rates allowed by law and will, in addition, receive the plant as a donation by reason of its ownership of the stock of the subsidiary.
>
> The plant site is to be acquired by a subsidiary of RFC and leased to the Wright Subsidiary, and the plant will be constructed and equipped with money loaned by the RFC directly to the Wright Subsidiary, the Wright Subsidiary in turn leasing the plant to the Parent Company at a rental sufficient to amortize the loan and pay the rental for the plant site. The purpose of this procedure is to obtain concessions from the Bureau of Internal Revenue with reference to depreciation for tax purposes. . . .
>
> I do not think that the RFC is justified in taking the position that the price to be paid for the engines is entirely a responsibility of the Army and Navy and that the depreciation to be allowed for income tax and other purposes is entirely the responsibility of the Bureau of Internal Revenue. RFC has set up its loan in such a way as to enable these concessions to be obtained. It is further agreeing to extend the maturity of its loan from five to eight years if this is necessary to enable the Wright Subsidiary to get the maximum depreciation allowed, although the result would be to decrease materially the payments per engine to be applied on the loan.[13]

Durr's memorandum had particular effect on RFC's chairman, Emil Schram. According to Durr,

> Several days after the adoption of the resolution authorizing the loan to Wright, Mr. Emil Schram . . . called me to his office and stated that he had been doing some further thinking about what I had said at the Directors' meeting and was inclined to believe I was right. He asked me to let him have a memorandum setting forth more fully my arguments in support of the lease arrangement, and I gave him a copy of my memorandum to Mr. Jones of June 29, 1940. Mr. Schram was convinced, and with his blessing we proceeded with the organization of the Defense Plant Corporation.[14]

Schram was determined that DPC not be a paper organization, as were the first two RFC defense subsidiaries, the Rubber Reserve Company and

the Metals Reserve Corporation. The presidents selected for these subsidiaries were RFC directors and longtime followers of Jesse Jones; indeed, Jones appointed Howard Klossner, a graduate of RFC's Examining
Division, to the Rubber Reserve presidency without consulting Schram.
These companies were operated out of the federal loan administrator's
office, with memorandums circulated to be read and initialed by the
directors, who attended no regular meetings. Before setting up the DPC,
Schram negotiated with Jones to make sure he would have a free hand.[15]

The RFC chairman told Durr he wanted to make DPC a "Boy Scout"
organization. In staffing DPC, Schram made a special effort to keep the
new subsidiary off limits to members or alumni of RFC's conservative
Examining Division. He chose John W. Snyder, former manager of RFC's
St. Louis agency, for the post of executive vice-president. Snyder, who
had made an enviable record at St. Louis, was an ardent defense advocate
and a colonel in the army reserve. Other sympathizers with the defense
effort, A. T. Hobson and Harry Sullivan, were appointed secretary and
treasurer. Clifford Durr, the general counsel, selected Hans Klagsbrunn
and S. W. Livingston as assistant general counsel. These men became the
nucleus of an unusually able and dedicated organization. They also had
considerable political strength. Snyder was a close friend of Senator
Harry S Truman. Durr, whose wife was a sister-in-law of Supreme Court
Justice Hugo Black, had warm ties to Senator Lister Hill and other
members of the Alabama congressional delegation. Schuyler Livingston
was the brother-in-law of Jerry Voorhis, a liberal California congressman.[16]

The new RFC subsidiary concluded its first agreement not with Wright
but with the Packard Motor Car Company. Toward the end of June,
NDAC had asked this auto company to manufacture, under license, Mer-
lin Rolls Royce aircraft engines for use by both Britain and the United
States.[17] Packard was willing to undertake the supply contract, but felt it
could not afford to risk its own funds in purchasing the necessary machinery and equipment. NDAC had consequently referred Packard to
RFC to discuss a possible loan. In these discussions, Henry E. Bodman,
general counsel for Packard, expressed dissatisfaction with the RFC loan
formula being urged by NDAC. Remembering the investigations following World War I, he stated that he did not wish to see his company run the
risk of embarrassment at some later date as the result of an arrangement
which would result in Packard gaining a windfall of machinery and
equipment in addition to profits on the motors.[18]

Because of the dissatisfaction of the Packard representative, Durr
suggested a lease agreement providing for the purchase of the necessary
machinery and equipment by DPC for lease to Packard. In return, Packard would pay a fixed rental. Following completion of the supply contract,
DPC would remove the machinery and equipment from Packard's plant

or, at Packard's option, would sell the machinery and equipment to Packard under a formula that would permit DPC to recapture its investment. Bodman approved this arrangement. In eliminating the possibility of a windfall to Packard, it also eliminated the possibility of future censure.[19]

This first lease was drawn up and accepted by the DPC Executive Committee on September 6, 1940. Three days earlier it had been signed by M. M. Gilman, president of the Packard Motor Car Company, subject to approval by the Packard Board of Directors. The agreement provided for the purchase of machinery and equipment by DPC to the extent of $8 million. This investment was considered sufficient to permit Packard to produce eight hundred Rolls Royce aircraft engines monthly. Since Great Britain was to receive each month twice as many engines as the United States, her share of the investment was $16 million. As rental on this investment, DPC was to be paid $1,500 for each engine delivered to the United States government. Because DPC retained title to the machinery and equipment, Packard was permitted no charge for depreciation or for use of the machinery in its price to the government other than the $1,500 per engine. The agreement also included an option by which Packard could purchase all, but not part, of the machinery at cost to DPC plus 4 percent per year interest, less 10 percent per year depreciation, or at cost plus 4 percent per year, less the amount in rentals paid by Packard to DPC, whichever was the greater.[20]

During the following six weeks, agreements were drawn up with three more firms. Two of these, with Continental Motors Corporation and Baldwin Locomotive Works, were intended to supply machinery and equipment necessary for the manufacture of tanks. Both companies were also entering into arrangements to manufacture tanks for Britain. Both agreements closely paralleled the Packard lease. As in the case of Packard, Knudsen was willing to accept these agreements providing for government title because the supply contracts were for defense goods that could pose no competitive threat within the industry after the end of the emergency.[21]

The other lease, with W. F. and John Barnes Company of Rockford, Illinois, was a departure. This small company made machine tools necessary for the manufacture of machine guns. It had been referred to DPC as a possible source of financing, not by NDAC, but, informally, by an officer of the Ordnance Department. The resulting $550,000 agreement was for land, building, and equipment. It included a "Construction Program" (buildings) and an "Acquisition Program" (equipment). As in the other three cases, the Barnes lease also contained a purchase option.[22]

Meanwhile, the proposed RFC loan to Wright hung fire. Durr had leaked the terms of the lease, so favorable to Wright, to some members of Congress, who shared his dismay. Nor was such a loan acceptable to the more liberal members of NDAC as Leon Henderson, David Ginsburg, or Donald Nelson. On August 1, 1940, the Tax and Finance Committee of the NDAC had held its first meeting for the purpose of formulating a new plant-financing mechanism that would draw upon private capital. At that meeting, Donald Nelson argued that permitting a defense contractor to acquire "a new or better plant, free," in addition to his profit, was "unwarranted and unnecessary." He held that such an arrangement would be "subject to justifiable criticism not only by the taxpayers, but by industry itself," for the defense contractor who acquired the plant as a windfall would be given an unfair advantage over its competitors.[23]

Conservatives like Biggers, Eaton, and Knudsen continued to be influenced by their ties to the business and financial community. They were sensitive to the cries of Emmet F. Connely, president of the Investment Bankers Association, who told an NDAC member early in August that substituting government financing for private capital was "a short cut to national socialism." They worked with members of the New York financial community, including Broderick Haskell, vice-president of the Guaranty Trust Company, and John Hancock of Lehman Brothers, in trying to come up with a contract that would open a wide door to private financing and would be responsive to the concerns of industry. Within government, they consulted with the Treasury Department, RFC, the War and Navy Departments, and the comptroller general.[24] The resulting compromise between the NDAC factions, the Emergency Plant Facilities Contract, proved far less effective than either faction had hoped.

On August 23, the NDAC made its first public announcement of its newly devised contract.[25] The Emergency Plant Facilities Contract (EPF) provided for construction of defense facilities by a private contractor when certified as necessary. Under its terms, the government agreed to repay the contractor for the cost of new facilities in equal monthly payments over a period of sixty months.[26]

These payments began in the month following completion of the plant and its entry into production. Repayment was adjustable to a briefer period if the emergency should end in less than five years. Because the contractor was to be reimbursed in full for its investment, the cost of the new facilities was eliminated from consideration in determining price for the supplies produced in the plant. Risk to the contractor, moreover, was reduced to a minimum because of its assurance that the government would ultimately pay for the facilities. Because the government would acquire title to the plant at the conclusion of the emergency, there was no possibility of a direct windfall gain.

The NDAC considered essential to the effectiveness of the EPF contract that the contractor's claim for reimbursement by the government be assignable to a bank or banks or to other financial institutions. This was necessary because few contractors would have sufficient capital to construct most defense facilities without outside financial aid. The banks, moreover, would be reluctant to undertake defense financing unless they could feel certain of recovering their loans. On October 9, 1940, the Assignment of Claims Act abrogated a statutory prohibition forbidding the assignment of claims against the government that had existed for almost a century.[27] Thereafter claims against the government could be assigned by the claimant to any bank, trust company, or other lending agent. As a result of this act, the borrower under an EPF contract could assign its claim to the banking institution that had financed construction. The sixty monthly reimbursement payments thus went not to the contractor but to the financial institution from which it had borrowed.

Certificates of necessity and of nonreimbursement or of government protection were also required in conjunction with the EPF contract. Through the amortization mechanism, the contractor was able to use the sums paid by the government as an offset for income tax purposes. The changes in the law with respect to procedure in qualifying for tax amortization affected contractors under EPF contracts in the same manner as if the contractor had used its own funds.

The EPF contract was meant to be attractive to private contractors in other ways. Although the contract specified that the government would reimburse the contractor for the cost of the facilities, the contract also gave the contractor the privilege of purchasing the facilities at the conclusion of the emergency. There were originally two formulas for purchase: either at cost less depreciation at rates of depreciation specified in the contract, or on the basis of an appraisal of the "fair value . . . which the Emergency Plant Facilities have to the contractor." If the contractor exercised the latter option, an appraisal binding upon the government was to be made by three appraisers. The "fair value" option was soon severely modified, in the light of criticism, so as to permit a negotiated purchase of the facilities but requiring neither arbitral proceedings nor forced sale. As modified, the contractor and the sponsoring government department had to be in agreement on "fair value" if a sale were to be concluded on any other basis than cost less depreciation. It was felt, rightly, that the original provision did not adequately protect the interest of government, for fair value to the contractor might be much less than the government could get through sale of the facilities to another firm.[28] Under the modified contract, the defense contractor was granted a right of first refusal to purchase or lease the facilities at the same price or rental at which the government was considering sale or lease to any other party.

To reassure those who feared future government operation of the plants, the government agreed, "so far as it lawfully may," to operate the facilities only for national defense or "for any purpose incident to the conduct and execution of any Act of Congress." The contract stated that the government would not use the facilities at any time "for business or commercial purposes."[29]

While the EPF mechanism was being perfected, no more defense manufacturers were referred to RFC. In addition to drawing the lease agreements already mentioned, the only other DPC activity during this period was the purchase of two plant sites. One was in Hamilton County, Ohio, for the proposed Wright plant. On the same day, September 12, 1940, the DPC board approved a similar resolution for the purchase of an aircraft plant site near Buffalo, New York, for the Curtiss-Wright Corporation.[30]

Aircraft manufacturers were anxiously waiting to seize the great opportunities the defense program offered. Still young and immature as an industry, they had no reason to fear the goblin of excess capacity. Their key problem was access to capital. As they endured inevitable delay while the EPF contract was being hammered out, they had a chance to consider the terms of the Packard lease agreement with DPC as a possible alternative.

Shortly after the EPF contract became available, executives of the Wright Aeronautical Corporation and the Bendix Aviation Corporation brought their EPF contracts to RFC for financing. RFC told both companies that it was not in competition with banks and that they should turn to the banks to finance their new facilities. Vice-President Gordon of Wright replied that he was not anxious to risk banker control of his company through large bank loans and that, as a result of his experience in Washington in the past few months, he preferred doing business with RFC. He further stated that, though NDAC had specified the EPF arrangement, he would much prefer a DPC lease similar to that with Packard. This mechanism seemed more attractive because of its simplicity.[31]

Edward R. Palmer, vice-president of Bendix, likewise preferred a DPC lease. Since Bendix was a manufacturer of airplane parts, some of which would be used in private aircraft, he was disturbed at that aspect of the EPF contract which would result in 100 percent reimbursement to Bendix for a plant not exclusively used for production for the government. Palmer feared possible future criticism embarrassing to his company if he took advantage of a contract that in his case would afford an extraordinary competitive advantage.[32]

Because of these feelings, Durr secured appointments for Gordon and Palmer with Jesse Jones so that they could discuss financing their plants through DPC. Following the interviews, Jones made arrangements for Durr to see Secretary of War Henry L. Stimson the next day, October 15, to determine the War Department attitude concerning having DPC construct these plants. Although Stimson was not present, Durr and Gordon, who accompanied him, did get a favorable response from the War Department officials to whom they talked. They were told, however, that the ultimate decision in the War Department in matters of plant financing rested with Assistant Secretary of War Robert P. Patterson, who was out of town and would not return until evening. On the following day, Patterson authorized DPC to arrange financing with Bendix but counseled delay on the more controversial Wright case.[33]

The problem remained of reaching an agreement with NDAC. Because the staff of the industrial commissioner was not in sympathy with the idea of government-titled industrial facilities, this promised to be difficult. Moreover, the NDAC was also interested in promoting its EPF contract. A meeting held in Jesse Jones's office on the morning of October 17 proved crucial. Several members of NDAC, including John D. Biggers and Frederick M. Eaton of Knudsen's staff, Leon Henderson, David Ginsburg, and Donald M. Nelson were present. So was Robert Proctor from the War Department. Proctor, a member of a prominent Boston law firm, Choate, Hall, and Stewart, had shared with Eaton in drafting the EPF contract. In a vigorous discussion of the comparative merits of EPF and DPC, Ginsburg broke ranks by pointing out deficiencies in the EPF contract, and Henderson's advocacy was lukewarm. Jesse Jones put his powerful support squarely behind the DPC lease which, he said, served the government's interest far better in its simplicity than did the EPF contract. Jones had found persuasive an analogy offered by Klagsbrunn likening the DPC lease to the equipment trust certificates used by railroads in financing additions to their rolling stock. Under equipment trust certificates the financing agency held title, and the railroads used the equipment free from restraint as long as they met their financial obligations. The meeting ended with each side agreeing that defense manufacturers needing plant financing could choose on a plane of equality between the EPF and DPC mechanisms. DPC was at last free to enter into leases with both Wright and Bendix.[34]

During the following two days, Durr and Klagsbrunn, in association with Harry Hotchkiss, the attorney for Wright, drew up a lease for the $57 million in new facilities required by Wright. Proctor was also present during the negotiations. At his insistence, several changes were made in the DPC lease form as developed in the Packard and subsequent leases. Chief among these was the introduction of a nominal rental. The War Department was trying to keep down the cost of its supplies by eliminating all charges for facilities in determining the price of the product. This adjustment created the problem of how DPC would recover its investment, for if only a nominal rental of one dollar per year were charged, DPC would ultimately have merely a depreciated plant as its investment. The damage done to RFC's image as a sound lending agency would hardly appeal to Jesse Jones.

DPC's attorneys proved equal to the challenge. Klagsbrunn conceived the plan of using a "take-out" arrangement to resolve the difficulty. Under the arrangement as evolved at this time, the War Department was to pay three-fifths of the cost of the plant by June 1, 1942. For the balance, it would give a "take-out" promising payment out of future appropriations when and if made. In turn, DPC agreed that title to the plant would pass to the War Department when the full cost had been paid. Jones added an amendment that an interest rate of 4 percent per year would be charged on the amount outstanding. There was no guarantee that Congress would advance the sums necessary for payment. If Congress did not, however, the take-outs would remove the stigma of loss from RFC.[35]

Following completion and signing of the Wright lease on October 19, 1940, the basic rental pattern for one of the two major types of lease agreements was established.[36] This type was used for manufacturers furnishing supplies directly to the government. DPC acquired facilities and leased them to a contractor for the manufacture of war supplies. The lease normally ran for five years, or for a lesser period if the plant were not needed to fulfill government contracts, at a rental of one dollar per year. The contractor also had the right of renewal if it had substantial unfilled government orders on hand at the end of the original period. Because of the nominal rental, the contractor agreed not to load any cost for facilities into the price charged the government for the supplies.

The second type of rental contract was also being formulated concurrently in the first of several Bendix leases. This agreement, drawn up in October, provided for construction by DPC and lease to Bendix of a plant at Philadelphia so that that firm might enlarge its output of aircraft parts.[37] It was made with a company that was not selling to the government directly but to aircraft manufacturers having government contracts. There was a strong probability, therefore, that not all the parts Bendix manufactured would be used in government aircraft. Because of its status as a subcontractor, Bendix agreed to pay DPC a substantial rental based on its volume of sales. The rate of rental for each lease was figured on a base that, at 90 percent of estimated capacity, would repay DPC for its investment, plus interest, over a five-year period. The rate of rental rose progressively in direct ratio with the volume of sales. DPC thus assumed the risk of partial nonrepayment on its investment by Bendix if orders were not sufficient to permit operation of the plant at capacity. In such a case, DPC would look to the War Department for reimbursement for the deficiency, in accordance with a War Department take-out agreement.[38]

Following the successful negotiation of these leases, DPC was in a position to expand. By the end of 1940, more than thirty leases had been negotiated for plant and equipment costing in excess of $250 million. The greater portion of these leases were made with firms manufacturing aircraft, aircraft engines, and parts. Among the largest were three plants for Curtiss-Wright Aircraft Corporation at Buffalo, Columbus, Ohio, and St. Louis for the manufacture of fighter aircraft for the War Department; a plant for Consolidated Aircraft Corporation at San Diego, California, for the manufacture of naval aircraft; and a plant for North American

Aviation Corporation at Dallas, Texas, for the manufacture of advanced trainer aircraft.[39] In lesser number, leases were entered into with firms producing such military and naval supplies as fuses, submarines and submarine tenders, scientific equipment, and 155-millimeter shells. At the beginning of 1941, DPC also took a step of great significance to the machine tool industry. It agreed to reduce risk and stimulate production by placing advance orders and operating a tool pool for manufacturers of arms, ammunition, and implements of war.[40]

EPF's conservative sponsors continued to mount a rear-guard action. Their hopes had been mirrored in a news story in *Business Week* early in October:

> Outright ownership by the government or the Defense Plant Corporation will be restricted to plants and equipment for which private manufacturers (who will operate them for the government) would have no probable use outside armament production. . . .
>
> To finance construction of new capacity for defense needs which are more or less in the line with commercial requirements but which call for much more than normal production, the Defense Commission has devised a so-called bankable [EPF] contract. . . .
>
> The clear intent of this plan is never to permit the government to use this capacity for commercial purposes.

To salvage as much as possible of these conservative goals, Proctor proposed late in October that the EPF contract be used exclusively to expand or create industrial facilities at nonstrategic locations, and that the EPF and DPC alternatives be equally available to contractors who were purchasing machinery only or were building complete plants at locations determined upon by the armed services for strategic reasons. Thus DPC would be limited to financing often small purchases of machinery or to the construction of plants at locations that would be less desirable for industrial use following the emergency. But Schram refused to accept the proposed limitation. Proctor next turned to a test of the legality of the "take-out" provision only to have its legality affirmed by the Office of the Judge Advocate General.[41]

EPF had too many deficiencies to be attractive. Contractors and bankers might, and probably did, hesitate to sign a contract that gave limited protection during the period of construction before the final cost certificate had been accepted and reimbursement payments began. Prior to acceptance by the government of the final cost certificate, neither the contractor nor the banker could be sure that all expenditures for the project would be accepted for reimbursement. Loans required for plant construction under these contracts were also frequently so large as to force banks toward or beyond the statutory limits of the amount they might lend to a single borrower. Moreover, some manufacturers, particularly in the young and rapidly growing aircraft industry, feared that banker control of their companies could result from such large loans.

As far as the government was concerned, the EPF contract was meant to have the advantage of attracting private capital into defense financing. The fact was, however, that the government department at the time of signing the contract had to set aside and freeze the funds needed for reimbursement for the full five-year period. If it failed to do so, the contract would not have been bankable with a private institution, because no bank would want to run the risk of repayment out of funds not yet appropriated. Early forms of the EPF contract provided that if at ninety days prior to the close of any fiscal year during the life of the contract sufficient funds were not earmarked for payment of all installments as they became due, the whole amount would immediately become payable. The EPF contract thus offered the government no relief with respect to the burden of defense financing. Instead, the armed services were in the anomalous position of paying interest to the banks when they were required by the contract to have sufficient funds on hand to pay the principal.

Because of this anomaly, Jesse Jones announced in mid-November that RFC would be willing to finance EPF contracts at 1.5 percent interest. This move caused great anguish in the financial community, for banks were hoping to charge 3 percent or more. His announcement was not effective in determining the EPF rate because interest was reimbursable, but a contractor wishing to make a good record would not want to pay much more. The low interest quoted in Jones's statement made EPF in further degree unpalatable.[42]

But the terms of contract were the greatest stumbling block. They were cumbersome, detailed, complex, and time-consuming. Before a contract could be executed, for example, every piece of machinery had to be listed. Once a piece of machinery was in place, it was exceedingly difficult to move the piece to another plant where the need might be greater. Government departments experienced great difficulty in flexing the contracts to conform to the changing requirements of national defense. In the words of one War Department attorney, the contract was "a monstrosity"; in the words of another, "the worst contract ever written."[43]

Despite these shortcomings, the bankers continued to beat the drums for EPF and private financing. In a speech to Chicago executives, Emmet F. Connely warned of the dangers of government financing: "Before this trend develops much further, it would be well if business men asked themselves what is going to happen to these new government-financed plants when the emergency ends. There will be people who will insist that the government make use of them." Concurring, the *Wall Street Journal* added its own word of warning: "Already too many have gone to Washington with hats in their hands—and hats not only of individuals but of

American cities and states and special groups seeking something for practically nothing; practically nothing, that is, except their future independence." In similar vein, P. D. Houston, president of the American Bankers Association, told a business audience: "If business is going to the government for the bulk of its credit now, it will be dependent on the government in the future."[44]

Because the EPF contracts were frequently too large to be handled by any one bank, the NDAC sent a financing specialist to New York late in November and to Chicago early in December. He discussed with bankers how they might handle large defense loans through the formation of banking syndicates. This was also the theme of the well-attended winter meeting of the New York State Bankers Association. They desired to find means by which the banks could give as quick and adequate service as the Defense Plant Corporation. Early in 1941, the American Bankers Association established a national network of committees to help speed private banking procedures in negotiating defense loans.[45]

A last-ditch effort to keep EPF alive occurred at the end of January 1941, when four of New York's biggest banks—Chase, National City, Guaranty Trust, and Bankers Trust—put forth a plan to ease defense financing by acting as a clearing house for defense contractors. They offered to give quick decision, preferably within twenty-four hours, on all contracts referred to them by the NDAC. If the decision was positive, they proposed to share the loan with the bank or banks with which the contractor ordinarily did business. "The objectives of the program," the *New York Times* reported, "are to facilitate the financing of as much defense work as possible within the framework of the commercial banking system, and at the same time provide manufacturers on defense work with the same speedy decisions they have been getting from the RFC."[46]

But this plan failed to strike home. Neither banks nor contractors could work up much enthusiasm for a plan that would place the New York giants in a favored position athwart the stream of defense financing. Consequently, contrary to the hopes of its sponsors, the EPF contract became almost obsolete. Overall, less than $350 million in industrial facilities were financed under the EPF contract during the defense and war periods.[47]

The failure of EPF to catch on cannot be attributed to a lack of promotion for EPF or to heavy publicity for DPC. Indeed, EPF was heavily promoted, while DPC operated, seemingly, under wraps. The NDAC, obviously, was not anxious to publicize DPC. News stories on groundbreaking for the new Curtiss-Wright plants at Buffalo and St. Louis and the Consolidated Aircraft plant at San Diego said nothing about DPC financing. The *New York Times* early in January 1941 erroneously reported that Wright's Ohio plant and an associated Otis Elevator plant for manufacturing airplane engine crankcases were EPF-financed.[48] DPC's contracts, amounting to more than $250 million by the end of 1940, were largely the result of word-of-mouth advertising among lessees who were pleased with the standard terms and the speed of action.

DPC probably was fortunate that it received so little publicity in these early months. If the DPC plan had been widely publicized, a more vigorous backlash from private finance would surely have developed, with Jesse Jones's own attitude uncertain. Jones was a conservative at heart, and the Defense Plant Corporation was an organization of mavericks within RFC. They were fortunate that Jones was appointed secretary of commerce in September, just as DPC was getting started. While learning the routines of his new position, he had to relax his careful scrutiny of RFC affairs. If he had recognized DPC's scope, he could readily have upset its smooth-running organization by moving in with his own partisans.[49]

Despite this risk and the military-style unwritten rule at RFC that Jones and the head of his information section must approve all publicity, Durr decided early in 1941 that DPC had to become better known if its lease mechanism was to be more fully used. He sought out his Oxford classmate, the syndicated columnist Ernest Lindley of the *Washington Post,* to urge Lindley to explore DPC's activities and to note Schram's important role. Fortunately, the story broke just as Jones was being belabored by the muckraking journalist Drew Pearson for dragging his feet in financing the defense effort. Schram commented that at a news conference in mid-January Jones "pretty nearly fell out of his chair" in amazement when Schram read off the long list of DPC projects. Jones found his defense against Pearson ready at hand in the record of the Defense Plant Corporation. He turned at once to preparing a report making use of it.[50]

With DPC effectively spotlighted at last, contractors found their way to its door in increasing numbers. They came sponsored by other government agencies, most frequently the War Department. The facilities they sought were usually for supply contracts relating either to aviation or to ordnance. In the spring of 1941, DPC also acquired a number of plants financed by Britain as part of the effort to help that beleaguered nation. By the end of April, the DPC overall investment in plant and equipment had grown to over $500 million.[51]

DPC was equipped to handle negotiations quickly and to speed the contractor on his way. At its origin, Durr had thoughtfully put in a by-law permitting two board members to function as an executive committee instead of waiting on the whole board to make decisions. A contractor who came early in the morning would be shown the appropriate standard lease form; if he was willing to agree to its terms (as most were), he could be headed for home with his lease by noon. DPC was streamlined for action.[52]

In the spring of 1941, the defense program entered upon a new phase.

On May 4, almost a year after his "50,000 planes" speech, President Roosevelt wrote Secretary of War Stimson asking that the heavy bomber program be stepped up to five hundred planes a month. He was calling for a nearly tenfold increase over current production. "I am fully aware," the president wrote, "that increasing the number of our heavy bombers will mean a great strain upon our production effort. It will mean a large expansion of plant facilities and the utilization of existing facilities not now engaged in making munitions."[53] The earlier phase had focused primarily on the expansion of aviation and ordnance facilities. The need for a similar expansion in such basic materials as aluminum, magnesium, and steel had been clouded over in debate. By the spring of 1941, there was no longer room for argument. The experience with the earlier expansion also strongly suggested that to an even greater extent the new phase should be financed through the Defense Plant Corporation.

There was some question whether the powers granted RFC in June 1940 were broad enough to encompass plant and equipment for the production of basic materials. As an RFC attorney phrased it,

> The terms "arms", "ammunition", and "implements of war" are not capable of any exact definition, and there are many articles and supplies vitally necessary for defense purposes which may not be embraced within their scope. Moreover, while it would seem clear that the manufacture of arms, ammunition, and implements of war would include parts and materials entering into such manufacture, whether produced in the same or different plants, it is not certain how far removed from the final process materials may be and still be properly included within the terms of the Act.[54]

Consequently, RFC decided to return to Congress for a clarifying amendment.

As in the preceding year, strong fears were expressed that if given additional power, RFC might create government corporations to compete with and undermine private industry. The conservative Senator John A. Danaher of Connecticut said he was "appalled at the grant of power solicited from us."[55] Representative Jesse P. Wolcott of Michigan charged that the bill, if enacted, "would grant such broad powers to the executive branch of the Government as to make it possible to establish a Fascist state in the United States."[56] Arthur Krock of the *New York Times* declared that the bill was "totalitarian" and "an alarming measure." He claimed that the powers requested were so all-embracing that, in effect, Jones was "asking for the dictionary."[57]

Despite the vigor with which such sentiments were expressed, the general temper in Congress tended to be sympathetic to the request for additional authority. Senator Prentiss Brown pointed out the necessity for the bill if RFC was to be able through its subsidiaries to build railroads, for example, to make the iron ore resources of Minnesota available in case the locks at Sault Sainte Marie were bombed.[58] Senator Taft, too, was amenable. The pending amendment he found to be "a sound amendment . . . probably justifiable under the present circumstances." In supporting the amendment, he stated

> Last year the Corporation came to Congress and requested authority to create corporations. The request was also unlimited at that time, and at my request, largely, the powers were cut down to those provided in existing law.
>
> I am not particularly concerned about the power to create subsidiary corporations by any method which may be prescribed. The subsidiary corporations already formed have done a very good job. Today we have committed $1,634,000,000 in that process, and I think those corporations are doing one of the most useful works in national defense.
>
> I believe that Mr. Jones had all the powers he desired under the Act as we amended it, and only today has he found that there are some other things he wished to do which cannot be done under the original authorization. I think it is a very good thing that when such additional powers are wanted, Mr. Jones should come back to Congress.[59]

The new measure became law on June 10, 1941.[60] Its effect was to permit RFC subsidiaries not only to engage in activities associated with the manufacture of arms, ammunition, and implements of war but also with respect to all goods and materials essential to national defense. The act, moreover, gave RFC subsidiaries new powers with respect to the production and ownership of railroad equipment and commercial aircraft and facilities for training aviators. In addition, under one all-purpose clause, the corporations were empowered, to the extent of $200 million, to follow the direction of the president and the federal loan administrator with respect to still other unspecified activities considered of consequence to the defense program. As long as their operations were concerned with national defense and all projects were entered into prior to January 22, 1947, the sole limitation placed upon the subsidiaries was that they not engage in five specifically designated projects that had been defeated in Congress during the past fifteen years.[61]

As a result of the new amendment, RFC was authorized by clause (3) of section 5d, when requested by the federal loan administrator, with the approval of the president

> to create or to organize, at any time prior to July 1, 1943, a corporation or corporations, with power (a) to produce, acquire, carry, sell, or otherwise deal in strategic and critical materials as defined by the President; (b) to purchase and lease land, purchase, lease, build, and expand plants, and purchase and produce equipment, facilities, machinery, materials, arms, ammunition and implements of war, any other articles, equipment,

facilities, and supplies necessary to the national defense, and such other articles, equipment, supplies, and materials as may be required in the manufacture or use of any of the foregoing or otherwise necessary in connection therewith; (c) to lease, sell, or, otherwise dispose of such land, plants, facilities, and machinery to others to engage in such manufacture; (d) to engage in such manufacture itself, if the President finds that it is necessary for a Government agency to engage in such manufacture; (e) to produce, lease, purchase, or otherwise acquire railroad equipment (including rolling stock), and commercial aircraft, and parts, equipment, facilities, and aircraft, and to lease, sell, or otherwise dispose of the same; (f) to purchase, lease, build, expand, or otherwise acquire facilities for the training of aviators and to operate or lease, sell, or otherwise dispose of such facilities to others to engage in such training; and (g) to take such other action as the President and the Federal Loan Administrator may deem necessary to expedite the national defense program, but the aggregate amount of the funds of the Reconstruction Finance Corporation which may be outstanding at any one time for carrying out this clause (g) shall not exceed $200,000,000.

RFC had by this time, with a few minor exceptions, the full range of powers it would exercise during the defense and war years.

The new legislation further increased the importance of DPC among the defense subsidiaries both in the scale of its operations and in its demands on RFC personnel. In fiscal 1942, the year following the new amendment, DPC was billed by RFC for $2,423,000 in salaries. This was approximately 21 percent of the RFC payroll amounting to $11,388,000 and equivalent to slightly less than 1,200 of the RFC staff numbering 5,664. By fiscal 1945, the size of the bill for DPC salaries had grown to $11,273,000—approximately 36 percent of the RFC payroll and equivalent to 4,550 employees.[62]

4

New Crisis

DPC suffered the last serious challenge to its authority almost immediately after the passage of the new amendment. The attack was launched surreptitiously by General Brehon Somervell, the ambitious and able head of the Construction Division in the War Department. Somervell viewed with dismay War Department negotiations for DPC to handle the construction of $500 million worth of additional facilities for the production of munitions. The suave and handsome general lobbied effectively among members of the House and Senate appropriations committees. He claimed that DPC was subverting the intent of Congress by taking over and supplementing appropriations granted the War Department and was creating a large and unnecessary duplicate organization for government construction. His attack led the Senate committee to invite the War Department to seek an additional $500 million to cover the expansion of ordnance facilities. The committee also added an amendment designed, in the words of Senator Elmer Thomas of Oklahoma, "to prevent the War Department from negotiating with the R.F.C. or any other agency in an effort to borrow money with which to construct defense plants." On a later occasion, reflecting some of the same feelings expressed by those who had opposed the recent additional grant of powers to the RFC, the Oklahoma Democrat made known his opposition to a possibly permanent RFC "if for no other reason, to manage these big establishments after this emergency is over, in a commercial way, so that they may continue to return, if possible, some financial compensation to the Government."[1]

The enactment of this crippling amendment brought Undersecretary of War Patterson to Congress to seek legislation limiting its effect solely to the $500 million appropriation for munition plants. The undersecretary had acquiesced in Somervell's drive for additional funds to allow War Department construction of these facilities, but he was anxious not to lose the future benefits of the DPC lease mechanism, particularly in the aviation industry. In a lengthy statement, he noted that the construction branches of the War Department were already overburdened with projects of a predominantly military character. DPC, by contrast, he argued, was particularly well set up to handle "essentially private industrial expansions," leaving "military appropriations and military men for military assignments." Reaffirming a judgment he had made a few months earlier, Patterson told members of the House Appropriations Committee: "We know that the Defense Plant Corporation procedure is flexible, efficient, and time-saving. We know that under it the Government interest is properly protected. We have had the finest cooperation from representatives of the Corporation. We are very anxious ... to utilize that Government agency in cases where it is determined by the Secretary or Undersecretary of War that such action will contribute to the successful accomplishment of the defense program." The legislation sought by Patterson was quickly enacted.[2] DPC's freedom to act was never again seriously threatened in Congress.

But the course of DPC did not run smooth. Internal tensions developed within the hitherto near-frictionless organization as a result of a shift in the center of power. Having discovered how important DPC had become, Jones could not abide its tendency toward independence. In reasserting control, Jones maneuvered Schram's appointment as chairman of the New York Stock Exchange, thus gracefully removing him as RFC's chairman and president of DPC. Sam Husbands, a director of RFC and longtime protégé of Jones in the Examining Division, succeeded Schram in June as DPC's new president. In the summer and fall of 1941, Jones himself took a leading part in the negotiations for the expansion of production of basic materials that characterized the second phase of industrial expansion.

Schram had been dedicated to the defense effort; Jones was much more skeptical of its urgency and more concerned that RFC's funds not be wasted. Schram had believed in standard contracts, fair and equal to all comers; Jones, accustomed to a lifetime of hard bargaining, preferred negotiating individual contracts, especially with large firms. Schram had worked easily with Snyder, Durr, Klagsbrunn, and others of the DPC staff; Jones, while open to suggestion, was far more authoritarian. As a result, Durr left DPC in mid-October to become a federal communications commissioner, six weeks before Pearl Harbor swept away all debate concerning the need for speed and the value of standard contracts.[3]

DPC's negotiations concerning synthetic rubber in 1940 and 1941 were a portent. By the summer of 1940, synthetic rubber had become a practical product capable of supplementing natural rubber if the supply of natural rubber was reduced or cut off. In June, Goodrich had introduced, with considerable fanfare at the Waldorf-Astoria, the "Ameripol" tire, which was more than half synthetic rubber costing sixty cents a pound. John Collyer, president of Goodrich, had just returned to the United States after spending ten years in England. His experiences there made him a passionate advocate of national defense. Later in June, he testified before the Senate Military Affairs Committee at its request, along with executives of Jersey Standard and DuPont, about the development of a substantial synthetic rubber program. Within a few weeks, an NDAC Committee of the Raw Materials Division recommended financing facilities sufficient to manufacture 100,000 tons annually. The NDAC turned to RFC to provide approximately $100 million. Late in August, Schram told Durr he believed the program would be a prudent defense move. Schram spoke of building synthetic rubber plants as similar to building a battleship—against potential need, even if never used. Shortly, a preliminary meeting was held between DPC officials, John Collyer of Goodrich, and an executive from Phillips Petroleum, the oil company that would manufacture the needed raw material, butadiene.[4]

No further attempt at negotiation was made until the following spring because Jones moved Schram aside and took over. Although he was willing to go along with a stripped-down version of NDAC's proposal, Jones considered any large expenditure rash, partly because he believed methods of synthetic rubber manufacture were still in the pioneering stage. He preferred to put his trust in stockpiling natural rubber through another RFC subsidiary, the Rubber Reserve Company. He had been encouraged in this view by Sir John Hay, head of the International Rubber Cartel, who was around Washington during much of the summer and fall of 1940. The cartel had helped maneuver the price of rubber from its depression low of about two cents a pound to approximately twenty cents in 1940. According to Jones, Sir John Hay was "not enthusiastic about our building synthetic rubber plants" to cut into his market. Because of his conservative bias, Jones usually favored decisions that would not threaten the stability of established enterprises. But even in stockpiling, he was in no hurry. He did not wish to tie up government funds in large amounts of rubber that might not be needed.[5]

It was mid-May 1941 before DPC signed agreements with the four major rubber companies—Goodrich, Goodyear, Firestone, and U.S. Rubber—for the construction of synthetic rubber facilities. Each was allotted $1.25 million for a pilot plant capable of turning out twenty-five hundred tons annually. John Collyer was enraged by this penny-wise, pound-foolish policy. Frank Howard of Jersey Standard likewise voiced his dismay when he heard of the decision. Howard wrote R. R. Deupree, the defense program's rubber executive, "I am sorry to say that I believe the handling of this synthetic rubber matter, up to this moment has not been a creditable one." During the summer, the financing of the plants was increased to permit each of the plants to produce ten thousand tons annually.[6]

Jones's skepticism about synthetic rubber continued undiminished. "It appears that none of the methods have been sufficiently proven to warrant the construction of expensive plants except in an extraordinary emergency," he wrote Roosevelt on September 16, 1941. The president agreed. A few days earlier, Ickes had written in his diary, "He [the president] said that if we ever started to manufacture synthetic rubber at a much higher cost than raw rubber brings, there will immediately go up a demand for a tariff to protect 'an infant industry' so that we will be saddling ourselves permanently with higher costs. I think that was a sound position to take."[7]

Supported by the White House, Jones made no further move. Progress on the synthetic rubber program continued at a snail's pace. None of the plants was in operation by the time of Pearl Harbor. Meanwhile, the stockpile of natural rubber had grown to 600,000 tons, with an additional 150,000 tons en route to the United States. The whole amounted to little more than a year's peacetime supply. It could not be increased because of Japan's rapid advance in Southeast Asia. After Pearl Harbor, the synthetic rubber capacity to be financed by DPC was raised quickly to 400,000 tons, but the damage had been done. Because of an excess of caution, the nation soon faced a rubber crisis.[8]

During 1941, DPC looked for guidance to the Office of Production Management (OPM), successor to NDAC. Organized in December 1940 and designed to bring greater efficiency to the defense effort, OPM drew primarily upon its headless seven-member predecessor for personnel.[9] A significant OPM concern during much of the year was increasing the production of three basic metals important for the nation's defense industries—magnesium, aluminum, and steel. In each case, it turned to DPC for the necessary financing.

Production of magnesium in the United States was still in its infancy. Magnesium was manufactured by a single firm, the Dow Chemical Company, which in 1939 turned out a little more than six million pounds at its Midland, Michigan, plant. In 1940, with private financing and spurred on by defense needs, Dow began tripling the size of its Midland plant and planning another of equal size on the Texas coast. Early in 1941, Dow was joined by a second producer, Todd-California Shipbuilding Corporation (later Permanente Metals), using an inferior process developed by an Austrian scientist. Permanente's enterprising promoter, the great wartime West Coast shipbuilder Henry J. Kaiser, financed his new venture with RFC loans that grew ultimately to $26 million.[10]

In mid-June 1941, OPM announced a program calling for a near-astronomic increase in magnesium production to 400 million pounds annually for use in aircraft and incendiary bombs. Because this huge amount far outran foreseeable peacetime demand, government financing was inevitable. OPM asked DPC to deal with seven manufacturers using almost as many different processes. Two of the large plants were scheduled for Dow and a smaller one for Permanente. The largest of all was assigned to Basic Magnesium, a lightly financed enterprise growing out of an amalgam of American and British interests that planned to use its own electrolytic process. After Pearl Harbor, plans for Basic Magnesium's plant were expanded to provide for a capacity of 112 million pounds annually. Mathieson Alkali was another of the designated firms that claimed to have it own special process. More powerfully than in the case of synthetic rubber, the question at issue was whether to move at once and gamble that the needed production could be achieved, regardless of cost and efficiency, or to proceed with caution. A secondary question concerned the postemergency use of these plants. In July, Roosevelt told Jesse Jones not to include purchase options in the contracts for their operation so that the government would be free to foster competition after the emergency.[11]

Jones moved slowly. Instead of permitting DPC to offer a standard contract, he insisted on bargaining with each firm, and instead of utilizing the DPC lease, at the direction of the president he drew up management-fee contracts under which the private firms manufactured and sold magnesium for DPC's account. The process of negotiation dragged on for several months. Two of the contracts were not signed until after Pearl Harbor.[12]

Expansion of aluminum production posed more serious problems. Unlike magnesium, aluminum had long been an important metal for industrial and consumer uses. Like magnesium, at the advent of the defense program its production was controlled by a single firm. This manufacturer, the Aluminum Company of America (Alcoa), was a powerful enterprise, a firm of great influence on the national scene. Because of its monopoly character, it had been under antitrust attack since 1937.[13]

In June 1940, production of primary aluminum amounted to approximately 400 million pounds annually. Obviously, more would be needed to support the "50,000 planes" program. The NDAC's Raw Materials Division put its faith in Alcoa, which, utilizing tax amortization, announced plans in October to boost its capacity to 690 million pounds annually by July 1942. In addition, in August 1940, Reynolds Metals Company entered the field. Reynolds, long a manufacturer of aluminum foil, became Alcoa's first competitor in the production of primary aluminum. Aided by a $16 million RFC loan, it began constructing an aluminum plant at Listerhill, Alabama, that would produce 60 million pounds a year.[14]

By the spring of 1941, defense officials could perceive that the aircraft program urgently required additional aluminum. Because the additional capacity seemed sure to run beyond national needs after the emergency, government financing seemed the only reasonable recourse. And because Alcoa had for so long been a powerful monopoly, New Dealers were anxious to bring new firms into the industry.

Toward the end of May—the month the stepped-up bomber program began—Knudsen wrote Jesse Jones formally seeking his help. Knudsen told the federal loan administrator that OPM was planning to expand the nation's primary aluminum capacity by an additional 600 million pounds, to be supplemented by Canadian imports of 200 million pounds annually. OPM sought to enlist the aid of DPC and RFC in financing this program.[15]

Jones, with his penchant for dealing with the "big boys," turned to Alcoa, which was fighting hard to maintain its monopoly. At a meeting of DPC and Alcoa officials in mid-July, the federal loan administrator withdrew to his private office with Arthur V. Davis, Alcoa's venerable board chairman, to hammer out terms. A week later he gave Sam Husbands and Durr a lengthy memorandum outlining his proposed deal. Reynolds was to be granted control of facilities capable of turning out 100 million pounds annually, and the balance of the increase would be provided from DPC plants built by and leased to Alcoa. The proposed terms bore little similarity to the standard leases DPC had used earlier. Also, they showed a strange solicitude for Alcoa's market position. Whenever demand was insufficient to sustain production at a level of at least 75 percent of capacity, the government was to make cuts in production in its plants twice as deep as those required in Alcoa's plants until Alcoa's production reached a permanent floor of 60 percent. At that point, the government would determine which of its plants should be kept in production to help meet any residual demand. Alcoa was to operate its government plants and handle the sale of their aluminum under a five-year renewable lease. The aluminum giant would be compensated by a 15 percent share of the net profits from the government plants. Alcoa would pay DPC the remaining 85 percent as rental. DPC would reimburse Alcoa in the event Alcoa incurred any loss. In addition, DPC was to finance at Hurricane Creek, Arkansas, a plant capable of manufacturing annually 400 million pounds of alumina, the intermediate product from which aluminum is made. This plant would also be operated by Alcoa.[16]

Although Sam Husbands, DPC's new president, found the proposed terms sound, Durr did not. He drafted a long memorandum indicating why he felt many of the terms were adverse to the government's interest. He argued that Alcoa was given too much control over the operation of the government plants, too much freedom in determining to whom and at what price the product was to be sold, and was being treated too favorably in the provisions for determining profits and guaranteeing that Alcoa would be free from loss. Durr questioned the legality of the terms under antitrust law. He also expressed surprise that three new West Coast plants at Tacoma, Spokane, and Los Angeles were apparently to be operated by Alcoa under the contract instead of by other companies proposed by OPM.[17]

Durr's statements in regard to antitrust law led Jones to seek out Attorney General Francis Biddle at a cabinet meeting and secure Biddle's reluctant assent to the terms. The federal loan administrator then dispatched Durr to the Department of Justice to help draw up the formal opinion Biddle had promised. The ripples this visit created caused Durr to be called back the next day to talk with Thurman Arnold, the rugged chief of the Antitrust Division and veteran of many a joust with Alcoa. Arnold's adamant opposition to the proposed deal caused Biddle to back down and, in turn, caused Jones to reduce the amount of new capacity offered Alcoa to 360 million pounds. After revision, it was agreed that Alcoa would serve as DPC's agent in building two of the three Pacific Coast plants, but all three would be operated by companies other than Alcoa. The cancellation clause covering the DPC plants operated by Alcoa was also modified to allow cancellation by either party if production fell below 40 percent of capacity for as long as six months. This change would later permit the government to break the lease and recapture the plants immediately following the war.[18]

It was mid-August before the contract with Alcoa was signed to build two Pacific Coast plants and to build and operate three large aluminum plants scattered across the nation and an alumina plant at Hurricane Creek, Arkansas. Even so, the criticisms by Durr and others did not abate. New Dealer Harold Ickes called the contract "damnable" and declared it "about the worst contract the government ever signed." Jones was outraged because his bargaining abilities were questioned when he appeared before the Truman Committee in the fall. But the contract was later amended to give DPC somewhat greater control over the operation of its plants.[19]

Meanwhile, DPC was having difficulty with the companies that had been chosen to operate the other aluminum plants. When Jones decided to let Alcoa build the plant at Los Angeles, in addition to those at Tacoma and Spokane, the designated operator for the Los Angeles plant, Bohn Aluminum and Brass Corporation, lost interest. Bohn was unwilling to operate a plant it had not built. Union Carbide and Carbon Corporation, OPM's choice for Spokane, also showed no enthusiasm. Thus Alcoa took over two more plants in addition to those it had originally received. Of the three operators OPM had selected, only Olin Corporation followed through—and only after it was permitted to build its own plant at Tacoma. This plant, with a capacity of 30 million pounds annually, was the smallest of the group. And Reynolds Metals, which had been authorized to expand its plant at Listerhill under DPC auspices, chose instead to use an RFC loan to finance the expansion and to build a second plant at Longview, Washington. Less than 10 percent of the new capacity (chiefly, the Reynolds plant at Longview) was available at the time of Pearl Harbor.[20] Because of the bickering, the other Pacific Coast plants were far from completion. Jesse Jones's penchant for dealing with established firms on an individual basis slowed negotiations and helped keep Alcoa in effective control of the aluminum industry during the war years. However, at the insistence of the president and Secretary of the Interior Ickes, Alcoa was given no option to purchase its government-owned company-operated plants. As in the cases of magnesium and synthetic rubber, the question of disposal of these facilities was postponed until after the emergency.[21]

Expanding the capacity of the steel industry posed another special set of problems. Unlike the young and immature aviation and magnesium industries, steel was old, established, and powerful. As in the case of aluminum, steel industry representatives were deeply entrenched and highly influential within the defense agencies.[22]

The threat of overcapacity bore heavily on the steel industry. During the depression, at bottom, its production in 1932 had fallen to little more than one-sixth of capacity. Having been burned so badly, industry executives were not anxious to add new facilities of doubtful profitability. Early in the defense effort, one of its most hard-bitten leaders, Eugene Grace of Bethlehem, admitted that "a substantial extension of facilities" would be needed for "armor plate, projectiles, guns, and other ordnance." But, he said, because these facilities would have "no commercial value, we are not warranted in spending our stockholders' money for the added plant."[23] Most leaders of the steel industry, like Grace and Tom Girdler of Republic Steel, were notably conservative in their political and social views. Many were deeply hostile to the New Deal.

Early recommendations for more iron and steel capacity for such urgent necessities as factories, machinery, ships, and railroad rolling stock, as well as armament, were frostily received. Industry leaders put little stock in a report of the National Resources Planning Board in December 1940 that the nation could use capacity sufficient to produce an additional 17 million tons of steel. They were much more pleased by a report in February 1941 prepared for OPM by Gano Dunn, chairman of a major engineering firm, J. G. White and Company, assisted by the American Iron and Steel Institute, who found that the nation's effective steel capacity was about 10 million tons greater than its probable needs for that year. But even though President Roosevelt was induced to say some strong words supporting Dunn's report, it did not hold up for long. Its critics pointed out that Dunn had achieved his optimistic finding by stating requirements at the bare minimum and assuming maximum production. Consequently, three months later Dunn reversed himself and called for an expansion of 13 million tons, particularly for such defense-related products as armor plate, deck plate, and heavy forgings. This statement of needed capacity was trimmed back to 10 million tons by OPM. Because of the armament character of much of the proposed product and the uncertain need for the additional capacity after the emergency, OPM turned to DPC during the summer and fall of 1941 for most of the financing.[24]

The proposed steel expansion differed from most others in that the government-owned facilities were built more frequently as additions or adjacent to private plants than as separately located new plants. Because of the intermingling, these facilities were known as "scrambled facilities." The land on which the government facilities stood was either purchased or leased from the private firm. Increased production could be achieved in this way more quickly and cheaply than through the construction of separate plants, but this procedure posed problems in disposing of the government facilities after the emergency. If the operator did not choose to buy the facilities at a price acceptable to the government, the government had few options. It could let the facilities lie idle if it owned the land or continued to hold a valid lease. When the lease expired, the terms usually required DPC to surrender the facilities or remove them and restore the property to its former condition.

Jesse Jones delegated to DPC's executives the negotiations with U.S. Steel, the first of the steel firms referred for financing. They experienced little difficulty in using their standard terms of contract for facilities costing $85 million at Homestead, Duquesne, and Braddock, Pennsylvania, to provide nearly one-fifth of the desired expansion. Later, similar contracts were drawn with Inland Steel and Republic Steel providing for smaller increases in the Chicago area.[25]

Bethlehem Steel was a different story. A reluctant and hard bargainer, it brought Jones to the negotiating table. Bethlehem extracted terms that differed significantly from those made with the other steel companies. These included eight thirty-five-year leases for scrambled facilities at four of its plants. Annual rental rates were set at 10 percent of the cost of the facilities during the emergency and 7 percent thereafter when the facilities were operated at capacity. If they were used less, rental rates were to be scaled down proportionate to the reduced rate of production. Bethlehem offered DPC concurrent thirty-five-year leases to the land on which the DPC facilities stood, but without access rights to those facilities. The operating leases were to be reviewed at the end of each five-year period. If, during the period, the facilities had been operated at an average of less than 25 percent of capacity, DPC could cancel the lease, but it had to remove the facilities and restore the property unless Bethlehem chose to buy the facilities at cost less depreciation. Unlike all other DPC purchase options, Bethlehem's did not require the company to pay interest on the principal from the time of the investment until the date of purchase.[26]

Because Jones himself recognized that the proposed agreement with Bethlehem "business-wise, . . . was none too good a contract," he had Sam Husbands inform Knudsen of the terms and seek his advice. Knudsen and Jones cleared the terms with the Supply Priorities and Allocation Board, the recently created supreme integrating defense agency, before Jones was willing to proceed further.[27]

Meanwhile, the DPC legal staff, and particularly Clifford Durr, its general counsel, had been watching the trend of events with mounting anguish. They had been dismayed at the course of the negotiations for synthetic rubber and were even more distressed at the company-by-company bargaining initiated by Jones in negotiating increased production of magnesium and aluminum. They put their trust in the standard lease terms devised the preceding year. These terms, which were the same for everyone, sped the decision-making process. Company-by-company negotiations, on the other hand, were conducive to delay and to bickering, as each company sought a better deal. Moreover, company-by-company negotiations were difficult for government negotiators—even Jesse Jones—who could not know as well as they ought the special characteristics of so many fields of enterprise.[28]

Durr had been distressed by the terms of the Alcoa lease. The Bethlehem lease was the last straw. On October 27, the day he resigned to become a federal communications commissioner, he sent Jones a memorandum detailing his vigorous objections to the Bethlehem lease terms. His general conclusion found its way into a Truman Committee report published three months later:

> From the outset DPC has endeavored to follow the policy of equality of treatment to all manufacturers, and by adhering to this policy, it has, to a large degree, won the confidence of the manufacturers and reduced the time required for negotiations to a minimum. If DPC should accept such a proposal as that submitted, the result would be to seriously delay, rather than expedite the defense program, for notice would be served upon all prospective lessees that better terms can be obtained by holding out than by cooperating. Moreover, it would be unfair to the manufacturers who have cooperated to give more favorable terms to a competitor.
>
> In times of emergency it would be fatal for the Government to concede that it is weaker than any of its corporations and that it must accede to their demands, however outrageous, in order to obtain arms and supplies with which to defend itself.[29]

Jones had sought to keep Durr from resigning. He esteemed Durr's acute legal mind but, even more, he was anxious that Durr not be free to discuss DPC affairs outside RFC. The Federal Communications Commission, Jones told Durr, was a poor place for a man of his abilities; Jones promised to find a better place for him in a year or two if Durr would stay on. But Durr would not. The two men parted on less than friendly terms. Durr respected Jones's business talent, but he could not abide the mismanagement of DPC's role in the defense program as he perceived it. Jones saw Durr as a troublesome and less than loyal subordinate. Years later, in a history of his service with RFC, Jones made no mention of Durr. He erased from the record DPC's principal architect.[30]

After more dickering, the Bethlehem leases were finally signed on February 2, 1942, nearly two months after Pearl Harbor. Hans Klagsbrunn, DPC's new general counsel, won at least one significant improvement by gaining access rights to DPC's facilities. This change was sufficiently disturbing to Bethlehem's rock-ribbed management that toward the end of 1943 it bought up the government-owned facilities at cost, having first determined that it could use the tax amortization mechanism to depreciate its investment. The purchase was made, said Eugene Grace, Bethlehem's chairman, "to prevent the government from 'being our landlord.' "[31]

Following Pearl Harbor, DPC activity became increasingly routinized. No longer was it possible to believe that the defense emergency might prove to be a false alarm. Nor was there time for individual bargaining with prospective lessees even if it were desirable. Construction crews working twenty-four hours a day building new factories became commonplace. Moreover, the increases in productive capacity after Pearl Harbor were usually merely additional rounds of expansion in industries that had experienced their first expansion during the defense period. The value of DPC authorizations during the first quarter of 1942 was fully four times as great as in the last quarter of 1941. So were DPC's machine tool pool orders for 1942, which underwrote virtually the entire machine tool production in the nation.[32] Thereafter both the wave of authorizations for plant investment and for machine tools slowly subsided.

Fully half of DPC's investment was for plant and equipment operated by major American corporations. They were chosen, not by DPC, but by the sponsoring agency. The top of the list (see Table 1) reads like a page from a bluebook of American enterprise—Alcoa, General Motors, United States Steel, Curtiss-Wright, Republic Steel, Chrysler, Ford, Anaconda, and others. Except possibly for a few aviation companies like Curtiss-Wright, United Aircraft, and Bendix, they were all big corporations by any standard prior to the war. And Curtiss-Wright and United Aircraft were two of the largest aircraft companies.[33]

DPC also financed expansions of plant and equipment for many smaller firms. They helped swell the number of DPC investments and, at times, were of critical importance. They included manufacturers of jewel bearings, ball bearings, searchlights, electrodes, dehydrated foods, frozen foods, medical supplies, and cordage. Of these, 350 represented investments of less than $100,000.

To a limited extent, DPC was involved with small business in at least two other ways. A law setting up the Smaller War Plants Corporation (SWPC) in June 1942 directed DPC to service the leases and loans made by that corporation. Ultimately, DPC serviced about 670 lease agreements for machinery and equipment valued at approximately $20 million. SWPC loans were serviced in the field through RFC loan agencies. Most of the loans were for working capital, but a part of some and all of others were

Table 1. Twenty-five Leading Companies Operating DPC Facilities during World War II (by amount of investment)

Company	Investment
Aluminum Company of America	$ 508,800,000
General Motors	470,500,000
United States Steel	372,000,000
Curtiss-Wright	358,100,000
Republic Steel	187,900,000
Chrysler	180,600,000
Ford Motor	172,500,000
Anaconda Copper Mining	170,200,000
Dow Chemical	150,700,000
United Aircraft	143,200,000
General Electric	137,100,000
Union Carbide and Carbon	134,500,000
Standard Oil of New York	103,600,000
Subtotal	3,089,700,000
Bendix Aviation	94,200,000
Goodyear Tire and Rubber	79,500,000
Koppers	74,000,000
Studebaker	73,700,000
American Rolling Mill	66,500,000
Continental Motors	65,900,000
Mathieson Alkali Works	60,400,000
Packard Motor	59,900,000
B. F. Goodrich	53,200,000
Nash-Kelvinator	53,100,000
E. I. du Pont de Nemours	50,700,000
Sperry	50,600,000
Total	$3,871,400,000

Source: Comptroller General of the United States, *Report on Audit of Reconstruction Finance Corporation and Affiliated Corporations for the Fiscal Year Ended June 30, 1945: Defense Plant Corporation,* 80th Cong., 1st sess., 1947, H. Doc. 474, 4:43.

for plant and equipment. At the close of the war, SWPC had disbursed more than $190 million in loans.[34]

During the summer of 1943, in conjunction with the War and Navy Departments, DPC inaugurated the use of what became known as the "rentra" lease. DPC used this means to lease, chiefly to small business, machine tools and other equipment that had become surplus to the needs of the war plants sponsored by the War and Navy Departments. Through nearly sixteen hundred rentra leases, over ten thousand machine tools were kept at work in the war effort.[35]

5

The Conduct of DPC Operations

DPC, like the other defense and war subsidiaries of RFC, was created in the pattern of RFC's prewar subsidiaries. It was a legal entity possessed of certain powers to perform specific functions. Physically, it was a fiction. DPC derived its authority, its board, its personnel, its office space, its supplies, and its money from the parent organization.

DPC operated through an administrative structure that was fluid and changing. This was primarily because it was an emergency corporation called into being to do an emergency job. Because it represented a new means of plant financing, its procedure and organization required experimental modification and elaboration in order to achieve greater effectiveness. Thus the original intent of DPC was to give each lessee maximum freedom in constructing, equipping, and operating its DPC-owned facilities. Although this idea remained dominant, DPC's administrative structure was nevertheless gradually expanded to give more adequate protection to the government's interest and also, in some ways, to give additional assistance to the lessee. Moreover, the very extent of DPC operations bore a direct relation to its organizational needs. The initial organization of a corporation created to handle a maximum of perhaps one hundred projects was obviously inadequate for a corporation that ultimately financed approximately twenty-three hundred projects and engaged in a number of collateral activities.

The board of directors was DPC's central governing body.[1] Composed originally of nine directors, it was streamlined in February 1941 to permit greater speed in decisions by a by-law that required only three directors for a quorum.[2] In addition, an Executive Committee, consisting of four specific members with any other board member eligible as an alternate, was empowered to act for the board at any time the board was not in session. Two members constituted a quorum of the Executive Committee.[3] During the early history of DPC, most business, even to the routine payment of bills, was submitted to the board for approval. As the war progressed, the board increasingly delegated its authority in specific matters to designated DPC officers and divisions.

Because of the frenzied period in which the corporation functioned and because of the shadowy nature of the corporation itself, some of

DPC's operational offices, divisions, and sections are at times difficult to discern. (For an organization chart as of fall 1943, see Chart 1.) All the offices and most divisions were established by the board, but some divisions and most sections subordinate to the divisions seem to have come into being without board action. The offices and most divisions, moreover, tended to be projections of established offices and divisions within RFC. Thus the Secretary's Office and the Treasurer's Office of DPC were presided over by officials who were both secretary and treasurer, respectively, of DPC and an assistant secretary and an assistant treasurer of RFC. Similarly, the general counsel of DPC was an assistant general counsel of RFC. Nathaniel Royall, who became chief auditor of RFC in mid-1941, was also chief auditor of DPC and of the other wartime subsidiaries.

Both the general counsel and the chief auditor of DPC were in charge of large staffs. In its earliest days, DPC was primarily an organization of lawyers, for its basic activity was the negotiating and drawing up of the lease or management and operation agreement. This work was particularly important while the forms of agreement were being evolved and the volume of new business was rapidly increasing. Even in the defense period, however, as construction and purchase activities got under way, an increasingly large proportion of the time of DPC attorneys was taken up with legal matters pertaining to the development and operation of the projects. Eventually the DPC Legal Division grew into a number of sections: lease, disbursement, real estate, contract, patent, and labor relations.[4] Each section specialized in the legal problems that confronted DPC in its designated sphere of activity. DPC attorneys were concentrated largely in Washington. In the field, DPC relied in great degree upon counsel of the RFC loan agencies.

Because DPC disbursed a great volume of funds, the Auditing Division soon acquired an importance almost as great as the Legal Division or the Engineering Division. In contrast to the legal establishment, most auditing personnel were in the field.

Initially, and for the first five months of DPC's existence, only engineers were assigned to the field. Auditing responsibilities, in addition to the general supervision of the project, thus devolved upon each engineer. The system worked poorly. Certifications for payment to the Federal Reserve banks from the engineers at the projects all too frequently failed to provide the information essential for identification of the items paid for when those bills ultimately were processed through the Federal Reserve banks to the DPC Treasurer's Office. Nor were the accompanying documents always in order.[5]

As a remedy, the DPC board on January 18, 1941, approved a memorandum requesting the assignment of a representative of the RFC Auditing Division to each project. According to this plan, the auditor and

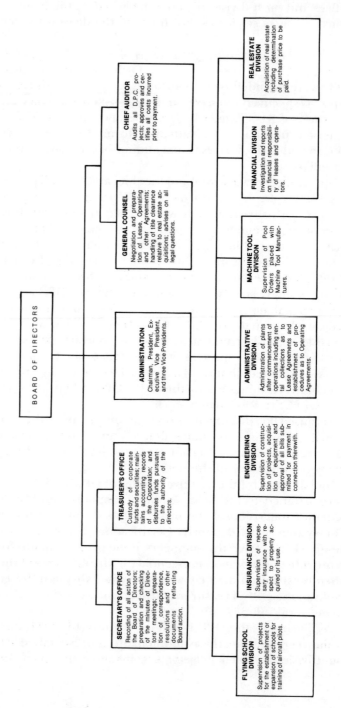

DEFENSE PLANT CORPORATION
(as of Fall, 1943)

Created by the Reconstruction Finance Corporation on August 22, 1940, pursuant to authority of Section 5d of the Reconstruction Finance Corporation Act, as amended. The Corporation's principal function is to finance the construction and equipment of plants making war materials and supplies.

BOARD OF DIRECTORS

SECRETARY'S OFFICE
Recording of all action of the Board of Directors; preparation and checking of the minutes of Directors' meetings; preparation of correspondence, resolutions and other documents reflecting Board action.

TREASURER'S OFFICE
Custody of corporate funds and securities; maintains accounting records of the Corporation; and disburses funds pursuant to the authority of the directors.

ADMINISTRATION
Chairman, President, Executive Vice President, and three Vice Presidents.

GENERAL COUNSEL
Negotiation and preparation of Lease, Operating and other Agreements; handling of title clearance relative to real estate acquisitions; advises on all legal questions.

CHIEF AUDITOR
Audits all D.P.C. projects; approves and certifies all costs incurred prior to payment.

FLYING SCHOOL DIVISION
Supervision of projects for the establishment or expansion of schools for training of aircraft pilots.

INSURANCE DIVISION
Supervision of necessary insurance with respect to property acquired or its use.

ENGINEERING DIVISION
Supervision of construction of projects, acquisition of equipment and approval of all bills submitted for payment in connection therewith.

ADMINISTRATIVE DIVISION
Administration of plants after commencement of operations including rental collections as to Lease Agreements and establishment of procedures as to Operating Agreements.

MACHINE TOOL DIVISION
Supervision of Pool Orders placed with Machine Tool Manufacturers.

FINANCIAL DIVISION
Investigation and reports on financial responsibility of leases and operators.

REAL ESTATE DIVISION
Acquisition of real estate including determination of purchase price to be paid.

SOURCE: RFC Statistical and Economics Division files

UA Cartographic Lab

engineer shared responsibility for certifying bills for payment to the Federal Reserve banks. The auditor made certain that bills were "proper for payment" and that the information for identifying the items was available for the maintenance of property records in the DPC Treasurer's Office.[6]

The new system was a great improvement over the earlier procedure. Nevertheless, one of its goals was not achieved for long, for the unforeseen volume of war work, combined with a shortage in personnel, forced the Treasurer's Office late in 1942 to forego its plans for keeping an itemized record of all DPC properties. This unfortunate breakdown in record keeping in many instances made more difficult, and even impossible, the determination of ownership and accountability after the war.[7]

The organizational structure of the DPC Auditing Division, like that of the other divisions, evolved gradually. Auditors at the projects at first had no intermediate level between them and Washington, but by early 1943 there were nearly one hundred subordinate offices located about the country. Each was headed by a project auditor supervising from one to twenty projects. These offices were gradually consolidated during the following year so that by the end of 1944 there were approximately forty field offices providing a higher degree of centralization.[8]

The Washington office of the DPC auditor also evolved gradually. In November 1941, the DPC projects were divided on a geographic basis into five groups. Each was under the jurisdiction of a supervising auditor. These auditors, or their assistants, frequently traveled about to check upon the conduct of auditing in the field.[9]

Engineering, the third important division, was the outgrowth of a huge expansion of the prewar Engineering Section of the Self-Liquidating Divison of RFC. Walter L. Drager, chief engineer of RFC and a longtime associate of Emil Schram, was appointed chief engineer of DPC on November 7, 1940. As the number of DPC projects grew, an increasingly large number of engineers were required to supervise the individual construction and equipment-purchasing programs. As the construction period drew to a close, this division assisted in preparing the DPC properties for disposal.[10]

Originally the Washington office of the Engineering Division of DPC also supervised land purchases, but later an independent Real Estate Division handled this phase of activity. The principal function of the Engineering Division throughout the war was supervising the formulation and letting of contracts for the engineering and construction of DPC plant projects. This phase of activity was handled by the Construction Contract Section, formally established in the Washington office early in June 1942. Personnel of this section supplied the DPC attorneys with engineering advice during the negotiation of contracts. The Construction Equipment Section, established in the Washington office early in July

1942, kept a card record of individual pieces of DPC-owned or rented construction equipment.[11]

The field structure of DPC's Engineering Division, like that of the Auditing Division, took shape gradually. For the first projects, supervising engineers from RFC's Self-Liquidating Division were sent to the field. As the projects grew in number, certain engineers of DPC's Engineering Division were given greater responsibilities and became known as division engineers. Some division engineers, to whom the supervising engineers were subordinate, were located in Washington. Others were located in the field. Still others supervised all DPC plants within particular fields of production, the so-called "industrial specialties."[12]

As the war progressed and as the number of projects (called "plancors," a coined word) far surpassed the wildest estimates of the defense period, the field organization of the Engineering Division was overhauled. In June 1942, the United States was divided into nine regions, each of which was placed under the jurisdiction of a regional engineer in the Washington office. At that time, the field structure of the Engineering Division was given the form it maintained until it was again revised during the summer of 1944 to accommodate the plant clearance program. These regions and the number of plancors in June 1942 were as follows:[13]

Number of plancors	Region	States
116	I	Maine, New Hampshire, Vermont, Massachusetts, New York, Rhode Island, Connecticut
55	II	New Jersey, Delaware, New York City, Long Island
50	III	Pennsylvania
105	IV	Ohio
100	V	Michigan
67	VI	Indiana, Illinois, Kentucky
33	VII	Maryland, West Virginia, Virginia, North Carolina, South Carolina, Tennessee, Alabama, Florida, Mississippi, Georgia
35	VIII	North Dakota, South Dakota, Nebraska, Kansas, Missouri, Iowa, Minnesota, Wisconsin
41	IX	Oklahoma, Texas, Utah, Washington, Oregon, Nevada, Arkansas, Louisiana, New Mexico, Colorado, Wyoming, Montana, Arizona, California, Idaho

One or more division engineers were subordinate to each regional engineer. Each division engineer was in charge of a field office, where he was supported by assistant division and head supervising engineers. The supervising engineers located at the individual plancors made up the bottom level of the hierarchy.

In addition, the Engineering Division maintained a separate organizational structure for the industrial specialities, which included aluminum, steel, shipbuilding, magnesium, high-octane gasoline, synthetic rubber, mining, and flying schools. Engineers with jurisdiction comparable to that of regional engineers were established in Washington for each of these specialties. Like the regional engineers, they had a subordinate supporting echelon of division engineers between themselves and the supervising engineers at the plancors. The industrial specialties were kept outside the normal organizational pattern because many construction and equipment problems were unique to each specialty.[14]

As projects were completed and began production of war supplies, the need for centralizing DPC administrative activity became increasingly apparent. In 1942, the DPC board established an Administrative Division. It depended in great degree upon personnel of the RFC loan agencies for assistance. The Administrative Division collected rents, discussed with lessees adjustments in rents, checked upon the payment of insurance and taxes, and laid down a more specific set of regulations for contractors operating DPC plants under management and operation agreements.[15] (See Table 2 for the number and location of leases administered by DPC, as of June 30, 1945.)

Other DPC divisions had more limited responsibilities. The Financial (Credit) Division, drawn from RFC's Examining Division, helped the DPC board in making decisions by investigating the status and responsibility of potential DPC lessees and management contractors. It also passed upon certificates of reimbursement which the lessees submitted to DPC for expenses incurred in construction and in purchasing machinery and equipment.[16] The Insurance Division made certain that DPC properties were properly insured and was responsible for collection in case of loss.[17] The Flying School Division supervised the civilian operators of sixty-two flying fields which DPC owned and leased for the primary flying training of cadets of the Army Air Forces.[18] The Machine Tool Division supervised the placing of machine tool orders with tool manufacturers under the three DPC tool pool programs.[19]

The activities of these various offices and divisions were integrated in weekly meetings presided over by DPC's executive vice-president.[20] This pattern endured until the spring of 1944, when changes in the internal structure began to be made to help with the emerging disposal program.

Each DPC project, however large or small, had a sponsor. Originally these were the armed services. During the defense period, the chief sponsor was the War Department, partly because it was the larger armed service and partly because its funds for construction were less adequate than those of the navy. During 1940–1941, the War Department generally used its own funds to build plants of a single-purpose, military nature, such as powder and heavy ordnance.[21] In constructing plants that

Table 2. Defense Plant Corporation: Distribution of Active Leases Serviced, by
Agency, June 30, 1945

Agency	Plancors*	Subleases	Rentras†	Swapcos‡	Totals
Atlanta	12		6	13	31
Birmingham	15		23	8	46
Boston	121	142	88	37	388
Charlotte	13	3	6	4	26
Chicago	213	386	277	50	926
Cleveland	288	166	291	68	813
Dallas	31	5	22	48	106
Denver	9		12	24	45
Detroit	172	815	237	3	1,227
Helena	3				3
Houston	38	30	14	8	90
Jacksonville	14		5	4	23
Kansas City	18	64	14	27	123
Little Rock	10				10
Los Angeles	79	96	42	30	247
Louisville	49	5	4	11	69
Minneapolis	23	1	46	68	138
Nashville	24	10	9	42	85
New Orleans	29	10	7	14	60
New York	235	433	228	90	986
Oklahoma City	17		12	21	50
Omaha	7		2	2	11
Philadelphia	90	88	82	21	281
Portland	23		3	1	27
Richmond	56	8	22	9	95
St. Louis	39	41	59	14	153
Salt Lake City	7			1	8
San Antonio	11		2	2	15
San Francisco	32	2	5	2	41
Seattle	14	5	2	4	25
Spokane	2	1	1	1	5
Washington	26				26
Totals	1,720	2,311	1,521	627	6,179

Source: DPC Rentals—General File, DPC files.
*Plancor is a coined word for a DPC project.
†Rentras are leases of plancor machine tools that had become surplus.
‡Swapcos are plant and/or machinery projects of the Smaller War Plants Corporation
administered by DPC/RFC.

were potentially convertible to postwar civilian use, it sought other methods of finance. Because the deficiencies of the Emergency Plant Facilities contract became manifest almost immediately, the DPC arrangement completely superseded the EPF contract as an alternate means. Although the ratio of DPC expenditure for the navy to all forms of navy plant financing was lower than the parallel ratio for the War Department, DPC was also the navy's prime alternate.[22]

During 1941, the number of government departments and agencies using DPC greatly increased. Late in the spring of 1941, the White House wrote Jesse Jones requesting that RFC assist the Maritime Commission in expanding repair facilities in private shipyards.[23] The Office of Production Management, the successor agency to the National Defense Advisory Commission, also sought DPC's aid in building up production in the steel, aluminum, and magnesium industries. Although these programs were in industries basic to war production, the materials they produced were far back in the process of manufacturing finished war supplies. Consequently, the services were unwilling to sponsor these programs. In time, OPM and its successor after mid-January 1942, the War Production Board, stood second to the War Department in the use made of the DPC mechanism because of the magnitude of these and other basic materials programs.[24]

The number of government agencies sponsoring DPC projects ultimately reached nineteen. For two of these, the War Department and the War Production Board, DPC authorized expenditures for plant in the amount of several billion dollars. For three other agencies (Rubber Reserve Company of RFC, Navy Department, and Petroleum Administration for War), DPC authorized expenditures of between half a billion and a billion dollars. For the Office of Defense Transportation and the Maritime Commission, DPC authorized expenditures in excess of $100 million. DPC authorizations in connection with the other twelve agencies aggregated slightly more than $100 million. A small minority of the projects were jointly sponsored, usually in conjunction with WPB (see Table 3).[25]

Because of changes in the names of war agencies and changes in their internal structure (as well as in the names of their internal components), it is difficult to give a summary statement of the route through which projects reached DPC from any one sponsor, to say nothing of the other eighteen. In all instances where a project was sponsored by an agency other than WPB (OPM), that agency coordinated with WPB. If the project was WPB-sponsored, WPB coordinated with the agencies that would use the basic material to be produced by the WPB project.

Probably projects of the Army Air Forces (AAF) offer the most valid example of procedure within DPC, since AAF-sponsored projects constituted more than one-third of DPC's total investment. These projects traveled, roughly, the following route: Each was formulated at Wright Field, Ohio, the Materiel Center of the Army Air Forces, where a supplier and a location for the additional facilities were tentatively selected. A supply contract was negotiated, and plans for the new facilities received a preliminary statement. From Wright Field the project moved for clearance, consecutively, to the plant facilities subdivisions of the supply staff divisions of Headquarters, Army Air Forces and of the War Department General Staff. After receiving clearance at these levels, the project was transmitted to WPB (OPM) for its consideration. If approved by the WPB subdivisions having jurisdiction over the creation and location of new facilities, the project was sent to the Office of the Undersecretary of War.[26]

Table 3. Dollar Value of DPC Authorizations, by Sponsoring Agency, August 22, 1940–December 31, 1945

Sponsor	Amount authorized
War Department	$4,156,536,000
War Production Board	2,396,612,000
Rubber Reserve Company	836,304,000
Navy Department	694,119,000
Petroleum Administration for War	525,713,000
Office of Defense Transportation	155,099,000
Maritime Commission	104,823,000
Department of Agriculture, Commodity Credit Corporation, Metals Reserve Corporation, Solid Fuels Administration, Civil Aeronautics Authority, Office of Strategic Services, Office of War Information, War Shipping Administration, Foreign Economic Administration, Treasury Department, War Relocation Authority, and National Housing Administration	103,326,000
Total	$8,972,532,000

At this stage, DPC was given notice if the project seemed suited to DPC financing. An "Appendix A" setting forth the preliminary statement of the necessary land and land improvements, buildings, machinery and equipment, portable durable tools and automotive equipment, and estimates of costs accompanied each request. After Pearl Harbor, even before the details of the supply contract had been fully agreed upon between the sponsor and its contractor, the contractor was frequently referred to DPC in an effort to save time.

In all cases the representative of the prospective war supplier was first directed to a DPC attorney. If need for the new equipment or the new plant was urgent, the DPC attorney might request at this stage a "letter of intent" from the Board of Directors even prior to negotiating an agreement. The letter of intent authorized the supplier to place orders for machinery and equipment and, in rarer instances, to commence plant construction.[27]

In normal circumstances, following his discussion with the DPC attorney, the representative of the supplier was referred to other DPC divisions. If the project involved the purchase of land and construction of facilities in addition to the acquisition of machinery and equipment, he was referred to the Real Estate Division. If special legal problems were associated with the purchase of land, an attorney from the Real Estate Legal Section of DPC was called in. In addition, the supplier's representative was directed to the Credit Division to provide financial data and to the Insurance Division to consider insurance matters. Likewise, the visitor was sent to the Engineering Division and to its Construction Section for preliminary discussions with respect to construction and to the Auditing Division for a discussion of matters pertaining to accounting records. Meanwhile, a member of the Credit Division was preparing a summary document on the project, the so-called "board sheet," for presentation, along with the agreement, to the DPC board.[28] Frequently, DPC was able to act upon the request of the sponsoring agency within twenty-four hours. A survey made in October 1941 revealed that 43 of 186 lease agreements had been negotiated and signed within a twenty-four-hour period. Only twenty-two cases—chiefly those in which the federal loan administrator had taken an interest—had required more than twenty days. This record was further improved during the war.[29]

After the lease agreement had been drawn up and a board sheet prepared, these documents were routed through the office of the DPC general counsel and executive vice-president for review before they went to the board. A Bureau of the Budget representative wrote of a DPC board meeting:

> The Board functions in a very informal fashion. The Chairman of the Board is nominally in charge of the meeting, but he moves in and out of the room and one of his subordinates will take over in his absence. For example, the Chairman of the Board of DPC is Sam Husbands.[30] When he would leave the room, John Snyder, Executive Vice-President of the Corporation, would carry on the meeting. The agenda of the meeting is prepared the night before by Husbands or Snyder and circulated to all those who will be present. Anyone on the staff of DPC who has a case that requires action by the Board presents that case at the Board meeting. Board members sit haphazardly around the table and in no way constitute a court on one side of

the room with those who present the cases on the other side of the room. Anyone may present a case to the Board, that is, one of the DPC lawyers, one of the engineers, or a member of the Credit Division will bring to the Board's attention whatever matters are necessary for action. The presentation of cases rotates around the table, and there is no confusion as one case is disposed of and another considered. As the men present their cases, they may, after they have concluded, leave the Board room or stay to comment on other cases that are coming up. Most of the discussion is carried on by the Board members and the official who presents the case, but in a few instances, non-Board members are called on for points of information or suggestion. Any action taken by the Board is promptly recorded by a clerk, and about every ten minutes a messenger carries this record of formal action to the Office of the Secretary of the Board, where decisions are sent out over the wires. Proceedings are unhurried, but there is very little time wasted.[31]

If the agreement negotiated with the supplier's representative was approved by the board, it went next to the company for approval. It was also referred to the sponsoring agency in cases in which the sponsor had agreed to bind itself to either full or partial reimbursement of DPC through a so-called "take-out" letter.

Following the return of the signed agreement from the lessee, the DPC board passed a disbursement resolution. This resolution prescribed procedures for fulfilling the terms of the agreement in regard to acquisition of the land, plant construction, and the purchase of equipment and authorized payment of the expenditures. These expenditures were payable by the Federal Reserve Bank in the district where the project was located from a credit established in the amount of the DPC commitment.[32]

From time to time amendments to the DPC lease and the related disbursement resolution proved necessary when the original authorization of funds for the project was too small or when the project was either enlarged or cut back at the request of the sponsor. In the former instance, the lessee made its request for funds directly to DPC for review and approval.

If the amendment provided for additional facilities, the matter was handled in the same way as if it were a new project. Requests for additional facilities required approval by the sponsor and (if the sponsor was other than WPB) by WPB, before submission to DPC. If the amendment provided for a cutback or cancellation of a project under construction, that request also came from the sponsor. DPC was obligated to follow the request of the sponsor, but, if necessary, could authorize additional expenditures to protect the government's investment.[33]

As DPC gained experience, it gradually standardized both its procedures and its lease and management agreements. In no other way could it have handled its volume of work effectively. Over time, it evolved five forms of agreement. DPC's intent in devising these forms was to protect its investment while freeing the initiative of industry in constructing and operating the plants. This was done by leaving industry free to exercise its superior know-how in carrying out the lease terms subject only to a minimum check by DPC. Wherever possible, self-policing by the lessee was substituted for direct DPC control. Moreover, DPC sought, through an explicit purchase option in most instances, to encourage the lessee to build an efficient plant at minimum cost and to maintain the plant well while in operation. Inclusion of the option encouraged the manufacturer to hope that the plant someday might become his. Although DPC sought standardization in these forms, it did not seek rigidity, for the forms were flexed when necessary to meet the problems of the individual lessee.

Forms 1 and 2, devised during DPC's evolutionary period in 1940, were the most common types of DPC lease agreements. The first form was used in conjunction with nominal rentals; the second was designed for leases with money rentals.[34] Variations of these forms were used in leases covering machinery only.

A third, more specialized, form of lease agreement was evolved in connection with the construction of plant and the purchase of equipment in the high-octane gasoline industry.[35] Still another form of agreement was devised for the synthetic rubber plants.[36] In both of these instances, the lease of DPC facilities was tied into the operating programs of other RFC wartime subsidiaries. Leases of aviation gasoline facilities were tied indirectly to supply contracts of the lessee with Defense Supplies Corporation. Facilities for the manufacture of synthetic rubber and its components were in all cases leased to companies manufacturing for the account of the Rubber Reserve Company.

For still fewer cases, a final form, a management and operation agreement, was drawn up, in which the contracting company agreed to operate a DPC plant for the account of DPC in return for a fee. This type of agreement was used primarily in instances where the element of risk to the potential operator was so large that the operator was unwilling to assume the status of lessee. Ultimately, thirty-nine of the total of more than twenty-three hundred projects fell into this category. The management and operation agreements closely paralleled the other forms of agreement. Although these agreements included special provisions establishing mechanisms for the payment of operating costs, for the payment of fees to the contractor for supervising construction and for management, and for controlling the disposition of the project, the document basically consisted of provisions governing construction and equipment and the respective rights and obligations of the two parties during construction and the term of occupancy.[37]

The terms of lease authorized the lessee to draw up plans for the construction and equipment of new plant, subject to approval by DPC and by the sponsoring agency or department. The lessee was also granted authority to subcontract in carrying out construction and in purchasing machinery, subject to DPC approval. DPC obligated itself to advance funds to meet the costs of construction and to pay promptly all bills for machinery. The lease provided, however, that in cases of payment of bills for machinery, the lessee was to certify to the need for the machinery, that prices were fair and reasonable, and that the bills were proper for payment. Overhead expenses of the lessee not directly associated with construction or the purchase of the machinery were excluded as charges against DPC, and a maximum figure for the cost of both plant and equipment was written into the agreement.

The agreement provided flexibility in the use of DPC equipment, for the lessee was authorized, after notifying DPC in writing, to transfer machinery and equipment to other lessee-owned plants. The lessee could also lease or lend machinery and equipment to its subcontractors, subject to the written approval of DPC and of the sponsor, but this machinery could be used solely for the production of war goods. The agreement specified that only charges paid by the lessee in operating the plant were to be figured into the price charged the government or a supplier of the government for war goods.

Termination of the agreement short of the date set for the life of the lease was possible at any time either party found that the plant and equipment were no longer of "substantial use" to the lessee in fulfilling government supply contracts. In such an instance, either party could inform the other of its desire for termination. The contract provided, however, that DPC would request or accept termination only with the consent of the sponsor, for in conformity with its role as a mechanism for the war effort, it took no action of a policy nature on its own initiative. In the event of the expiration, termination, or cancellation of a lease governing the use of DPC machinery within a plant owned by the lessee, DPC was obligated to remove the machinery within sixty days. If it did not do so, the lessee was authorized to remove and store machinery at DPC's expense.

Most agreements carried a purchase option giving the lessee the right to purchase all, but not part, of its leased facilities. Exceptions were made for projects representing about one-fourth of DPC's total investment where it was thought socially desirable to keep the hands of government free in determining postwar policy.[38] In the case of nominal rentals, the purchase option provided that the lessee might purchase the DPC facilities it operated within eight months of the execution of the lease at the actual cost of the facilities. Thereafter, and for a period up to ninety days following the termination, expiration, or cancellation of the lease, the lessee could purchase the facilities at cost less depreciation. In the case of leases involving money rentals, the terms were slightly more complicated. Throughout the life of the lease, the lessee could purchase the facilities at cost plus interest at 4 percent per year less rentals and less interest on the rentals at 4 percent per year. If the lessee chose to exercise the option after the first eight months, however, DPC required the lessee to purchase at cost less depreciation if the latter alternative would yield DPC a greater return.[39]

Depreciation was calculated in both cases on the basis of rates adapted from those used by the Bureau of Internal Revenue in determining allowances for depreciation for income tax purposes. They were, in fact, somewhat higher than those of the Bureau of Internal Revenue because of the excessive wear and tear resulting from the tempo of operations during a war period. The National Defense Advisory Commission drew up these rates in connection with one of the purchase clauses contained in its Emergency Plant Facilities contract.[40] DPC, in turn, appropriated them for its option provision.

Although the lessee could exercise its purchase option only with respect to the whole of the DPC plancor during the ninety-day option period following termination of the lease, it could also negotiate for all or any part of the facilities. DPC agreed not to sell the plant and equipment to any other party for an additional ninety-day period without first having made the same offer to the former lessee. A few of the leases that contained no purchase options, particularly the synthetic rubber leases, also contained the right of first refusal in some form.

All DPC leases contained rental provisions that varied from nominal rentals of one dollar per year to rentals designed to repay over a five-year period the entire cost of the facilities plus interest. The rentals were assessed and collected in a number of different ways depending, chiefly, on the nature of the market for the product.[41]

One dollar per year leases were used most frequently in the case of large DPC plants where the lessees were manufacturing solely for the government and were adding no rental charge in determining the price for the product. Such rental arrangements had the advantage of simplicity. They kept the cost of the facilities totally separate from the cost of supplies and left the problem of repayment for the facilities solely between DPC and the sponsoring service department or agency. In June 1945, a total of 1,658 projects, exclusive of flying schools, were in operation on a rental basis. Of this number, 199 were being operated under one dollar per year lease agreements. These 199 projects averaged approximately $15 million each in investment.[42]

A second type of rental—"depreciation rental"—was written into the lease agreements if subcontractors or contractors sold in a competitive market. In such an instance, when it was not possible to determine the ultimate destination of the product—for example, an airplane part that might wind up in either a civilian or a military aircraft—a money rental was charged sufficient to cover the cost of depreciation on the facilities.

This rental was fair because otherwise the manufacturer would have an advantage in the civilian market over competitors who had to consider depreciation of their plant and equipment as a factor in determining price for their output.

The third type of rental—"full rental"—was used particularly during the defense period when DPC was concentrating more seriously on recovering its investment, plus interest, over a five-year period. The rental charged per year was intended to approximate 22 percent of the cost of the facilities. Protests by officials of the Office of Price Administration at the effect of such large rental payments upon prices helped to discourage its use.[43]

Methods used in figuring money rentals varied widely. The most common method was to pay a fixed percentage of the cost of the facilities as rent. Another common method was to take a percentage of gross or net sales that, figured at 80 percent of the estimated capacity, would give the rental return desired. Other methods included fixing charges per unit produced or using some unit of weight or measure, such as per pound, gallon, or ton. In cases where no other base seemed feasible, rentals were figured in terms of machine hours or kilowatts of electricity used. Percentage-of-cost rentals tended to be used if the manufacturer could feel sure of his ultimate market; percentage of sales or of production were used when fear of a reduced supply contract made the manufacturer reluctant to accept a percentage-of-cost rental.[44] (Table 4 shows classification of leases according to the basis of rental, as of June 30, 1945.)

"Take-out" letters, designed to protect DPC from loss, were initiated with the Wright and Bendix agreements of October 1940 and were continued throughout the war. In general, take-outs were received from permanent government departments or agencies, such as the War Department, Navy Department, and Maritime Commission, that could expect appropriations from Congress in the postwar period. Take-outs were also submitted by the Rubber Reserve Company to cover the extensive synthetic rubber program on which DPC had embarked. They were usually not received from impermanent war agencies, which were created for a specific purpose and could look forward to only a short life. Approximately two-thirds of the value of DPC's investment was covered by take-outs.[45]

The take-outs, which were not a part of the lease but an accompanying document, varied as to the rental terms of the specific lease agreement. In cases of dollar-a-year rentals, the first few take-outs specified that the War or Navy Department would pay 60 percent of the cost of each sponsored project by June 30, 1942, and would pay the balance from future congressional appropriations when and if made. In December 1940, at the request of Undersecretary of War Patterson, DPC agreed to reduce the initial payment on future agreements to 40 percent. The rate of interest

Table 4. Defense Plant Corporation: Classification of Leases Serviced according to Basis of Rental, with Rent Returns, as of June 30, 1945

	Number	Estimated Cost	Total Rent Received
Plants on $1.00 per year rental	199	$3,106,952,973	$ 640
Plants on percentage of expenditures rental	930	1,146,950,362	136,491,062
Plants on percentage of sales and/or production rental	529	1,849,482,162	329,100,250
Machinery leases (rentras)	1,521	23,556,606	2,329,970
Subleases (under plancors)	2,311		2,330,555
Flying Schools (8 now in operation)	62	41,686,071	48,295,038
Total Active Cases	5,552	$6,168,628,173	$518,547,514
Terminated leases (plancors)	200	$ 376,519,033	$ 19,759,740
Terminated leases (rentras)	118	1,659,008	101,610
Terminated leases (subleases)	188		147,485
Total DPC Cases Serviced	6,058	$6,546,806,214	$539,556,349

Source: DPC Rentals—General File, DPC files.

on the amount of the deficiency, originally 4 percent per year, was also reduced at this time to 1.5 percent. Subsequently, early in 1942, the amount of the firm commitment was increased to 50 percent, where it remained for the balance of the war.[46]

The terms of the take-outs varied between the services in instances when a depreciation rental was charged. Under such conditions, the navy take-out provided for a 40 percent firm commitment and a 60 percent deficiency. The War Department, in contrast, generally bound itself to pay from current appropriations two-fifths of the difference between the estimated cost of the project and the estimated return from rentals and to pay the remainder out of future appropriations.

The take-outs also provided for the transfer of title to the sponsoring department or agency on property for which DPC had been reimbursed in full either from rent or payments by the sponsor. This occurred in fourteen instances during and after the war. The largest transfer, a $25.5 million smokeless powder plant at Memphis, Tennessee, consisted of two plancors that had been sponsored by the Ordnance Department of the War Department. Transfers could also have occurred in several other cases where DPC had been fully reimbursed, but the sponsors chose not to act.[47]

Payments required from the sponsors by the terms of the take-outs were met faithfully, but, except in cases where the sponsor took title, additional payments were rarely made. Consequently, as a means for recovering the DPC investment, the take-outs proved of little value.[48]

6

Extent and Fields of DPC Plant Financing Activities

DPC's plant financing included projects in the thousands and expenditures in the billions. So numerous and diverse were the projects that thus far little systematic effort has been made to deal with their number and diversity. Rather, the intent has been to make clear the various processes and procedures by which those projects came into being. The individual projects are relevant only to World War II; the processes, on the other hand, could potentially be useful in a new emergency.

The extent of DPC operations offers impressive evidence of the effectiveness of the processes and procedures used. DPC fields of activity, for example, included plant and equipment for manufacture of airplanes, of aircraft engines and aircraft parts, and of aviation gasoline. They included flying fields, which DPC owned and leased to civilian contractors for training pilots. They included metals essential to the manufacture of war supplies: aluminum, magnesium, pig iron and steel, tin, nickel, copper, lead, and zinc. DPC also helped enlarge the nation's machine tool plant—a necessity for any large general expansion of industry.

DPC's investment in other facilities was also of major magnitude. It built and equipped plants for the manufacture of guns, shells, and tanks. It supported the great expansion in production of chemicals, such as alcohol, toluene, sulphuric acid, oxygen, and acetylene, that were vital in many cases both to the manufacture of munitions and to general industry. It supplied the plant for nearly all the huge new synthetic rubber development and made substantial investments for expanding the radio and communications industry. DPC built and equipped shipyards and erected plant for the manufacture of ship parts. It also invested smaller sums in such activities as the manufacture of jewel bearings and diamond dies, hemp, processed foods, and medical supplies.

DPC made sizable investments in still other and more miscellaneous fields. These involved the construction or purchase of several pipelines, especially the "Big Inch" and "Little Big Inch," of tugs and barges, and of tank cars for the transportation of oil and petroleum products. They included the purchase of trucks and trailers for lease to haulers of dry freight, of passenger buses and streetcars, and of troop sleeping cars and kitchen cars. They also included construction of housing adjacent to government war plants and flying fields.

Tables 5 and 6 show the extent and timing of DPC financing and the various major categories of investment.

Aviation.   No industry in World War II required as great an expansion to meet war needs as did aircraft. John D. Biggers, director of the Division of Production, Office of Production Management, told a House committee early in 1941:

> We think of the automotive industry as the industrial miracle of the twentieth century, but please consider that we are faced with the herculean task of building up the aircraft industry in three short years—1940, 1941, 1942—from the small beginning to a more gigantic output than the automotive industry obtained during 30 years of spectacular development. In other words, airplane production in 1939 was about equal to the automobile production of 1910. But the airplane production of 1942 must substantially exceed the $3,000,000,000 of automobile production obtained in 1940.[1]

The necessity for expansion became even greater with the advent of war. Most aircraft companies were relatively small enterprises before the war and did not have funds for expansion. Nor were many banks anxious to participate in the financing of facilities of doubtful peacetime utility unless the terms were highly favorable and, consequently, adverse to the government. Ultimately, almost three-fourths of the expansion was financed through DPC.[2]

DPC's first lease agreement was signed in September 1940 with the Packard Motor Car Company for equipment to permit Packard to manufacture three thousand Rolls Royce airplane engines for Britain and for the United States government. This order was later expanded manyfold.[3]

A more important effort to break the airplane engine bottleneck was made when DPC executed a lease agreement with the Wright Aeronautical Corporation in October 1940 for a new plant at Lockland, Ohio. The plant, built within 142 days from the beginning of construction, was in production within a year after the lease was signed. Including later expansions, it consisted of thirty buildings containing 161,775 pieces of machinery and equipment scattered over 247 acres.[4]

Fourteen of the fifteen largest airplane engine plants constructed during the war were wholly or partially DPC-financed. The largest, a plant at Chicago operated by the Chrysler Corporation, covered 476 acres and represented an investment of nearly $170 million.[5] Overall, DPC disbursed approximately $1.357 billion for airplane engine plants.

DPC also entered early into the creation of new facilities to meet aircraft

Table 5. RFC Authorizations for Defense and War Facilities, June 25, 1940–December 31, 1945, by Date of Authorization and Use of Funds (thousands of dollars)

Date of Authorization	Amount Authorized				
	Total	Construction	Equipment	Land (DPC Projects)	RFC Loans to Construction Contractors
Total	$9,783,004	$3,371,115	$6,159,166	$142,802	$109,921
1940:					
3d Quarter	31,380	14,147	16,785	425	23
4th Quarter	289,626	92,052	191,755	4,344	1,475
1941:					
1st Quarter	185,501	45,458	136,904	1,742	1,397
2d Quarter	282,057	116,628	155,043	10,351	35
3d Quarter	679,226	213,575	453,443	11,226	982
4th Quarter	636,138	170,373	439,513	26,097	155
1942:					
1st Quarter	2,599,098	727,149	1,836,971	27,752	7,226
2d Quarter	1,616,729	454,778	1,136,708	11,792	13,451
3d Quarter	552,426	242,979	289,649	7,370	12,428
4th Quarter	378,579	255,056	107,346	4,984	11,193
1943:					
1st Quarter	690,872	464,427	205,528	9,893	11,024
2d Quarter	276,041	44,037	221,591	3,941	6,472
3d Quarter	284,323	210,858	61,276	4,247	7,942
4th Quarter	254,521	91,320	153,929	3,855	5,417
1944:					
1st Quarter	263,056	109,166	141,429	3,320	9,141
2d Quarter	175,882	13,482	150,347	2,433	9,620
3d Quarter	111,909	27,553	81,353	1,648	1,355
4th Quarter	45,824	6,886	36,005	673	2,260
1945:					
1st Quarter	285,987	52,213	227,533	4,530	1,711
2d Quarter	115,284	9,973	98,317	1,751	5,243
3d Quarter	26,582	8,357	16,457	397	1,371
4th Quarter	1,963	648	1,284	31	

Source: RFC Research and Statistics Division.

assembly needs. On October 25, 1940, it signed lease agreements with Curtiss-Wright for construction of aircraft plants at Buffalo, Columbus, Ohio, and St. Louis. In each of these cases the expenditure authorized ranged between $12 million and $15 million. A week later, DPC drew up a lease agreement with Consolidated Aircraft Corporation for construction

Table 6. RFC Financing of Defense and War Facilities (Defense Plant
Corporation), as of December 31, 1945

Field of Investment	Authorizations (in millions)	Disbursements (in millions)	Disbursements (GAO)
Aircraft engine	$1,678	$1,420	$1,357
Aircraft assembly	680	602	592
Aircraft parts	825	706	665
Flying training facilities	71	54	
Aviation gasoline	324	245	237
	(272)*	(191)*	
	(55)†	(55)†	
Aluminum	842	702	684
		(31)†	
Magnesium	449	398	428
		(26)†	
Iron and steel	1,148	947	951
		(109)†	
Metals and minerals	178	149	138
	(8)‡	(5)‡	
Machine tools	91	71	92
Ordnance	495	383	285
Industrial chemicals	214	132	
Synthetic rubber	1,056	783	740
Radio and communications	120	88	81
Ships and parts	201	138	132
Miscellaneous plants	142	91	
	(280)†		
Transport	423	336	301
		(44)†	
Housing	29	27	
Miscellaneous	6	4	299
	(196)†		
Disbursements on RFC loans for facilities not elsewhere included (est.)	___	(90)§	___
DPC Total	$8,972	$7,276	$6,982
Total by other Means	($810)	($542)	
RFC Total	($9,783)	($7,818)	

Source: RFC Research and Statistics Division. The first two columns are from a
table prepared by the RFC Research and Statistics Division as of December 31,
1945. The third column (Disbursements—GAO) is from an audit of the Defense
Plant Corporation, completed in November 1946, as of June 30, 1945: Comptroller General of the United States, *Report on Audit of Reconstruction Finance Corporation and Affiliated Corporations for the Fiscal Year Ended June 30, 1945: Defense Plant
Corporation,* 80th Cong., 1st Sess., H. Doc. 474, 4:71. The figures used in the text of

this chapter for disbursements by category are usually from the GAO report as probably more accurate.

*Defense Supplies Corporation loans or advances.

†RFC loans.

‡Metals Reserve Corporation loans.

§The additional $90,000,000 in disbursements on RFC loans for facilities was comprised of a large number of small loans in practically every field of investment listed above except synthetic rubber.

of a $14.5 million plant at San Diego, California, for the manufacture of navy planes. Each authorization was subsequently greatly increased.

The construction record of the Consolidated Aircraft plant suggests the speed with which many DPC projects were completed. Even prior to signing the lease, Consolidated had placed orders for a portion of the machinery and equipment. The plant was put into partial operation in June and into full production on October 20, 1941. Although originally intended for the manufacture of navy aircraft, the larger part of the output went to the army. The Consolidated plant at San Diego ultimately turned out 6,725 B-24s—approximately one-fifth of all medium-range, four-engine bombers produced in the United States during the war. In addition, the San Diego plant produced an aggregate of 3,083 other aircraft, including B-32 very heavy bombers.[6]

The giant among aircraft assembly plants was the Ford-operated B-24 plant at Willow Run, Michigan. Costing approximately $86 million, it included a complete assembly plant in a two-mile-long building. DPC investment in aircraft assembly plants by the conclusion of the war totaled $592 million.

The third phase of manufacturing required for getting airplanes into the skies and keeping them there was that of providing a vast supply of aircraft parts. On October 18, 1940, DPC entered into the first of several lease agreements with Bendix Aviation Corporation. The expansion thus begun was extended to include a large number of other companies. Because these manufacturers required much less capital for individual plants than was necessary for either the manufacture of aircraft engines or aircraft assembly, DPC financed expansions for many relatively small firms in this phase of war production.[7] Its investment in parts manufacture amounted finally to approximately $665 million.

Aviation Gasoline. Each thousand new combat aircraft created additional requirements for the potent and highly combustible hundred-octane gasoline necessary for their effective operation. The number of combat aircraft manufactured increased from 11,106 for the eighteen months through December 1941 to 24,864 in 1942, 54,077 in 1943, and 74,135 in 1944. Another 35,157 were turned out during the first seven months of

1945.[8] Production of hundred-octane gasoline was required in an even greater ratio of increase.

During the fall of 1941, production of all aviation gasolines was running at about 40,000 barrels per day. By the spring of 1945, this figure had increased to 566,000 barrels daily, 523,000 of which were hundred-octane gasoline. To achieve this expansion, nearly $900 million was invested in new facilities. Of this amount, approximately $237 million was in DPC-titled plant. The balance was privately owned.[9] Here also, however, the role of RFC was significant. DPC's sister subsidiary, Defense Supplies Corporation (DSC), loaned or advanced nearly $191 million to private oil companies for facilities expansion, and RFC lent $55 million to another refining corporation.[10]

Beginning in 1942, at the request of the Petroleum Administration for War, DPC entered into a series of agreements. In one case, DPC built a complete hundred-octane gasoline refinery, the Abercrombie-Magnolia plant at Sweeney, Texas, costing approximately $28 million. In nearly every other instance, DPC-constructed facilities were additions to existing refineries. These agreements were estimated to have swelled aviation gasoline production by approximately eighty thousand barrels daily.[11]

Flying Training Facilities. At the request of the War Department, in the fall of 1941 DPC purchased forty-four private pilot training schools with which the Army Air Forces had contracts for the first stage of flying training for air cadets. As a result, the AAF gained a larger degree of control over the schools without committing its personnel or funds, both of which were in short supply. DPC could also better control the profits made by the schools through periodic adjustments in the rental rates.[12]

The number of these DPC flying schools later grew to sixty-two scattered across the southern United States from Florida to California. They provided primary flying training for most American military pilots, as well as several thousand British and other foreign pilots. For DPC the program was a bright spot, for it more than paid out. DPC disbursements of $41.9 million were less than the $48.4 million it received from rentals and the sale of some of the airfields.[13]

During 1943, DPC undertook an aircraft purchase operation closely allied in purpose to the flying field program. It authorized an expenditure of $25 million to buy aircraft from individual private owners for lease to the Civil Aeronautics Authority. The CAA used these aircraft to give preliminary flying training to civilians in order to increase the flow of pilot trainees into the armed services.[14]

Aluminum. Aircraft production and other requirements, including munitions, created a demand for more aluminum in the defense period than existing facilities could supply. As in aircraft production, the need promised to outrun peacetime requirements. Private expansion by Alcoa, the longtime aluminum monopoly, provided part of the necessary increase; a smaller amount was provided when Reynolds Metals Company, aided by RFC loans, invaded the field. But, as noted earlier, the bulk of the expansion was gained from plants financed and owned by DPC and built and operated by Alcoa.

Following Pearl Harbor, the demand for primary aluminum again shot upward. The War Production Board called for an enlargement in the capacity of the Alcoa-operated alumina plant at Hurricane Creek, Arkansas, and for the construction of a new billion-pound alumina plant at Baton Rouge, Louisiana, to help bring about an increase of 640 million pounds annually in primary aluminum. In order to achieve this increase, WPB requested the expansion of three Alcoa-operated DPC plants and the construction of three additional plants. There was no time to debate who would operate the new plants. In each instance, WPB named Alcoa. To speed construction, DPC issued letters of intent during the prolonged negotiation of leases. Its overall investment in the alumina and primary aluminum programs amounted to approximately $250 million.[15]

Because of private expansion by Alcoa, RFC loans to Reynolds, and DPC's financing of government-titled plant, peak production of primary aluminum was achieved in October 1943. This production, at an annual rate of 2.257 billion pounds, was actually in excess of needs. The DPC plants were responsible for slightly more than half of this amount.[16]

DPC disbursed an even larger sum for the construction and equipment of aluminum fabricating facilities. In some instances DPC built complete plants; in others it supplied equipment for lessee-owned plants. Expansion in this field was particularly necessary to provide aluminum fabrications for aircraft. By the end of the war, DPC had expanded capacity in aluminum extrusions by 30 percent; in castings by 25 percent; in forgings by 45 percent; in tubing by 40 percent.[17] The DPC investment in this phase totaled more than $400 million.

A further and much smaller area of DPC activity grew out of the fear of German submarine interference with bauxite shipments from Dutch Guiana to the United States. Late in 1941, at the request of OPM, DPC authorized an experimental project to determine whether alumina could be derived from alunite.[18] During 1942, when the submarine menace became real, three more experimental projects were authorized to explore other possible sources of alumina. Approximately $17 million was invested in these projects, and an additional $5 million expended in operating costs. Although no need developed for so desperate a substitute, three of the plants were successful in producing alumina.[19]

Magnesium. The problem of securing a supply of magnesium adequate to defense needs was similar to that of aluminum. Like aluminum, magnesium was an important metal in aircraft production. It also was much used in the manufacture of incendiary bombs and flares. And even more than aluminum, the production of magnesium, which was still in its infancy, called for government financing.

Through negotiations recounted earlier, production of this "war baby" was expanded fortyfold. DPC's share of the financing amounted to $295 million, which was more than three-fourths of the whole. In January 1944, when magnesium was being turned out at an annual rate of 491 million pounds, the DPC plants were providing 431 million. DPC also invested in excess of $33 million in magnesium fabricating plants.[20]

Steel. As noted previously, a steel industry expansion program emerged in the summer of 1941 only after prolonged controversy. OPM and its successor, WPB, sought to provide this increased capacity partly through private initiative and partly through government construction. Approximately $1.3 billion was invested in new facilities during the war by the iron and steel industry. Of this amount, RFC loans accounted for $109 million. The Kaiser plant at Fontana, California, was wholly built with RFC money, and $12 million was advanced by RFC for the smaller Sheffield plant at Houston, Texas. In carrying out this expansion, private industry availed itself, in the main, of the tax amortization privilege. The remainder of the new capacity, except for approximately $250 million in projects directly financed by the Navy Department, War Department, and Maritime Commission, was constructed by DPC. DPC's investment in additional iron and steel plant and equipment amounted to about $951 million.[21]

Of DPC facilities in all fields, the most costly was the gigantic Geneva Steel plant at Geneva, Utah, in which DPC invested more than $200 million. The plant was constructed without fee by the United States Steel Corporation and was operated without fee under a management contract by a specially established subsidiary, the Geneva Steel Corporation. Despite shortages and other delays in construction, Geneva Steel began production in October 1943, within two years of the signing of the contract. The Geneva plant, called by *Fortune* "perhaps the finest steel mill in the world," was a completely integrated enterprise capable of producing a wide array of products. Covering sixteen hundred acres, it included eleven miles of railroad, raw material facilities, coke ovens, blast furnaces, and steelmaking and finishing equipment.[22]

In addition to Geneva and other large plants, DPC made numerous additions to private facilities. Negotiation of these projects was occasionally troublesome, for iron and steel companies were sometimes reluctant to sell DPC land on which its share of intermingled or scrambled facilities would be located. If the problem could be solved in no other way, DPC settled for a lease sufficiently long to permit normal depreciation of the facilities. DPC invested in excess of $110 million in scrambled facilities.[23]

In sum, DPC financed over 40 percent of the expansion in the nation's steel ingot capacity, 44 percent in blast furnace, 37 percent in coke, and 43 percent in sinter capacity. It participated in the expansion of virtually every segment of the steel industry. It invested in a total of 205 plants and added 6,226,460 of the 15,300,000 tons of new steel ingot capacity created during the war. Stated another way, DPC facilities added to the pig iron and steel plant of the United States an annual output roughly equivalent to that of prewar France or Japan.[24]

Other Metals and Minerals. Although another RFC wartime subsidiary, Metals Reserve Corporation, was the principal agent in increasing the supply of such vitally needed metals as tin, nickel, copper, lead, and zinc, Defense Plant Corporation was called on to build smelting and other necessary facilities. Most plants built for processing these metals were sponsored by WPB; a small fraction were sponsored by the Metals Reserve Corporation.

As early as the summer of 1940, the State Department and the Advisory Commission to the Council of National Defense discussed with RFC the feasibility of constructing a tin smelter in Texas to process Bolivian ores. No such smelter had existed in the United States since World War I. DPC entered into negotiations with N. V. Billiton Maatschappij, a Dutch company with long experience in tin smelting, Tin Processing Corporation, a New York subsidiary of the Dutch company, and Metals Reserve Corporation. In February 1941, an agreement was reached providing for a DPC-constructed tin smelter to be operated at Texas City by the Tin Processing Corporation. During the war, it produced more than ninety thousand tons of fine tin, or about 40 percent of all new tin consumed in those years.[25]

DPC played an important part in processing a number of other metals and minerals. It invested more than $32 million in a troublesome project at Nicaro, Cuba, for facilities designed to produce 32 million pounds of nickel annually. The corporation made several important investments, chiefly in Arizona, for plant and equipment in the copper mining industry. It also made sizable investments in one or more plants in various locations for the production of such metals and minerals as lead, zinc, chrome, vanadium, beryllium, molybdenum, graphite, manganese, tantalum, fluorspar, coal, cyanite, antimony, and silica. DPC's overall investment in plant and equipment for processing these metals and minerals amounted to almost $138 million.[26]

Machine Tools. Production of machine tools in sufficient quantity was basic to all defense and war industry. No great increase in defense and war production was possible without a nearly comparable increase in the plant and machinery for manufacturing the machines needed to turn out the supplies. A portion of the necessary expansion was provided by the industry, using private capital and stimulated both by orders and by tax amortization. But this was not enough.

DPC was the primary agency called upon to fill the gap. Mainly under the sponsorship of the War Department, it supplied the investment necessary for constructing 35 new machine tool plants and for purchasing additional machinery for another 131 plants. Its investment in the machine tool industry, nearly $92 million, was slightly larger than the amount of expansion privately financed.[27]

DPC was called upon to stimulate machine tool production not alone through the construction of new plant and acquisition of equipment, but also by placing advance orders for machine tools in a major pooling operation. It also operated smaller pools in cutting tools and gages. These pools were so important that they are discussed in the following chapter.

Ordnance. Many ordnance plants, such as powder plants, were potentially useful only in wartime. Usually, the armed services constructed and controlled these plants directly, although early in the defense period the War Department also considered alternative forms of financing. Other types of ordnance, such as tanks, could be manufactured in factories more readily convertible from or to civilian industry. Under War or Navy Department sponsorship, DPC was involved in the construction of plant and the purchase of equipment for the production of a wide variety of ordnance.

Prior to the development of an extensive American defense program, the allied nations, chiefly Britain and, in lesser degree, France, had made substantial investments in American ordnance facilities to supplement their production at home. As the United States began to gird for defense, one potentially available source of military supplies was these foreign-financed plants. Moreover, if the United States purchased these plants and permitted Britain and France to share in the product, Britain and France would derive sorely needed dollar exchange.

During 1941, at the request of the War Department, DPC acquired a number of British-owned ordnance and aircraft engine facilities. In March, it bought four large machine gun factories and the British-owned, Du Pont-constructed Tennessee Powder Company at Memphis, Tennessee. This Memphis plant was designed to produce 160,000 pounds of smokeless powder, 80,000 pounds of TNT, and 16,000 pounds of DNT daily.[28] In June, by letter of the president, RFC was ordered to purchase any British plant when requested to do so by the secretary of war or the secretary of the navy.[29] In handling these purchases, DPC spent approximately $100 million.

In addition, DPC made numerous other investments in ordnance facilities. It constructed plants and purchased equipment for the production of tanks and tank engines, machine guns, howitzers, cannon, antiaircraft guns, height and range finders, fire control instruments, shell casings, cartridge casings, fuses, bombs, armor plate, and steel helmets. DPC put about $285 million in 108 plants which it either constructed and equipped or for which it purchased machinery.[30]

Industrial Chemicals. Industrial chemicals had many uses for war industry. Some, like toluene, were important ingredients in high explosives. Others, like alcohol, served a long list of war needs, including smokeless powder, chemical warfare gas, and synthetic rubber. By 1944, synthetic rubber alone was using half again as much industrial alcohol as the 217 million gallons produced in 1941.[31] As in other fields of industry requiring expansion, DPC proved to be a major resource.

DPC's assistance in increasing alcohol production was probably its most significant contribution in the chemical field. The need for this industrial agent required a near tripling of the supply available in 1941. At the same time, as a result of competing demands for sugar, industrial alcohol plants on the East Coast using molasses as a base were being deprived of their raw material. Because of DPC investment, by the fall of 1942, six of these East Coast plants were converted from molasses to grain for manufacturing alcohol. Distilleries, particularly in the Midwest, were diverted from the manufacture of beverages to the supply of industrial alcohol. Since 190-proof alcohol was desired and since many of the distilleries were reluctant to finance the costs of conversion and of new equipment, DPC met these costs in numerous cases. It increased alcohol production further through the construction of new plants. A plant in Philadelphia with a capacity of 55 million gallons annually was the largest of these facilities. Another, at Omaha, Nebraska, had a capacity of 22.75 million gallons. The total DPC investment of about $39 million provided additional capacity of 246 million gallons per year.[32]

DPC financed new plants and supplied additional machinery for old plants for the production of many other industrial chemicals. These DPC projects producing munitions-related chemicals, such as toluene, sulphuric acid, oleum, and potassium perchlorate, were usually sponsored by the War Department. Many other chemical projects were sponsored by the War Production Board, including the production of oxygen, acetylene, DDT, ammonia, caustic soda, chlorine, superphosphate, freon, anhydrous aluminum chloride, and phthalic anhydride. DPC disbursed approximately $93 million for plant and equipment in conjunction with these projects.[33]

Synthetic Rubber. The fall of Singapore and the Philippines early in 1942 and the consequent cutting off of the prime source of natural rubber in the East Indies placed an enormous burden upon the American war economy. The debate, recounted earlier, concerning the wisdom of entering upon large-scale production of synthetic rubber ended abruptly. After Pearl Harbor, the token synthetic rubber program was quickly revised upward several times until by May 1942 the total planned production was in excess of eight hundred thousand tons annually. This amounted to about one and a quarter times the national rubber consumption in 1940. Day-to-day supervision of these plants, costing nearly $670 million, was the responsibility of DPC's sister subsidiary, the Rubber Reserve Company.[34]

In addition to its investments in the basic synthetic rubber industry,

DPC invested smaller amounts in plant and machinery for the fabricating of essential items. It disbursed nearly $6 million for plant and equipment for the manufacture of rubber soles and heels and more than $65 million for auto and truck tires.[35]

Radio and Communications. DPC projects in the radio and communications industry were sponsored chiefly by the army's Signal Corps. The total investment, approximately $81 million, included six of the thirteen largest government-financed radio and communications plants and a seventh financed jointly with the Army Air Forces. DPC provided equipment for lease to manufacturers operating ninety-seven other plants.[36]

DPC facilities produced a wide variety of supplies. Among the more important were radios and radio equipment, including tubes, batteries, motors, generators, field telephone wire, and radar equipment. Among the more unusual were two short-wave transmitters constructed under the sponsorship of the Office of War Information for use in broadcasts to the Orient.[37]

Ships and Shipyards. DPC's role in connection with shipbuilding was relatively minor. Early in 1941, the navy briefly considered using DPC to construct between $50 million and $60 million in ship repair facilities, but after its appropriations were increased it chose to finance these facilities directly. In certain instances, DPC did finance facilities for building tankers, cargo ships, tugs, barges, and for ship repair at the request of the Maritime Commission, the Navy Department, or the War Department Transportation Corps. Its investment of $20 million was of slight importance, however, in comparison with the approximately $1 billion invested directly by the navy and the Maritime Commission.

DPC was used in greater degree for plant and equipment to manufacture ship engines and parts. In this field, it financed construction of eighteen plants costing approximately $90 million and invested an additional $23 million in machinery leased to forty-four plants. Sponsors for these projects were chiefly the Maritime Commission, the navy and, to a lesser extent, the War Department.[38]

Miscellaneous Manufacture. In addition to the various categories already mentioned, DPC invested widely in facilities for the production of many types of military supplies more difficult to classify. These investments ranged among items as various as jewel bearings, ball bearings, cranes and hoists, diesel engines, hydraulic presses, forging machinery, searchlights, electrodes, dehydrated foods, frozen foods, medical supplies, and rope.

Its investments in new plant or in equipment for the production of these and other supplies totaled approximately $74 million, divided among some two hundred different plants.[39] Six were for the new miracle drug, penicillin, which DPC financed to the extent of about $7 million. Forty-one others, costing nearly $12 million, processed hemp. These were sponsored by the Commodity Credit Corporation of the Department of

Agriculture.[40] Still another project was sponsored by the WPB to process yucca fiber for rope.

Transportation. DPC assisted the war effort not alone through its investments in manufacturing but also in transportation facilities. Chief among these were its financing of pipelines, particularly the "Big Inch" and "Little Big Inch." But the corporation also invested substantially in tugs and barges, buses and streetcars, troop sleeping and kitchen cars, and truck and railroad equipment.

DPC activity in pipeline investment grew from the nation's need in 1942 to find some means to replace tanker delivery of oil from the Gulf of Mexico to the East Coast. Formerly, tankers had accounted for about 95 percent of the deliveries. In 1942, however, tankers were being harried by German submarines and were also being pulled from peacetime routes to serve new ones made necessary by war.[41] Since railroads, the first alternative to tankers, were already heavily burdened, DPC authorized construction or purchase of six pipelines at the request of the Petroleum Administration for War. Four were relatively small. Two of these were in the Southeast: an eight-inch line from Carrabelle to Jacksonville, Florida, that saved the water run around Florida for an estimated thirty-five thousand barrels daily of gasoline and light oils[42]; and another eight-inch line that extended an existing pipeline for gasoline and light oils originating in the Texas-Gulf area from its former terminus at Greensboro, North Carolina, to Richmond, Virginia.[43] The third and shortest of the lines ran from Tiffin to Doylestown, Ohio, connecting systems of the Shell Oil Company and the Standard Oil Company of Ohio. The fourth, a fourteen-inch and sixteen-inch line, ran from Corpus Christi to Houston, Texas. Already in existence as a natural gas pipeline, it was purchased and diverted to the status of a crude oil feeder line for the "Big Inch."[44] These four lines cost approximately $16 million.[45]

The two other lines were giants, extending nearly fourteen hundred miles from the East Texas fields to New York and Philadelphia. The first, a twenty-four-inch line, was authorized in June 1942 and was completed in August 1943 at a cost of $77 million. The second, a twenty-inch line, was authorized in February 1943 and finished in March 1944 at a cost of $62 million. Together they could deliver about five hundred thousand barrels of petroleum and refined products daily—equal to approximately one-third the average daily deliveries to the East Coast during 1941 by all methods. The "Big Inch" was used for crude oil; the "Little Big Inch" provided gasoline and light petroleum products.[46]

The pattern of construction and operation of the DPC pipelines was similar in nearly all cases. To supervise construction, DPC contracted with a pipeline company that in most instances was newly created and jointly owned by a number of oil and pipeline companies. Thus the War Emergency Pipelines, Incorporated, was jointly organized by eleven major oil and pipeline companies to supervise construction of the "Big Inch." For its supervision of construction of both the "Big Inch" and "Little Big Inch," War Emergency Pipelines received no fee. Following completion of the lines, DPC leased the lines to a sister RFC subsidiary, Defense Supplies Corporation. DSC, in turn, drew up management contracts for operation of the pipelines with the companies that had supervised construction, or, in the case of Humble Pipe Line Company, had sold a line to DPC.[47]

DPC also helped solve the problem of oil transportation by expenditures amounting to approximately $80 million for the construction or purchase of tugs, towboats, and barges. Nearly $67 million of this amount was spent for steel-hulled tugboats and wooden barges. These projects were sponsored by the Office of Defense Transportation. Purchases of tugs and towboats and the conversion of barges for use in hauling petroleum products were made primarily under sponsorship of the Petroleum Administration for War.[48]

Four barges, constructed under sponsorship of WPB at a cost of approximately $14 million, were unique among DPC projects. They were equipped with thirty-thousand-kilowatt-hour electric power plants and were designed to supply mobile power to war industry along inland waterways in an emergency. The barges were operated by the U.S. Army Corps of Engineers for the account of DPC.[49]

Another important area of DPC activity was financing additions to the nation's severely strained passenger transportation facilities. To help meet transportation problems in certain cities swollen with war work, DPC provided more than $4 million for streetcars and buses.[50] It invested nearly $21 million in troop sleeping cars and kitchens to supplement regular railroad equipment for troop transportation. In conjunction with war programs, DPC also invested nearly $11 million in constructing iron ore docks at Escanaba, Michigan, and $4 million in railroad trackage for mineral transportation in upper New York state.[51]

Housing. Many DPC projects, for a variety of reasons, were located away from cities sufficiently large to house their workers. Consequently, DPC invested more than $27 million in twenty-nine emergency housing developments scattered across the nation. The two largest were a $7 million project located at Henderson, Nevada, near the magnesium plant operated by Basic Magnesium, Incorporated, and a $5 million project at Columbia, Utah, adjacent to the Geneva Steel Plant.[52]

DPC's investments ranged from minor to massive and across the nation. Overall, they comprised about 30 percent of new facilities brought into being to help fight against the Axis. These dominantly commercial-type facilities were a crucial 30 percent, possibly achievable in no other way and certainly in no such sure and simple manner. They testify to the critical importance of the innovative means devised by the architects of the Defense Plant Corporation (see Table 7).[53]

Table 7. Defense Plant Corporation: Number of Plants and Other Projects and Amount Disbursed, by States, as of October 31, 1945

States	Number of Plants and Other Projects	Amount Disbursed (in thousands)
Total	2,300	$7,275,256
Alabama	19	76,642
Arizona	19	94,040
Arkansas	13	85,583
California	129	323,242
Colorado	6	6,362
Connecticut	70	140,534
Delaware	7	2,851
District of Columbia	4	3,311
Florida	14	11,056
Georgia	13	4,004
Idaho	1	156
Illinois	136	638,252
Indiana	97	364,625
Iowa	22	16,199
Kansas	13	48,644
Kentucky	52	151,528
Louisiana	31	227,893
Maine	2	293
Maryland	45	41,499
Massachusetts	80	81,136
Michigan	213	664,708
Minnesota	28	22,909
Mississippi	6	2,044
Missouri	36	158,797
Montana	3	12,412
Nebraska	7	12,945
Nevada	5	150,327
New Hampshire	3	1,046
New Jersey	135	280,979
New Mexico	6	9,370
New York	169	525,526
North Carolina	9	12,471
Ohio	250	702,222
Oklahoma	21	48,595
Oregon	29	42,511
Pennsylvania	202	571,370
Rhode Island	14	6,307

continued

Table 7.
continued

States	Number of Plants and Other Projects	Amount Disbursed (in thousands)
South Carolina	11	7,934
Tennessee	30	62,136
Texas	108	650,384
Utah	19	239,714
Vermont	6	4,396
Virginia	10	15,171
Washington	30	131,131
West Virginia	16	91,606
Wisconsin	61	140,281
Wyoming	4	11,944
Scattered	88	337,173
Outside United States	8	40,997

Source: RFC Research and Statistics Division.

7

The DPC Machine Tool Pool

No problem confronting defense planners was more critical in the latter months of 1940 than that of securing an adequate supply of machine tools. Knudsen stressed the need: "Big guns just don't sprout overnight. It takes months to get started, [but] once you get going the momentum takes you a long way."[1] The output of machine tools would powerfully influence the extent and pace of the defense program.

Almost at once, RFC was called upon to assist in the solution of this difficult problem. On July 2, 1940, the president signed a bill giving him authority to stop exportation of machine tools essential to the national defense program. Shortly thereafter, the National Defense Advisory Commission asked RFC to lend $10 million to tool manufacturers whose tools were stopped at the docks while a substitute national defense purchaser was selected. The RFC board authorized such loans, but none proved necessary.[2]

RFC's later financing of the machine tool industry through DPC and DPC's operation of a pool of tool orders is of no such transient interest. Overall, DPC's machine tool pool was responsible for almost half of all tools manufactured from 1941 through 1945 (see Table 8).

Table 8. DPC Machine Tool Pool Orders and Shipments, 1941–1945

Year	DPC Pool Orders	Shipment of DPC Pool-Ordered Tools	Total Production of Machine Tool Industry
1940			$ 440,000,000
1941	$ 284,000,000		775,000,000
1942	1,361,000,000	$ 751,000,000*	1,320,000,000
1943	223,000,000	807,000,000	1,180,000,000
1944	29,000,000	109,000,000	502,000,000
1945	48,000,000	32,000,000	407,000,000
Total	$1,945,000,000	$1,699,000,000	$4,184,000,000

Source: RFC Statistical and Economic Division.
*Combined figure for the years 1941–1942.

For a number of reasons, the defense program required DPC's assistance to help bring about a rapid expansion of the machine tool industry. One was that some tool builders had sad memories of their World War I experience. They had expanded and operated at capacity during the war period, but their contracts were canceled after the armistice, and a famine had supplanted their short-lived feasting. Some had overbuilt. Executives of one of the largest machine tool firms, Warner and Swasey of Cleveland, Ohio, as late as 1940 could see from their offices a five-story plant not operated since World War I which they had dubbed their "World War folly." Also, machine tools were durable and usually multipurpose. The ordinary tool could have a useful life of fifteen years or more. Excessive sales today could jeopardize the size of tomorrow's market.[3]

Other difficulties centered around the nature of the machine tool industry and its methods of doing business. It was composed of relatively small firms of limited capital resources employing highly skilled labor. Within the industry, considerable subcontracting was practiced. The period necessary to construct a tool could be six or more months. In addition, in 1940 the machine tool industry was deluged with orders, many from abroad. Some tool manufacturers had a backlog that would take eighteen months or more to fill.[4]

As in many other fields of production, the problem of expanding plant in the machine tool industry was handled in part by private financing, stimulated by larger orders, tax amortization, or other incentives, and in part by DPC construction and lease agreements. This expansion was accomplished gradually over a period of years. To accelerate the rate of expansion, however, it was necessary for tool manufacturers to feel sure of a market for tools they produced without firm orders. They also needed additional working capital with which to build up inventories of materials for construction of still more tools.

Peacetime procedures required that a manufacturer who ordered tools accept liability for payment either for the machine or for the cost incurred in the partial manufacture of the machine plus a reasonable profit if the order were canceled. This procedure was not universally practicable during a war. From the beginning of the defense period, a substantial proportion and increasingly more new plant was government-titled. New procedures had to be developed for placing orders for tools for government plants and for coordinating orders with plant construction so that tools would be available when the plant was ready. Moreover, procedures had to be modified for prospective defense contractors expanding or retooling private plants. Some contractors possessed more know-how than credit and consequently seemed dubious risks to machine tool manufacturers. Some, too, were reluctant to accept liability for machine tool orders before a supply contract was signed. Or, if signed, a defense contractor was uncertain whether the terms of contract might not be modified before his new plant got into production, requiring additional machinery or making unnecessary equipment already on order. Since the government needed the know-how of the contractor and maximum production from the machine tool manufacturer, both parties were in an excellent position to try to avoid some of the more extreme risks in placing orders for tools.[5]

Consequently, in December 1940, NDAC requested RFC to establish a pool of machine tool orders on which RFC would bear the risk until purchasers were found. The intent was, in every instance, that the ultimate purchaser be an enterprise, government or privately owned, engaged in defense work. Emil Schram, president of DPC, replied that during 1941 DPC would be willing to "place orders for machine tools for use in the manufacture of arms, ammunition, and implements of war up to an aggregate of $35,000,000." At the end of May 1941, DPC agreed to an additional $200 million to support the heavy bomber program.[6]

The DPC pool operation, here begun on a modest scale, reached its peak in 1942, when a vast majority of all tool orders were placed through the pool. Thereafter, as new plant construction fell off, tool orders also subsided. They were revived to a limited extent only in December 1944 and early 1945 at the time of the Battle of the Bulge.

Under the pool system, the tool manufacturer was guaranteed a market and a price for each item. The machine tool industry was accorded a stability that was conducive to maximum production and also a stimulus for the construction of new facilities. The system also assured defense officials that, provided the pool orders were well planned and priorities properly granted, machine tools would be ready when needed in defense and war plants.

Following Pearl Harbor, two related pools were organized for gage and for cutting tools. The gage tool pool, authorized to a maximum of $50 million, was set up toward the end of January 1942,[7] and the cutting tool pool, authorized to a maximum of $180 million, was established early in the following month.[8] Like the machine tool pool, these pools for nondurable tools guaranteed a price and a market for tools on order. As in the case of machine tools, the existence of the cutting and gage pools helped to bring about plant expansion in those specialties.

Orders for gage and cutting tools differed somewhat from those for machine tools. Unlike the latter, which were specific orders, gage and cutting tool orders were placed automatically to cover a manufacturer's estimated production for a specified period ranging from two to six months. They were intermittently increased to offset shipments. Thus the orders were kept constant, ensuring a fixed backlog of gage and cutting tools until the pools were canceled.[9] By the conclusion of the war, thirty-three cutting tool orders had been issued, aggregating $78,144,000.[10] Ninety-six gage tool orders aggregating $15,962,000 had also been made.[11]

All three pools helped manufacturers in another way. For most of the period of machine tool pool operation and throughout the period of the minor pools, DPC backed its pool orders with a 30 percent cash advance, in accordance with an OPM request made the day following Pearl Harbor.[12] The 30 percent advance provided additional working capital for tool manufacturers at a time when their own resources were strained by the pressure of orders and by heavy investments in additional facilities. Originally, the 30 percent advance, which was given without interest, was returned to DPC at the time a purchaser was found for the tool. Late in January 1942, this pattern was changed, for tool manufacturers who needed working capital were finding it impossible to get a similar advance from the ultimate owners of the machinery.[13] Thereafter, the 30 percent advance was not returnable to DPC until the date of invoice or shipment of machinery, whichever was earlier. The procedure of allowing a 30 percent advance was continued until June 1943, when pool orders had almost ceased.[14] It was used less frequently after pool operations were revived on a limited scale late in 1944. In the case of gage and cutting tool orders, the 30 percent advance was nonreturnable during the life of the pools, because the size of the orders in each pool remained constant. The total advances on pool orders of all types amounted to approximately $420 million.[15]

After a period of almost complete suspension, machine tool pool orders were revived to some extent at the end of 1944 to supply additional tools for use in ammunition plants and, in lesser degree, in rubber tire factories. The first stimulus to revival grew out of a possible shortage in production of ammunition arising from the huge needs of the European theater and the second from the increased flow of synthetic rubber available for tires.[16] Neither program was large. In December 1944, DPC estimated that total pool orders issued through August 1945 would be less than $70 million. In fact, although orders were placed for $51,365,000 in tools for manufacturing ammunition, only $15,300,000 were delivered. The balance of the orders were terminated.[17]

In preparing for this program, DPC took steps to make certain that orders were not placed when idle tools could fill the need. No order was issued without first having been referred to the Surplus War Property Division of DPC to determine whether the tools desired might be in DPC's surplus stock.[18] In addition, DPC field engineers and lessees were apprised of the general nature of the machine tool needs. On December 26, 1944, Jesse Jones telegraphed all DPC lessees: "Will you arrange for an immediate spot inventory to determine the machine tools in your possession which you can make available? Defense Plant Corporation's supervising engineer will submit to your firm a list of the types of machine tools urgently needed and will transmit to us your list of available tools. I am sure you want to do everything you can to meet this emergency."[19] After WPB, DPC, and the armed services jointly set up a "machine tool trading pit" early in 1945, no order for a new tool costing in excess of $3,000 was issued without first screening the order at the pit.[20]

Production of new tools under pool orders continued until just after the surrender of Japan.[21] Up to that time, advance purchase commitments had been issued totaling nearly $1.95 billion. Of this amount, DPC was forced to accept delivery of less than $3 million for lack of substitute purchasers. Nearly $2 million worth of these tools were turned over for sale as surplus property and the balance sold as scrap.[22] In a study completed in 1946, the General Accounting Office was unable to see the machine tool record as quite so perfect. It criticized DPC for flawed accounting and forecast a loss of "something over $12,000,000."[23]

Nonetheless, DPC was notably successful in underwriting much of the risk for tool manufacturers and thereby securing maximum production. Where necessary, through its liberal policy of advances, it also supplied an important supplemental source of working capital. As a result, tools were available when and where needed. Following the war, Secretary of War Robert P. Patterson observed prophetically: "In the mobilization of industrial America for World War II the fundamental problem was to provide, when needed, machine tools and other production equipment, including gages, metal cutting tools and industrial specialties. To accomplish this purpose the pool order mechanism was developed. Pool orders proved very successful and assisted in meeting war requirements efficiently, and, therefore, will probably be used in connection with any future emergency."[24]

8
Winding Down

By 1943, concerns over postwar disposal of the vast industrial plant built in response to war needs began to outweigh the earlier concerns for increased war production. The need for demobilizing the war economy, however, evoked little of the crusading zeal that had accompanied its mobilization. Echoes of earlier debates can be heard, but the balance in the debates had changed. Ideas on how to effect demobilization ran across a spectrum from using demobilization to achieve social and economic reform to the restoration of business as usual. The highly visible contribution of business to production had greatly strengthened the forces toward the conservative end of the spectrum. The main thrust behind wartime planning for demobilization was to interfere as little as possible with the economic and social structure, while at the same time seeking to avoid a recurrence of the Great Depression.

It is possible to think that different leadership might have made some difference. In January 1945, for example, President Roosevelt sought to replace Jesse Jones with Henry A. Wallace as secretary of commerce and federal loan administrator. Jones and Wallace had feuded bitterly during the war over procurement of essential raw materials outside the United States. Jones and most of the business community saw Wallace as a dangerous and impractical visionary; Wallace and the New Dealers considered Jones a man of narrow business values, a haggler over pennies, and an apostle of the status quo. Jones and his Senate allies were strong enough to block the confirmation of Wallace as secretary of commerce until the office of federal loan administrator was split off from the cabinet post. Conservatives were not eager to see Wallace become secretary of commerce, but they were even more determined that he not be federal loan administrator. The latter office dominated the powerful RFC, which the conservative Senator Harry Byrd had described as "a fourth branch of the Government" because of its huge size and many functions.[1]

The office of federal loan administrator passed quickly from hand to hand. Within a week after the confirmation of Wallace as secretary of commerce on March 1, a moderate New Dealer, Fred M. Vinson, formerly director of the Office of Economic Stabilization, was appointed federal loan administrator. Vinson served less than a month before he succeeded James F. Byrnes as director of the Office of War Mobilization and Reconversion.[2]

To succeed Vinson, the press mentioned as likely candidates Harold Smith, the highly efficient director of the Bureau of the Budget, Leo T. Crowley, chairman of the Foreign Economic Administration, and Donald M. Nelson, former chairman of the War Production Board. Within the White House, another candidate, Clifford J. Durr, was being given serious consideration. "Durr knows the loan operations of the government as does perhaps no other genuine Roosevelt man in Washington," wrote James G. Patton, president of the National Farmers Union, in a warmly supportive letter. Henry Wallace and Secretary of the Treasury Henry Morgenthau were pushing for him, as was Senator Lister Hill of Alabama. No final decision appears to have been made before Roosevelt's death on April 12.[3]

There is irony in the strong possibility that Durr would have been appointed federal loan administrator except for the death of the president. Surely Jesse Jones would have been far from happy to see his former quarrelsome subordinate succeed to a position of such power. But Durr was probably fortunate not to have secured the appointment. By April 1945, general policies governing surplus disposal had already been laid down, and he would have had to have acted within them. Durr would have had little opportunity to generate and implement bold improvisations like the DPC mechanism in the defense period. Probably the best he could have done would have been to be more sensitive to the interests of small business, to which, like Henry Wallace, he was deeply devoted, and to forestall where possible any trend toward monopoly.

President Truman sought out John W. Snyder, his old friend and Durr's capable but more conservative DPC colleague, to become federal loan administrator. With Truman's approval, Snyder quickly moved to terminate RFC's principal wartime subsidiaries "in the interest of simplification and operating economy." As of June 30, 1945, these subsidiaries were folded into RFC. DPC became the Office of Defense Plants.[4]

The change was symbolic. It signalized the end of DPC as a plant-financing agency and portended the end of the Office of Defense Plants as the administrator of DPC's former industrial facilities. The task of disposing of the DPC properties was not unique but a part of the total problem of the disposal of surplus property of all government agencies. Because of this fusion and also shortcomings in record keeping, the pace of divestment was slow. Inadequate records have made it virtually impossible to perceive accurately the extent of the government's recovery of investment from the DPC properties.

The formulation of policy and the subsequent conversion to peacetime use of the vast increment in government-titled industrial facilities was a difficult process of great economic and social significance. Approximately

$16 billion in plants and equipment were involved. This figure may be compared with the $39 billion reported as the value of the nation's industrial plant in 1939, but such a comparison would be erroneous. Replacement of the prewar plant in 1944, according to the Brookings economist A. D. H. Kaplan, would have cost approximately 40 percent more than its value in 1939. Plant built during the war, by contrast, was overvalued because of the dominance of military considerations in emphasizing speed of construction over costs, strategic over economic locations, and construction of facilities providing large outputs of products like high explosives, ships, and aircraft for which there was a limited peacetime market. On the other hand, plants built during the war were generally more efficient. Balancing off these various factors is difficult. Probably the effective increase in the nation's peacetime productive capacity represented by these new facilities was about 15 percent.[5]

The DPC investment of approximately $7 billion encompassed the major portion of commercial-type facilities most attractive for peacetime use. Largely through DPC, the government held title to 90 percent or more of the synthetic rubber, aircraft, and magnesium industries, owned 55 percent of the nation's aluminum capacity and the bulk of the nation's machine tools, and had significant ownership in a variety of other industries.[6] A committee of the House of Representatives studying postwar economic policy stated, "How these Government facilities are distributed and the uses to which they are or are not put, can have a decisive influence on the character of American industry—or indeed the character of the economic system under which we live."[7] The ways these plants were transferred from wartime to peacetime service held the potential for economic and social change. Actually, the range of meaningful debate was not great, and the outcomes were distinctly conservative.

The debate over policy went on for about two years. An early effort to sample the public mind was made by Princeton's Office of Public Opinion Research in the spring of 1943. It reported that nearly half of its sample (46 percent) believed that the government plants should be sold to their wartime operators. The second largest group (26 percent) wanted the government to keep and operate the plants; this group grew to 46 percent in the replies to a companion question asking what government should do if the wartime operator was not interested. Fully 80 percent also believed that the government should favor small business in disposing of government-titled plants in order to forestall further concentration of ownership in industry.[8]

Social purpose influenced the thinking of numerous commentators deeply interested in the fate of the government plants. Clifford Durr, appropriately, was one of these. In a paper presented in December 1942 at the annual meeting of the American Economic Association, he urged that the facilities be disposed of in such a way as to enhance competition and that "consideration should also be given to the retention of some of the plants for operation as yardsticks." The yardstick principle, made famous in debates over the Tennessee Valley Authority, was also endorsed by James G. Patton, president of the National Farmers Union. J. Raymond Walsh, a well-known labor economist and director of research and education for the CIO, told a Senate committee that his organization wanted a plant disposal program that was not demoralizing to any industry. But, he emphasized, the CIO was anxious that as much as possible of "this new American domain" be kept in production and also used to fight monopoly.[9]

Harold Ickes, in a speech to the Commonwealth Club of San Francisco, showed again his unusual ability to think the unthinkable. Ickes was determined that the government plants he believed so vital to the industrial development of the West be kept in production after the war. Professing fear that rich monopolies would buy up plants at low prices and stifle production, Ickes sketched out an alternative in which government would set up a giant holding company, with a subsidiary company for each industry group. World War II veterans would receive the stock as a bonus and as a rough equivalent to the homesteads on the public domain to which Civil War veterans had been entitled. After these enterprises had been properly financed and were functioning smoothly, the government would withdraw, leaving their continued operation to the veterans. This novel idea for "giving ten million young persons shares of stock in the America for which they risked their lives" struck a few sparks, but Ickes never developed it further.[10]

Business leaders, their prestige enhanced by the production achievements of wartime, were undoubtedly heard more sympathetically by most members of Congress. These businessmen reflected the fears so frequently expressed prior to Pearl Harbor concerning government title as a threat to free enterprise and excess capacity as a threat to profits. R. S. Smethurst of the National Association of Manufacturers, in testifying before the same Senate committee as had J. Raymond Walsh, the CIO economist, urged that "all Government-owned plants and equipment [be] made available for private operation as promptly as possible." He also asked for legislation expressing the "unequivocal policy" that "the Government not own or operate directly or indirectly any enterprise which competes with privately owned trade or industry." Smethurst's business colleague, A. C. Mattei, representing the U.S. Chamber of Commerce, wanted officials charged with the disposal of government facilities to be advised by "industry committees." If facilities were not needed for military purposes and were not purchased by industry, he argued that they should be scrapped. The Senate Special Committee on Post-War Economic Policy and Planning, led by the conservative Walter George of Georgia, echoed much of these views in its report issued in February 1944.

It called for the speedy sale of as many government plants as possible where this would not result in "ruinous competition" and "the production of more goods than the market could absorb at reasonably competitive prices." Instead of scrapping plants not sold, the committee recommended that these facilities be used for storage. The committee also urged a disposal policy that would not strengthen or encourage monopoly.[11]

The Truman Committee took a more moderate position in its *Third Annual Report* released in March 1944. It gave priority to putting "the best and most important . . . plants" in standby status as insurance in the event of a future emergency, but called for use of the remainder to meet the needs of the peacetime economy. The committee asserted that "a very large proportion of the . . . plants can produce useful peacetime articles and can continue to provide employment . . . if we have the courage and intelligence to utilize the vast industrial resources which we have already created." The committee opposed closing plants "for fear of competing with established interests." It asked only that the plants be disposed of at fair prices.[12]

While these hearings were being held and reports made, a much heralded report by Bernard Baruch and John M. Hancock on *War and Post-War Adjustment Policies* brought the government to the brink of action. This report, presented on February 10, 1944, by the nation's most distinguished senior statesman and his longtime investment banker associate, had been solicited three months earlier by James Byrnes, director of the Office of War Mobilization. It was a sweeping survey of all aspects of the problem of surplus disposal, written for impact in simple statements and printed in different-sized types. The report emphasized the need for speed, the desirability of getting fair market prices, and the conduct of all transactions with "goldfish bowl" visibility.[13]

Baruch and Hancock called for the appointment in the Office of War Mobilization of a surplus property administrator who would chair an advisory surplus property policy board representing all departments and agencies concerned with the problem of surplus: War, Navy, Treasury, RFC, War Production Board, Bureau of the Budget, Food Administration, attorney general, Federal Works Agency, State Department, and Foreign Economic Administration. Disposal would be channeled through four major divisions: consumer goods, capital and producer goods, ships and maritime properties, and food.[14]

Capital and producer goods, they suggested, should be handled through a single RFC subsidiary formed from a consolidation of all of its war-related subsidiaries. The choice of RFC was appropriate not only because of the magnitude of its wartime investments but also because its loan agencies would provide a ready-made national net of disposal outlets. Baruch and Hancock were opposed to government operation of surplus war plants in competition with private industry, to sales that would promote monopoly, and to the "deliberate destruction of *useful property.*" They favored equal opportunities to purchase and preference for local ownership free from subsidization. In special cases, they believed leasing might be desirable, for example, to assist a smaller enterprise to use a plant it could not afford to buy or to permit multiple tenancy in a large plant for which no purchaser could be found. But in identical language and type, Baruch and Hancock twice averred, *"Leasing must not become a hidden device for the Government to compete with private plants; it must not be a hidden device for subsidies—by any name—to anyone.* Once plants leave the Government's hands they must stand on their own feet competitively."[15]

There can be little doubt that the Baruch-Hancock report was in tune with business thought and feeling. When *Fortune* asked a cross-section of executives a few months later whether they favored speed in getting government plants into private operation to avoid unemployment, as opposed to seeking a maximum return for the government or, as a third alternative, sales to enhance competition, the replies from the executives favored the first alternative by 43 percent as against 26 percent for the second and 29 percent for the third. The same group of executives, by a majority of nearly three to one, favored sale at a fair price to a big company over lease at a fair rental to a smaller competitor. A later question regarding the disposal of western steel and light metal plants elicited a response of 68 percent supporting sales to buyers who, with favorable terms, were reasonably certain to operate the plants without subsidy. Dominant business opinion, reflected in the Baruch-Hancock report, clearly did not wish to see plant disposal used as an instrument to effect economic and social change.[16]

In submitting their report, Baruch and Hancock recommended to Byrnes that Will Clayton be appointed surplus property administrator. Clayton, an articulate and able businessman, was serving as assistant secretary of commerce to Jesse Jones. Even more than that of Jones, his career was a rags-to-riches story. He was born on a cotton farm in Mississippi; his formal education had ended with the eighth grade. In 1904, at the age of twenty-four, he joined two of his wife's relatives in forming Anderson, Clayton and Company, which he built into the world's largest cotton factoring firm. In November 1940, Clayton came to Washington as deputy federal loan administrator to help his good friend and fellow Houstonian, Jesse Jones, with what proved to be a too conservative stockpiling of strategic materials. He continued to have a strong hand in the operations of several of RFC's wartime subsidiaries after he became assistant secretary of commerce.[17]

The president did not wait for congressional legislation to implement the Baruch-Hancock report. Instead, impressed by their emphasis on the need for speed, he established the Surplus War Property Administration in the Office of War Mobilization by Executive Order 9425 on February 19, 1944, four days after Byrnes had received the report. On February 21, Byrnes appointed Clayton surplus war property administrator, and on March 2 the first meeting of the Surplus War Property Policy Board was convened in the RFC Board Room. On March 6, Sam Husbands, president of DPC, was appointed director of surplus war property for RFC, and a month later, Hans Klagsbrunn, DPC's executive vice-president, became his deputy director. Early in June, Clayton chose Mason Britton, former chief of the Machine Tools Division in OPM and former vice-chairman of the McGraw-Hill Publishing Company, to take charge of the disposal of machine tools. The next month, Britton was made assistant administrator with jurisdiction over all capital goods, industrial plants, and real estate.[18]

These months following the Baruch-Hancock report were occupied primarily with planning and shaping the pattern of control of the disposal process. Planning was more important with respect to machine tools than plants because a small number of machine tools, virtually all DPC-owned, were already being released as surplus. These tools were not being acquired by their wartime users under the terms of the standard option in the DPC lease. They were the vanguard of a flood, for the nation's machine tools had doubled in numbers during the war years. Of the nine hundred thousand new tools, approximately two-thirds were government-titled. They were modern; they worked at great speeds and to higher tolerances than the older tools; but they were also more costly. Much peacetime work did not require such efficiency. If these tools were to replace older tools and to increase output, greater price concessions would have to be made than were allowed in the uniform depreciation provision in the DPC lease.[19]

This step was taken on August 9, 1944, when the surplus war property administrator issued SWPA Regulation 3, later known as the Clayton formula. It called for a 15 percent discount on the cost of standard new tools and depreciation at 2.5 percent per month for the first six months and at lower rates thereafter so that standard tools that had been used for two and a half years could be purchased for 50 percent of cost. Special-purpose tools and tools no longer manufactured were reduced an additional 25 percent from the price for a surplus standard tool.[20]

The purchase option with respect to most DPC plants was showing similar shortcomings. "In our opinion, the purchase rights running to the builders or operators of the plants built by the RFC [DPC] have very little value to them," Jesse Jones wrote Harold Smith, director of the Bureau of the Budget, in August 1943. The cost of most plants had ballooned as the result of such wartime practices as round-the-clock construction, involving overtime, the substitution of less desirable construction materials, and costly delays with labor idle because of shortages of materials. The plants had also suffered hard wear in war production. Three months after writing Smith, Jones told the George committee that DPC was seeking a new formula that would be "fair to the Government, and fair to private industry." One line of thought was toward a sale price equal to the cost of reproduction, less depreciation and whatever other costs were required to ready the plant for peacetime use. But because virtually no plants had been declared surplus, there was no need to issue a regulation in 1944 governing plant sales.[21]

Will Clayton would have preferred to have carried on under an executive order that allowed him a high degree of independence, but Congress was unwilling for him to do so. Since he could not forestall legislation, he sought to shape it to conform to his own desires. After discussions with his Advisory Board, Clayton drew up a bill introduced in the House late in June by Representative William Colmer of Mississippi, chairman of the Special Committee on Post-War Economic Policy and Planning. It was relatively short and simple, emphasizing both speed and high recovery of costs in disposing of surplus and allowing the administrator substantial freedom. The bill listed among its specific goals increasing peacetime production, avoiding dislocation of the economy, discouraging monopolistic practices, and preserving and strengthening the competitive position of small business. It limited the authority of the administrator in disposing of plants solely with regard to synthetic rubber and aluminum facilities that had cost the government more than $5 million. Before taking any long-term action with respect to any plant in these two categories, the administrator was required to submit disposal plans for congressional approval.[22]

The Senate proved less willing to go along with Clayton's ideas. Thus the bill enacted into law in October was a much more complex and cumbersome measure than he and Byrnes desired.[23] It expanded the objectives to include a much wider range of social and economic goals and wrote in a series of priorities. Agencies of the federal government were given the first priority to acquire facilities. If none were interested, state and local governments and nonprofit private agencies and institutions stood next in line. Small business and veterans were also granted priorities. To protect the rights of small business, the Smaller War Plants Corporation had representatives in the regional offices of each disposal agency who could purchase facilities on their own initiative. SWPC was authorized to make loans to assist small firms to acquire, convert, and operate the former war facilities. It also helped veterans who were likely candidates for small business. These priorities reflected serious social and economic concerns, but they were also certain to slow the disposal process.

The Senate wrote in still other restrictions and regulations. Instead of limiting freedom of action in disposing of plants solely to synthetic rubber and aluminum facilities, the final bill listed a total of twelve industrial categories for properties costing the government more than $5 million—aluminum; magnesium; synthetic rubber; chemicals; aviation gasoline; iron and steel; pipelines; patents, processes, and inventions; aircraft; shipyards; transportation; and radio and electrical equipment—that required the submission of disposal plans to Congress. In eight of the categories, no property of this size could be sold or leased for a term longer than five years until thirty days after Congress had received the report unless the property was a "scrambled" facility operated as an integral part of a privately owned plant and incapable of separate operation. In addition, any transaction involving a plant or other property costing the government $1 million or more, or patents or inventions regardless of cost, was subject to a review by the attorney general to determine whether the transaction violated antitrust law. This review could take as long as ninety days.

Finally, instead of consolidating authority in a single administrator, the act provided for an independent three-member Surplus Property Board to establish policy. Separating policy making from operational authority was for Clayton the last straw. He denounced it as "unworkable" but agreed to stay on in a caretaker role until the Surplus Property Board took over. Clayton resigned in December just before Robert Hurley, a former governor of Connecticut, took office as the first of the board members. Another month passed before the other two members, Edward H. Heller, a San Francisco banker and corporation executive, and former Senator Guy M. Gillette of Iowa as chairman, took up their new duties.[24]

The Surplus Property Board proved as ineffectual as Clayton had prophesied. In spite of efforts by Baruch and others to encourage the board to act, it moved with glacial slowness. None of the board members was experienced in the administrative processes of the federal government. The complex statement of goals and procedures in the Surplus Property Act helped make the board too wary of error. After several months marked by uncertainty in policy making and frustrations because of inadequate staff, Gillette asked to be relieved. President Truman appointed his friend and supporter Stuart Symington as Gillette's successor, with the understanding that amending legislation would be introduced to abolish the board and make Symington administrator. The amendment became law on October 1, 1945.[25]

Like Clayton, Symington was a successful businessman, though on a much smaller scale and with markedly different origins. Born into a wealthy family, he graduated from Yale in 1923 and worked in family business firms for a few years before moving out on his own. In 1945, he was president of the Emerson Electric Company in St. Louis, which he had rescued from bankruptcy just prior to World War II by such unorthodox tactics as profit sharing and cooperating with a Communist in developing good labor relations.[26]

Symington was appointed in the interim between the victory in Europe and the victory in Japan. These events greatly increased the amount of surplus awaiting disposal and, consequently, the need for action. In the three months between June 30 and September 30, 1945, inventories of plant, equipment, and surplus aircraft assigned to RFC for disposal had almost doubled, growing to $3.757 billion. Although Symington served little more than six months, he gave surplus disposal a sharp shove forward. He filed all but two of the long-delayed reports required by Congress describing plans for a disposal program for each of the industrial categories listed in the Surplus Property Act of 1944. He also fought a notable battle with Alcoa. Alcoa's monopoly in the manufacture of primary aluminum was ended when it finally yielded and agreed to grant royalty-free licenses of its patents for use at the large government-owned alumina facilities in Arkansas and Louisiana.[27]

The energetic administrator stressed speed in shifting wartime plants and machines into peacetime production. Their production, he argued, need not be "an economic worry," but, on the contrary, "an economic blessing." The increased production would be "a most effective curb on inflation" and would help generate the high national income necessary to service the war-bloated national debt. It would also help maintain the full employment of the war years.[28]

In order to widen the range of potential purchasers for government plants, the lame-duck Surplus Property Board, with Symington as chairman, issued Special Order 19 on September 9, replacing the old formula of reproduction cost less depreciation and conversion costs with a more favorable formula for purchasers that emphasized "fair value." Fair value was defined as "the maximum price . . . a well-informed buyer . . . would be warranted in paying if he were acquiring the property for . . . a profit-making purpose [representing] the most productive type of use for which the property is suitable." The new formula took into account values in land, buildings, and equipment only to the degree that they were useful to a purchaser. It authorized the disposal agency to call on qualified persons, including appraisers, for help in determining fair value. In cases where offers did not meet the figure established for fair value, the disposal agency was authorized to consider a lesser offer and easier terms if the purchase or lease conformed to goals of the Surplus Property Act.[29]

Symington sought to consolidate and routinize all disposal activities in a single agency. In November 1945, he effected the transfer of the disposal of surplus consumer goods from the Department of Commerce to the RFC and in January consolidated all of RFC's surplus responsibilities in one of its lesser-known wartime subsidiaries, the Petroleum Reserves Corporation, which had been renamed the War Assets Corporation. General Edmund B. Gregory, quartermaster general of the army during World War II, was chosen as chairman of the board of the new disposal agency. By Executive Order he assumed sole responsibility for surplus disposal on February 1, 1946, the day after Symington resigned as surplus property administrator to become assistant secretary of war for air. Gregory presided over the transfer of responsibility for surplus disposal from the War Assets Corporation to an independent agency, the War Assets Administration (WAA), toward the end of March. When General Gregory resigned in July 1947, his successor was Major General Robert M. Littlejohn, formerly chief quartermaster in the European theater. Littlejohn, in turn, was succeeded by Jess Larson, an attorney and deputy administrator of the War Assets Administration, after Littlejohn resigned in November 1947.[30]

While policy was being worked out at a higher level, DPC and, later, RFC's Office of Defense Plants, were engaged in the mundane activities of preparing their plants and equipment for eventual disposal. DPC's days of excitement were over. Its officials could carry on in an efficient, workmanlike way, but their opportunities for daring innovation epitomized by the DPC lease were long gone. The climate was no longer receptive to novel ideas even if such ideas could be generated. It was a time for small steps and small thoughts.

Nevertheless, the efficient organization led by Sam Husbands, DPC's president, and Hans Klagsbrunn, its executive vice-president, continued to receive the respect it merited from government officials in the executive branch and in Congress concerned with the problems of conversion from war to peace. Representatives of the George committee reported in September 1943 that DPC had "the best information in Washington" for planning for the disposal of war plants. Three months later, a survey made by the Bureau of the Budget found planning, apart from DPC, either deficient or nonexistent in considering the meaning of disposal and conversion of government plants for peacetime production. Within DPC, the report singled out individuals like Klagsbrunn for "giving considerable thought to arrangements for disposal of plant and equipment that would both protect the government's interest and promote the welfare of the civilian economy."[31]

During 1944, DPC polled its lessees operating scrambled facilities or DPC machinery in lessee-owned plants to determine their interest in acquiring the facilities or machinery either through the purchase option or through negotiated purchase of the whole or part. The replies received from more than three-fourths of the lessees indicated an interest in acquiring less than one-tenth of the value of the DPC investment. DPC also gained an insight into the magnitude of its plant clearance program. The replies revealed that 3.5 million square feet of storage space would be required to house the undesired DPC machinery in addition to the nearly one million square feet of space which lessees were willing to make available in their own buildings.[32]

Later that year, DPC polled 376 firms operating 586 of its plants. Of the

326 replies, 116 firms operating 160 plants indicated lack of interest or uncertainty. The remainder said they were interested either in using the purchase option or in leasing, while a few expressed interest in an extended lease only. The replies were more sanguine than the final decisions. Fortunately, the replies were substantially discounted by the DPC headquarters.[33]

Because of the high costs of plant construction and the relatively minor degree of inflation during the war period, the option privilege proved of slight importance, as had been surmised. By the end of 1946, only 51 plants costing $49 million had been sold under the option clause. The option was even less attractive to lessees of machinery and equipment, for the Clayton formula offered a considerably larger reduction from original cost than did the depreciation rates fixed in the DPC lease. Consequently, only in unusual circumstances did a DPC lessee exercise its purchase option to acquire machine tools. As of April 30, 1947, only five sales for a total of approximately $5 million were recorded on the books of the RFC treasurer.[34]

The limited desire of lessees for DPC machinery alerted DPC to its problem of plant clearance. Under the standard lease terms, DPC was obligated to complete the removal within sixty days after it had received a request in acceptable form from the lessee. If DPC did not do so, then twenty days thereafter the lessee could remove and store the machinery at DPC's risk and expense. Careful advance planning was essential if this vast volume of work was to be handled efficiently. The planning was especially difficult if a prime contractor had scattered DPC machinery and equipment among a large number of subcontractors.[35]

During the spring of 1944, the Engineering Division structure was expanded through the creation of a series of newly titled senior division engineers. The geographic jurisdiction of these engineers was made identical with that of the RFC loan agencies, with which the engineers were instructed to cooperate in planning plant clearance. The engineer was responsible for ascertaining whether the lessee desired to exercise its purchase option and, if not, what equipment the lessee might wish to purchase or lease. The loan agency would then take over and carry on the negotiations, leaving to the engineer and his superiors responsibility for the eventual removal of the remainder of the machinery.[36]

Advance planning, although beneficial, was not more successful because of factors beyond DPC control. Some lessees, after listing what they wished to purchase, revised their lists once or several times. Others were loathe to make lists while they were still engaged in war production. Many were not sure what machinery they wanted or lacked the manpower to make the necessary surveys to determine their needs at a time when their supply contracts were still large.

Plant clearance would have been a greater problem after the war if RFC had not adopted the lenient policy of writing interim leases after termination for lessees desiring to continue to use its machinery. RFC's encouragement of requests for partial plant clearance also helped spread the burden of clearance activities. Through April 1945, a total of 171 requests were received for plant clearance. Thereafter the number increased to a peak of 632 in December. The number of requests continued high in the early months of 1946, but gradually subsided. By the end of June 1946, machinery valued at $475 million had been removed.[37]

RFC gave first priority to plant clearance of lessee-owned plants, but toward the end of the war the Office of Defense Plants (ODP) began developing an "owned plants removal program." ODP had recognized that the "expeditious clearance of RFC-owned machinery and equipment from RFC-owned plants was also important to successful reconversion. When such plants were sold or leased, they could not go into production until the unneeded property was removed." Of the $2.194 billion in machinery and equipment in RFC-owned plants, $210 million was moved out during the fiscal year 1946. After the War Assets Administration became an independent agency on March 25, 1946, RFC removed surplus machinery and equipment from its owned plants solely at the direction of the War Assets Administration.[38]

In helping speed reconversion, DPC's first consideration had to be preparing for the flow of machine tools from lessee-owned plants, but over the long haul preparing its own plants for sale was more important. More capital was invested in these plants than was tied up in scrambled facilities or in tools in lessee-owned plants.

As early as March 1944, DPC was diverting the best of its engineers to make an industrial survey of each plant. Guided by a set of twenty questions, the engineer reported on its physical and economic characteristics, sought to determine its most attractive postwar possibilities, and, if it was a very large plant, the prospects for multiple tenancy. In October, DPC distilled this information in a *Briefalogue,* which it published in an edition of thirty-five thousand copies. The *Briefalogue,* providing succinct descriptions of 879 plants and plant sites, was distributed widely not only from the Washington office and the loan agencies but also through the U.S. Chamber of Commerce, the Council for Economic Development, and the American Association of Railroads. Banks neighboring the plants were made another channel of distribution to arouse local interest. Four-page brochures giving more detailed information on specific plants were also printed and a larger, revised edition of the *Briefalogue* was published in August 1945, coincident with the surrender of Japan.[39]

But this was only a part of the preparation for disposal. The Washington office made comparisons of construction costs and operating costs between different plants producing the same product, undertook individual studies of certain giant plants like Basic Magnesium at Las Vegas, Nevada, and Geneva Steel at Geneva, Utah, subsidized research in an effort to find new uses for magnesium, and sought to determine the competitiveness of its plants within each industry. To centralize these efforts, DPC borrowed an economist, Frederick E. Berquist, from the Department of Justice.[40]

Another type of study was begun early in 1945, when Louis H. Bean, assistant chief of the Real Estate Section, was assigned responsibility for determining the current reproduction cost of individual plants. The purpose of these studies was to squeeze out the excess costs of wartime construction in order to arrive at reasonable figures for negotiating sales. Bean was authorized to hire outside consultants to help prepare these appraisals.[41]

Simultaneously, a Plant Utilization Section was organized in the Engineering Division to make "engineering studies of the potential uses of DPC-owned plants and facilities." The Plant Utilization Section sought to provide an additional basis for negotiation by determining the "fair value" of a specific plant to a prospective purchaser. The section also tried to find peacetime uses for special-purpose war plants in order to encourage their conversion to civilian production.[42]

These several types of studies were integrated by a Plant Utilization Committee, of which Berquist was chairman. Since the studies were intended as advance planning, their full effect could not be realized until the plants had been declared surplus. This did not occur in many instances until after RFC was no longer the disposal agency. Nearly all the personnel of these sections were later transferred to the War Assets Administration at its inception in March 1946.[43]

Only a small part of DPC's huge investment in land, plants, and machinery were sold while RFC was responsible for surplus disposal. This investment stood at $6.982 billion as of June 30, 1945. Before these properties could be offered as surplus, they had to be released by their sponsoring agencies. In addition, the termination process, involving the settlement of outstanding contracts and purchase orders, had to be completed. An even greater hurdle was the provision in the Surplus Property Act forbidding disposal of properties in eight industrial categories that had cost the government more than $5 million until thirty days after a report for that category had been filed with Congress.[44]

As the war approached its climax, sponsors began gradually to release DPC facilities. This development became notable, however, only near the date of Japan's surrender. On July 28, 1945, the Navy Department gave its consent, with certain exceptions, to the disposal of navy-sponsored DPC property when that property was no longer being used for manufacturing naval supplies. A similar letter was received from the War Department on August 20, 1945. Nine days later, WPB released 146 of its projects. During succeeding months, the War Department relinquished additional plants.[45]

The disposal of so much property could never have been easy, but the climate in which disposal took place and the variety of goals laid down in the Surplus Property Act contributed to difficulties in transferring the surplus from government into private hands. The speedy demobilization of the armed forces, civilian employees as well as men in uniform, slowed the process of determining which War and Navy Department plants should be declared surplus and, after these decisions were made, of preparing the plants for disposal. Similarly, within RFC there was an exodus of a good many of its more experienced and talented executives. Within a year after V-J Day, for example, both Sam Husbands and Hans Klagsbrunn were gone. Attractive opportunities in the postwar boom in the private sector were a powerful incentive; so was the fact that the top annual salary in federal civil service of $10,000, established during the depression, was maintained into 1948 during a time of soaring prices.[46]

The combining of economic and social goals in the Surplus Property Act also caused problems. The goals of discouraging monopoly and aiding small business, fostering postwar employment, avoiding dislocations in the economy, and supporting independent new enterprises competed for attention alongside the desire to obtain a fair return from sales for the government. During the Seventy-ninth Congress, ending with the close of 1946, the Committee on Military Affairs War Contracts Subcommittee (renamed the Subcommittee on Surplus Property) was the Senate watchdog over surplus disposal. Senator James E. Murray of Montana, chairman of the subcommittee early in the Congress, was succeeded by Senator Joseph C. O'Mahoney of Wyoming. Senator Murray was also the devoted chairman of the Special Senate Commitee on Small Business. His colleague, Senator O'Mahoney, was well known for his work as chairman of the Temporary National Economic Committee, which just prior to World War II had carried on an important investigation of monopoly and of big business practices and power. During the war, O'Mahoney had served as chairman of a subcommittee on industrial reorganization for Senator George's Special Committee on Post-War Economic Policy and Planning. Murray and O'Mahoney, like Senator Edwin Johnson of Colorado, Harold Ickes, and others, were vigorous advocates of the industrial development of the West.[47] When their Senate subcommittee investigated the progress of plant disposal early in 1946, it lashed out at RFC for what it perceived as balance-sheet mentality: "The statistical data developed by RFC have . . . primarily been used to prove that RFC is doing an outstanding job in recouping for the public purse a high percentage of the original investment. . . . Undue emphasis on this particular objective, however, is not conducive to the development of a balanced industrial plant in line with all the stated objectives of the Surplus Property Act."[48] A few months later, Representative Estes Kefauver, chairman of the Monopoly Subcommittee of the House Committee on Small Business, charged the War Assets Administration with failing to use the disposal process to strengthen the competitive position of small business.[49]

The Congress elected in November 1946, with a Republican majority, was of a quite different mind. In the Senate, responsibility for overseeing the disposal of surplus property was transferred to a newly created five-member subcommittee of the Committee on Expenditures in the Executive Department. The conservative bias of its members—Homer Ferguson of Michigan, Bourke Hickenlooper of Iowa, Joseph McCarthy of Wisconsin, John McClellan of Arkansas, and Herbert O'Connor of Maryland—was almost a guarantee that its yardstick would be strictly financial. The subcommittee noted that the rate of return from the sale of surplus was going down much more rapidly than the payroll of the War Assets Administration. They considered the WAA a bureaucratic agency that was outliving its usefulness and put virtually no stock in the agency's claim that its work had been slowed because of the numerous goals laid down in the Surplus Property Act.[50] In the emerging climate of the Cold War, Jess Larson, the administrator of the War Assets Administration, probably felt more secure when he told the House Armed Forces Committee in May 1948 that his agency had always given "paramount consideration" to the needs of national defense in addition to the various objectives of the Surplus Property Act.[51] As Baruch had told the Surplus Property Board in May 1945, "No matter what you do . . . , there will always be a minority—and a very noisy one—who will say you did the wrong thing."[52]

The disposal of surplus plants and equipment was neither neat nor swift. Sometimes plant and equipment were sold together; more frequently, a large part of the machinery was sold separately. Because RFC and its successors, the War Assets Corporation and the War Assets Administration, sold plants and equipment, sometimes together and sometimes separately, regardless of source, it is not always possible to discern what proportion of the total sales were of property formerly owned by DPC. But rough estimates can be made.

Three bench marks can be supplied—January 31, 1946, seven months after the demise of DPC as an RFC subsidiary; September 30, 1947, more than two years after V-J Day; and December 31, 1948. In the period of uncertainty climaxed by the first of these dates, little was accomplished. RFC received $123,953,000 for 130 plants and sites that had cost the government $180,941,875. Of these plants, 118 had been owned by DPC, 10 by the War Department, and 2 by the Navy Department. Nearly half of the DPC plants had been sold to their wartime operators. An additional 41 plants, representing an aggregate investment of $213,178,000, had been leased for from ten months to seven years. With two exceptions, these had formerly been DPC plants. As in the case of plants sold, their wartime operators had leased nearly half of these plants.[53]

The most thorough survey of the disposal of government plants was undertaken by the War Assets Administration in the summer of 1947 at the request of the Bureau of the Budget. This survey reported on all sales of government plants costing more than $500,000 in which machinery was sold with the plant. It showed a higher ratio of RFC plants sold to plants available than for the other three major owners—the War Department, Navy Department, and Maritime Commission. More than 60 percent of the DPC plants had been sold (462 of 737) in whole or in part, compared to slightly less than half for the other three owners. The sales of DPC plants also yielded a higher return on investment (50 percent—$832,000,000 on property costing $1,663,000,000), compared to from 12.5 percent (Maritime Commission) to 35 percent (War Department). For all agencies, smaller plants were most readily sold.

The War Assets Administration estimated that slightly under $5 billion in plants and plant sites remained under government title. Of this amount, $2 billion in plants was being retained by the owning agencies, chiefly the War Department. The War Assets Administration had responsibility for disposal of slightly more than $2 billion, with the remainder being subject to lease or sale by the owning agency under national security restrictions. As of September 30, 1947, $942 million (110 plants) of this inventory were under lease.[54]

The third bench mark, December 31, 1948, marked the date the WAA released a representative list of 495 plant disposals. Although lacking dollar figures, the list provides information on the prior owning agency, the wartime operator, the peacetime operator, and the wartime and peacetime products made at each of these plants. DPC had owned 367 of the plants. Of this number, 199 had been acquired by the wartime operator, and 197 were manufacturing the same or similar products to those in wartime.

A random sample of 28 of the former DPC facilities indicated that the recovery of cost ranged from 6 percent to 82 percent. In most cases, the price paid approached WAA's determination of fair value. In at least one-quarter of the cases, there was only one bidder, and two of the properties were "scrambled." In at least one-third of the cases, WAA refused to accept the initial bid, and in one case it accepted a lower bid in the belief that the successful bidder would be more certain to keep the plant open and would provide a larger payroll.[55]

Three months later, at the end of March 1949, WAA published a list of plants that were under lease. The report listed eighty-six plants, of which seventy-eight had formerly belonged to DPC. An analysis of a sample of sixteen of the DPC plants reveals a government investment ranging from $200,000 to $27,350,000. Twelve of the lessees had been wartime operators. Ten were manufacturing the same products as in wartime, and in four other cases the new products were closely allied to the old.[56]

The disposal process relating to DPC properties can also be looked at from the perspective of major industrial categories. Those directly or indirectly tied to the aviation industry were by all odds the most important. Nearly three-fifths of the DPC investment as of June 30, 1945, was linked in one way or another to that industry. The bulk of this investment was in aircraft plants—airframe and assembly, engines, and parts and accessories. Most investments were in amounts of under $5 million, but sixty-four plants, ranging upward from $5 million to $169 million for the giant engine plant operated by Chrysler outside Chicago, accounted for 85 percent of the total outlay. The sheer size of many of these plants worked against their easy transfer into private ownership. So did the fact that the high clearance and wide bays of airframe plants caused heavy maintenance costs for light, heat, and air conditioning.[57]

Following the war, the aircraft industry was sharply cut back. Between 1937 and 1944, the industry had been expanded more than one hundred-fold to become the nation's largest—four times as large as the peacetime automobile industry. After V-J Day, the total output of the aircraft companies shrank in 1946 to about 6 percent of its wartime peak. The Senate investigating committee earlier known as the Truman committee urged the War Assets Administration "to use every means possible to speed the lease or sale of these plants to aircraft manufacturers" in order to build a strong postwar industry, but peacetime prospects were too bleak for aircraft companies to be deeply interested.[58]

Most aircraft plants were sold or leased to major firms outside the industry, including International Harvester, General Motors, General Electric, Western Electric, Westinghouse, and Electrolite. Because these firms were usually interested in the plants rather than their equipment, vigorous efforts had to be made to clear the plants of machine tools. Special-purpose tools suitable for little else than their wartime use were frequently destroyed and sold as scrap, but some general-purpose tools were bought by General Motors, Packard, and Studebaker to help round out their assembly lines.[59]

The magnitude of the disposal problem posed by the aircraft plants helped the War Assets Administration to view with favor plans advanced by three new firms seeking to enter the auto industry—Kaiser-Frazer, the Tucker Corporation, and the Playboy Motor Car Corporation. This attitude also conformed to the goal in the Surplus Property Act of encouraging competition, but the outcomes were hardly encouraging. Playboy, which had hoped to manufacture a low-priced sports car in an aircraft assembly plant in Buffalo, was never able to find sufficient financing to get its enterprise beyond the planning stage.[60]

The widely publicized Tucker Corporation was little more successful. The Tucker promoters dreamed of a radically new car, the "Torpedo," which they planned to build in the aircraft engine plant in Chicago operated by Chrysler during the war. In spite of friendly cooperation by WAA officials, Tucker also failed to get under way because of inadequate financing. Indeed, Tucker was indicted, but not convicted, for mail fraud in the sale of his company's securities.[61]

Only Kaiser-Frazer was able to break into the auto industry. It lasted only a few years. Henry Kaiser, the ebullient West Coast entrepreneur, had joined forces with Joseph Frazer, former head of Graham-Paige, a well-known prewar auto firm, to manufacture three cars, the lightweight Henry J. and two larger cars, the Kaiser and the Frazer. They hoped to use plentiful aluminum to a considerable extent, and as the site of manufacture secured a ten-year lease on the large airframe plant at Willow Run, Michigan, which they later purchased. Their inability to continue more than a few years suggests that greater financial resources and operations on a larger scale were essential for effective competition against the entrenched auto makers.[62]

The disposal of government aviation gasoline plants paralleled in some respects and on a smaller scale the similar problem with respect to aircraft plants. Government involvement in financing the fourteenfold increase in the production of aviation gasoline was much smaller. Most of the new facilities had been financed by refiners using the tax amortization privilege, but 30 percent, approximately $238 million, had been provided by DPC. Nearly all of these facilities were additions to refineries, enabling them to turn out larger quantities of basic gasoline and of components necessary to achieve the octane rating required for high-performance fuel. Because so many of the facilities were scrambled, bids were usually limited to the owner of the interlocked refinery. Because tax amortization had permitted substantial windfall gains to competitors and because the demand for aviation gasoline was sharply reduced, the government sold the DPC facilities for a lower percentage of its investment than it received from almost any other major industrial group. The recovery from the sale of DPC aviation gasoline facilities prior to September 30, 1947, was little more than 30 percent compared to 50 percent for all DPC plants.[63]

Another related part of the winding down process was the transfer into private ownership of the government's substantial investment in aluminum and magnesium plants. The investment in facilities for ore refining, manufacturing pig aluminum, and its fabrication amounted to $684,168,000. Except for a small reduction plant operated by Olin Industries at Tacoma, Washington, all DPC plants in the first two stages of manufacturing aluminum had been operated by the Aluminum Company of America (Alcoa). In March 1945, after prolonged litigation, Alcoa was adjudged a monopoly in federal court. The leverage provided by this decision helped the government to break Alcoa's hold on the industry, for early in 1946 Alcoa was forced to deliver its patents on a royalty-free basis to operators of the government-owned alumina plants at Hurricane Creek, Arkansas, and Baton Rouge, Louisiana. This outcome gave Reynolds Metals Company the courage to expand further its beachhead in the industry by leasing and later purchasing several government plants. About the same time, Kaiser entered the industry in the same way on what was to prove, in contrast to automobiles, a profitable new venture. By

1956, Alcoa's share of the primary capacity of the industry had been reduced to 43 percent. Kaiser ranked next with 27 percent; Reynolds followed with 26 percent; and Anaconda, a latecomer, had 4 percent. In that year, the production of aluminum—1,609,000 tons—was eight times larger than in 1940. Aluminum manufacturers had developed a range of new uses supplementing and supplanting wood, steel, and copper in various aspects of construction, transportation, the manufacture of consumer durables, and the transmission of electric power. A few of the government's aluminum plants failed to find purchasers, chiefly because of uneconomic locations. The recovery of costs was about 20 percent less than the average for DPC plants because of uncertainty as to the extent of demand for aluminum and also because of the government's desire to encourage competition.[64]

Magnesium was a different story. Prior to World War II, Dow Chemical was its sole manufacturer. Because magnesium had a very thin market, the wartime expansion of magnesium facilities was financed by government to a greater extent than was true in any other industry except synthetic rubber. DPC's investment in plants using a variety of processes amounted to $428 million. Unlike aluminum, there were no major new entrants in the magnesium industry after the war. The plant of Basic Magnesium at Las Vegas, Nevada, largest of the magnesium facilities, was far too large and inefficient for continued use. Ultimately, it was sold as a multipurpose plant to an agency of the state of Nevada for payments of as much as $24 million over twenty years, depending upon the amount the agency collected from rentals. Because of inadequate demand, most of the magnesium plants were placed on standby or dismantled.[65]

Unlike DPC's investments in facilities for aviation gasoline, aluminum, and magnesium, its investments in iron and steel were related less to the aviation industry than to armament and the generalized needs of a war economy. And unlike the relatively young, high-risk aviation, aluminum, and magnesium industries, steel was a major mature industry that was fearful of expansion because of heavy excess capacity during the depression. Because of the industry's reluctance to build new facilities, particularly for such items as heavy steel plates, DPC became the medium for almost half of steel's wartime expansion. DPC's total investment amounted to $950,548,000. More than half the amount invested in thirty-four plants or parts of plants costing more than $5 million was in four facilities: the huge and highly efficient integrated steel plant at Geneva, Utah, operated by U.S. Steel; large additions to U.S. Steel plants at Homestead, Braddock, and Duquesne, Pennsylvania; and two steel plants in the Chicago area operated, respectively, by Republic Steel and Inland Steel.[66]

Because of its size and western location, the disposal of Geneva Steel attracted particular attention. Indeed, Senator O'Mahoney of the War

Contracts Subcommittee declared that the outcome with respect to Geneva Steel would tell much about the whole disposal process. Initially, three steel companies expressed interest—U.S. Steel, Colorado Fuel and Iron, and Kaiser. Henry Kaiser, the most colorful and successful of wartime entrepreneurs, had used his shipyard profits and an RFC loan to build an important new steel mill at Fontana in southern California. But the Kaiser interests made no firm bid for Geneva, and for a time U.S. Steel also dropped out. When a decision was reached in the spring of 1946, Colorado Fuel and Iron and U.S. Steel were the only two significant bidders. Colorado Fuel and Iron offered to lease Geneva for from fifteen to twenty-five years with an option to purchase if the government would lend $48 million for construction of additional facilities, but the rental proposed was inadequate to cover either depreciation or interest on the loan. U.S. Steel, by contrast, offered to pay $40 million plus $7.5 million more for the inventory at the big Utah plant, to invest an additional $18.6 million in new facilities, and, in conjunction therewith, to build a sheet and tin-plate mill downstream at Pittsburg, California, near San Francisco, costing $25 million. It claimed it could not pay more because of the high cost of rail transportation to West Coast markets nearly a thousand miles away, where it would be competing with cheaply delivered waterborne steel from the East. U.S. Steel's assessment of the prospects for Geneva may have been correct, but the sale clearly indicates the problem for the government of a paucity of buyers when selling large plants.

U.S. Steel was willing to pay the government's figure for fair value, $65,013,000, for the facilities it had operated in Pennsylvania. Republic and Inland acquired the facilities near Chicago for approximately 75 percent of fair value.[67]

Synthetic rubber, as a virtually war-created high-risk industry, was almost wholly DPC-financed. DPC's total investment in the synthetic rubber industry was $793,695,000. Of this amount, $648,485,000 was in thirty-four large plants costing from $5 million to $60.3 million. DPC leased these plants at a nominal rental without a purchase option. They manufactured components of synthetic rubber for the account of another RFC subsidiary, the Rubber Reserve Company which, in turn, channeled the rubber into government-approved uses. In 1945, the industry manufactured 820,000 tons. Because synthetic was inferior to natural rubber for most uses and because of the significance of synthetic rubber for national defense, the surplus property administrator delayed declaring the rubber plants surplus until a national policy could be formulated. The policy, announced in 1946 in conformity with the request of the Army-Navy Munitions Board, called for the maintenance of facilities capable of manufacturing 500,000 tons annually. This quantity was later increased by congressional statute to not less than 600,000 tons of general-purpose and 65,000 tons of special-purpose rubber. About one-third of this capac-

ity was standby. The plants continued to be operated under lease from
RFC, with utilization of the rubber being assured by mandatory regulations issued by the Department of Commerce requiring minimum pro-
portions in various types of tires and for other purposes.[68]

The government investment in synthetic rubber was ultimately recaptured. During the war, the Rubber Reserve Company realized a profit of
$120.8 million on its sales. Following the war, the disposal agencies re-
ceived $41.5 million in selling off excess facilities prior to September 30,
1947, that had cost $112 million. After the development of "cold rubber"
had transformed the synthetic product from an inferior to a superior
rubber for tire making, Congress moved in 1953 to transfer the remaining synthetic rubber plants into private hands. When the transactions
were completed in 1955, the buyers had paid $284,850,000 for twenty-six
plants, a sum that exceeded the government's residual net investment by
$25,885,000. In retrospect, it appears that the rubber and oil companies
could have afforded to pay even more. According to a *Fortune* article, in
the year following divestment the industry earned 20 percent before taxes
on the capital invested in the former government plants. By 1960,
twenty-nine additional plants had been built to supplement the production of those acquired from the government. The partnership of government finance and control combined with private know-how had carried
an industry from infancy to maturity.[69]

The government enjoyed a similar satisfying experience in disposing of
six DPC-financed pipelines in which it had invested $155 million. Two of
the lines, "Big Inch," a twenty-four-inch crude oil carrier from Longview,
Texas, to Linden, New Jersey, and "Little Big Inch," a twenty-inch products line running from the refinery complex at Baytown, Texas, to Linden, were responsible for $139 million of this amount. The original
intention was to keep these big lines in petroleum service. But the return
of tankers to coastal sea lanes in more than adequate numbers and fears
concerning the impact of the pipelines on competition in the oil industry,
particularly in refined products, led the government to reopen the bid-
ding in 1947. In the second round, natural gas companies seeking efficient means to reach eastern markets with their cheap fuel were permitted
to bid on a parity with the oil companies. The bid accepted for the two
lines, $143,127,000 by the Texas Eastern Transmission Corporation, was
$77 million higher than the top bid on the earlier round. It was sufficient
to permit the government to recapture the approximate total cost for both
lines. During the war, the Defense Supplies Corporation, another RFC
subsidiary, had cleared $109,069,000 from its purchase and sale of oil that
had passed through the lines. In cost recovery and economic meaning for
the nation, no DPC facilities surpassed the big pipelines and the synthetic
rubber plants. The four smaller lines also found buyers, though at less
favorable prices.[70]

Other DPC fields of investment included chemicals, ordnance, radio and electrical equipment, ship construction, and motor vehicle plants, but, except for machine tools, none of these matched in importance the industries already discussed. Overall, they accounted for an investment of an additional $1.1 billion. The average rate of return on cost for the still minor fraction of facilities in these fields that had been sold prior to September 30, 1947, ranged from a low of 24 percent for nonferrous metal (excluding aluminum and magnesium) to a high of 97 percent for machine tool facilities. In each case, the sums were very small.[71]

DPC's wartime importance in machine tools derived much less from its investment in facilities than from its machine tool pool through which it underwrote nearly half the increase in production by guaranteeing a market and supplying working capital. Two-thirds of the pool tools wound up in government ownership. Many were in DPC plants. As war production began to fall off in 1944, a trickle of tools became available as surplus. The trickle became a mighty stream following the conclusion of the war. In November 1945, it was estimated that as many as seven hundred thousand tools costing $1.8 billion might become surplus. The extent of DPC's contribution to this surplus cannot be stated precisely, but it can be suggested. More than half of DPC's investment in the aircraft industry of $2.6 billion was for machinery and production equipment. Purchasers of larger plants, with at times literally acres of tools, proved usually least interested in acquiring them.[72]

Surplus disposal was the greatest threat faced by the postwar machine tool industry. Because of this threat, Will Clayton and his successors were especially concerned for the industry's welfare. Clayton's first assistant, it may be recalled, had been in charge of OPM's Machine Tool Division. When Symington was surplus property administrator, he called on a Metalworking Machinery Industry Advisory Committee composed of eleven representatives of major tool firms for counsel. Some of the special-purpose tools, like heavy presses or other equipment designed for the production of munitions, military tires, or aircraft engines, posed no problem. They could be destroyed and sold for scrap. But the general-purpose tools, the lathes, planers, milling and grinding machines, cutting tools and gages, commanded a wide market.[73]

The huge amount of tools required a large number of outlets. In addition to government outlets, the successive disposal agencies sought to enlist the aid of the tool industry's manufacturers and dealers. Early in 1945, DPC made an agreement to channel all surplus cutting tools through the original manufacturers, who would restore the tools to first-class condition. The manufacturers were reimbursed for this service and, in turn, agreed to use the restored tools to fill one-quarter of their orders, receiving a commission of 17.5 percent. For other, more durable tools, the government built up a net of more than seventeen hundred dealers and manufacturers who received a commission on sales, first of 12.5 percent and later 15 percent. To help small business firms, tools were sold for as little as a 15 percent down payment, with the balance payable over five years at 4 percent interest.[74]

As might be surmised, the percentage of recovery of costs was greater on earlier sales. The $34 million of tools sold in 1944 recovered 74 percent of the original cost; the $257 million sold in the eighteen months prior to June 30, 1946, yielded 50 percent of cost; the $401 million sold during the calendar year 1946 returned about 40 percent. In the last quarter of that year, in order to speed the disposal process, WAA pulled many tools from under the Clayton formula for sale at reduced fixed prices. Early in 1947, WAA went further. It pushed sales to educational and public health institutions, usually at 5 percent of fair value, and made plans for scrapping most older tools. Overall, the disposal agencies had sold about 170,000 tools through March 1947.[75]

WAA's aggressive marketing cut into the market for new tools, bringing cries of alarm from machine tool manufacturers. During 1946, the industry had been able to sell only $375 million of new tools. At the end of February 1947, its unfilled orders amounted to $145 million. At that time, the WAA inventory of about 200,000 tools represented about five times the value of these orders. About 180,000 more tools were expected to become surplus. The industry was reporting a rise in the cancellation of orders, which it attributed to the competition from surplus tools.[76]

No doubt both WAA and the machine tool industry were pleased when in the emerging climate of the Cold War, Congress passed a law in August 1947 providing for an industrial reserve of plants and machine tools for national defense. WAA could be pleased to see its disposal task made easier, and the machine tool industry could appreciate the prospect of diminished competition.[77]

As far back as 1940, in arguing for what became the DPC lease, Clifford Durr had maintained that government title to war plants would assure an adequate industrial reserve for national defense following the war. This insight gained support during the war. Undersecretary of War Patterson, for example, appearing before the War Contracts Subcommittee of the Senate Committee on Military Affairs in July 1944, urged that DPC aircraft plants not taken over by the industry should be transferred to the Army Air Forces for standby or storage. A few months earlier, the Truman committee had made a similar recommendation for the army and navy to put major government-owned plants on standby as protection against needs in a subsequent emergency. After the war, the War Department and joint agencies of the army and navy made known their desires for specific plants for aircraft and ordnance production and for a reserve of 63,717 tools valued at $350,444,000. The idea of setting up a machine tool reserve was approved by the director of the Office of War

Mobilization and Reconversion in November 1946, but it was without legal force until the president signed a bill in August 1947 authorizing an industrial reserve of both plants and tools. This program was further defined in the National Industrial Reserve Act of July 2, 1948.[78]

Meanwhile, the joint army-navy machine tool program (JANMAT) had gotten under way on a small scale early in 1947. Plans for the reserve ran as high as 183,000 tools costing approximately $625 million. At the time of the Korean War, the machine tool reserve numbered about 150,000. The tool reserve had sopped up a considerable portion of the surplus tools and, in doing so, made them no longer a competitive threat for the machine tool industry.[79]

Similarly, the acts of 1947 and 1948 had provided for a national industrial reserve of plants certified by the armed services as essential to national defense. These plants could be sold or leased, subject to a national security clause requiring their conversion to war production if necessary in times of a national emergency. If they were not sold or leased, they were placed on standby in a custodial reserve. Plants disposed of under the national security clause, numbering 145 in all, had been almost wholly DPC-owned during World War II. They ran across a broad spectrum from facilities in basic industries—aluminum, magnesium, and steel—to aircraft, ordnance, and shipbuilding plants. An additional 100 plants, valued at close to $1 billion, which the War Assets Administration had been unable to sell or lease, were placed in custodial reserve with the Federal Works Agency, the chief predecessor of the General Services Administration.[80]

By midyear 1949, the disposal of surplus plants and tools had been largely accomplished. The fact that the nation did not fall into a postwar depression but, on the contrary, enjoyed a boom helped generate and maintain a substantial demand for production facilities. The national industrial reserve handled much of the rest.

9
A Trial Balance

In evaluating DPC, two related questions can be asked: How effective was the Defense Plant Corporation? How well did it serve the national interest?

Surely a central part of the answer is in the quality of DPC's performance. But this is not the totality. Another part relates to the extent of recovery of its vast investment. Still others are the significance of the disposal of its plants and equipment in expanding peacetime production, in opening up new opportunities for enterprise, and in stimulating the economic development of regions hitherto lightly industrialized. Finally, a comparison should be made of the relative merits of the two principal means used to bring the war-related commercial-type facilities into being—DPC and tax amortization.

The performance of an emergency agency like DPC is virtually certain to be flawed. Such an agency is born and acts in a situation of crisis, which itself may also be increasing in magnitude. Emphasis is not on perfection, but on success in dealing with the emergency. Some of the actions taken can be questioned at the time and, even more, later on. But a balanced judgment requires that shortcomings should not be permitted to obscure the extent of the achievement.

DPC, surely, had its shortcomings. As an emergency agency without parallel, it was doing what had never been done before. It was put together in haste in less than ideal circumstances to give speedy implementation to decisions by other government agencies and departments. Some of its policies and actions were criticized during the war. Still other criticisms came later, particularly as the result of a searching examination of RFC and its wartime subsidiaries undertaken by the General Accounting Office (GAO) in 1946 in response to an act of Congress.[1]

During the war, at least three areas of criticism arose regarding specific lease terms—the payment of real property taxes, the problem of breaking loose idle machine tools from under the leases for use elsewhere, and the variety of money rentals. These were also examined, along with other perceived operational deficiencies, in the detailed report of the General Accounting Office.

Probably the sharpest dispute between DPC and the armed services during the war revolved around the payment of local property taxes by the lessee. Because these taxes were paid, they had to be included as a charge in figuring the cost of supplies produced under the supply contract. The services, secure in their tax immunity with respect to the plants they owned, considered DPC's interpretation of its tax obligation under the RFC Act as an unwarranted burden on the federal taxpayer, especially since the vast majority of states exempted federal property from taxation either by statute or by constitutional provision. To avoid these tax payments, both services seriously considered paying off DPC under the take-out letters and assuming ownership of their sponsored projects.[2]

DPC viewed the matter differently. It objected to disturbing its amicable relations with local communities. DPC pointed out that its commercial-type facilities, in contrast to much of the arsenal-type facilities of the services, were usually located in heavily populated areas. Their presence in old, established communities was beneficial to the communities but created problems in providing the plants with water, sewage, fire protection, transportation, and other communal services. Most communities were cooperative in relaxing building codes to speed construction.

DPC argued that some tax payment was appropriate in return for the assistance received in getting the plants into operation. Moreover, the tax load was often lessened because of DPC's success in gaining reductions in tax assessments because of inflated war costs. DPC also usually was successful in excluding heavy machinery, sometimes classified as real property, from the tax base. DPC officials maintained that freeing the projects from all taxes would place a heavy burden upon the local communities and risk loss of goodwill.[3]

Both services ultimately accepted the practice of a limited payment of taxes. They did so not because of a shortage of funds to purchase the plants under the take-outs, but principally because paying off the balance would have required them to take on the DPC administrative burden. A lesser reason may have been that the addition of their sponsored DPC projects to their directly owned plants could have seemed to Congress a startlingly large agglomeration of industrial properties. They ran less risk of attracting congressional attention with many of their properties DPC-titled.[4] The advantages of community assistance and goodwill and the general success of DPC in keeping taxes at modest levels make it appear that the concern of the services over taxes was exaggerated.

Concern over difficulties in breaking loose machine tools from under the lease for use elsewhere was of greater consequence. The omission of any provision permitting transfer of machine tools except to sublessees was done deliberately early in the defense period at the insistence of contractors and of the War and Navy Departments. Many contractors, it will be recalled, were drawn into the defense program in the belief that through exercise of the purchase option the DPC facilities each was building and operating would ultimately become its own. One of the strong points of the DPC program was this stimulus of pride in potential ownership that induced defense contractors to install special equipment, which they would have done more reluctantly, or not at all, if they had felt that at the conclusion of the defense period title could pass to competitors. Nor were contractors anxious to run the risk of arbitrary action by some subordinate government agent who might deprive them of tools essential to the fulfillment of their contracts. The army and navy, too, wished to avoid a situation in which production might be disrupted through possible development of a system of overriding priorities for tools already in use.[5]

There was one condition in which contractors were willing, even eager, to release idle DPC machine tools. This occurred when rentals were based on a percentage of cost of the project, for the manufacturer was not eager to pay rent on idle tools. When rentals were based either on a percentage of sales or of production, or were nominal, the situation was different because the manufacturer would gain nothing from the release of the tools. He therefore was apt to seek to retain the tools for possible future use on other government contracts or as a protection against production difficulties on present contracts that contained penalty provisions for nonfulfillment.[6]

As the war progressed, concerted efforts were made to keep machine tools active. Early in 1943, the armed services joined with DPC and WPB in an agreement that if machinery were idle and needed elsewhere, specific items of machinery would be released to the service requesting the transfer. Lists of idle machine tools were compiled by such major units as the Army Air Forces, Ordnance Department, Signal Corps, the Chemical Warfare Service in the War Department, and the Bureau of Aeronautics in the Navy Department. Those, in turn, were converted into a master list by the Tools Division of WPB. When tools were transferred from a DPC project under WPB Directive 13, which resulted from the agreement, the original take-out continued to govern the tools, insofar as DPC was concerned. The initiative in designating DPC machinery as idle rested with the sponsors.[7]

A more important contribution to the solution of this problem, the "rentra" lease, was devised by the services and DPC during the summer of 1943. This new lease freed tools from under plancor leases with a minimum of effort and avoided the negotiation of a new plancor lease. The rentra was intended to cover the needs of the smaller contractors of the services who needed a limited amount of machinery and who were not DPC plancor lessees.

Initially, the new procedure was used to effect transfers not exceeding $50,000 in value. The transfer of machinery, at the request or with the consent of the armed service, freed the original lessee of all obligations pertaining to the machinery. The rentra lease, negotiated by DPC with the new party at a rental of 1 percent per month of the original cost, was terminable at the request of the service. These provisions were subsequently modified to increase the value of machinery that could be transferred to $100,000 and later $500,000.[8]

The new program ultimately resulted in 1,557 rentra leases of more than ten thousand tools valued at nearly $38 million. Because the program required the cooperation of already overburdened field staffs and the Washington office, it was not always administered smoothly. Two or more weeks frequently elapsed between the time the supervising engineer was notified of the impending transfer of tools and his ability to supply the Washington office with a detailed description of each item. Often there were further delays before the lease was sent to the appropriate regional loan agency for servicing. The loan agency did not always collect these relatively small monthly rentals when due, which brought forth criticism from the General Accounting Office in its postwar survey of DPC operations.[9]

Following a survey of DPC properties by field engineers and lessees in December 1944 to ferret out idle machine tools, DPC took a final step to utilize its tools more efficiently. Its officials conferred with the services and WPB to determine the feasibility of establishing an interagency organization for transferring idle tools where needed. An Inter-Agency Review Committee was organized, with the chief of the Machine Tool Section of DPC as chairman, to receive statements of need and lists of tools reported as surplus. All applications for new equipment having a unit price of more than $3,000 were screened against these lists for possible substitutions. If found, idle tools were sent to new destinations within a few hours or days, in contrast to weeks, as formerly. Both economy and efficiency were thus achieved.[10]

Through these means, the machine tool problem was substantially alleviated despite the unqualified character of the lease. Persuasion by the services and consciousness on the part of the lessees themselves of the need for keeping machine tools at work helped bring about a high degree of cooperation late in the war. Nevertheless, a more direct means for achieving transfers would have been desirable. Perhaps the lease should have contained a provision permitting withdrawal of tools from a project on certification of need by an officer of high rank, say, at the cabinet level. This would have provided greater flexibility while at the same time affording protection from the anarchy that could have ensued if the power to order transfers were exercised at too low levels by individuals in programs that were fiercely competitive. Such a provision also need not have unduly alarmed contractors. Contractors, on the other hand, would justly have feared any provision making the transfer of machine tools too easy.[11]

A further criticism of the DPC lease, made during and after the war, concerned the wide variation in the bases used for determining rentals. Nearly half of DPC's investment was leased for nominal rentals of a dollar per year. Rentals in the remainder were calculated as a percent of cost or sales, or, in a few cases, of net income or the volume of production. Similarly, there were variations in the time periods for which rental payments were due. Some were due monthly, others quarterly, and still others annually.[12]

These variations brought DPC substantial goodwill because of its willingness to flex its terms within limits to conform to the desires of the lessees, but they also made administration of ultimately thousands of leases (including rentras) much more difficult. Each lease had to be read carefully to determine its content. Moreover, because DPC personnel were so heavily burdened, probably too great faith had to be placed in self-policing by lessees. Lessees, for example, were far more likely to call DPC's attention to situations suggesting the need for a rental adjustment in the interest of the lessee than they were to a similar situation suggesting the need for an adjustment in the interest of the government.[13]

The General Accounting Office also criticized rental practices under various forms of the DPC lease on more specific grounds. The GAO pointed out that in instances of nominal rental the contractors and subcontractors were required to use the facilities solely to fill government contracts, but DPC frequently failed to determine independently, particularly in cases of subcontractors, that this obligation was being met. The same requirement existed for sublessees under percent of sales and volume-of-production rental agreements. Here, too, violations could occur without DPC's knowledge. DPC usually relied on audits by independent public accountants with respect to these latter rental patterns to help ascertain whether rental payments were in the correct amount, but it did not always examine the audits carefully to make sure that they were fully adequate for its needs. In at least one instance, the twenty-five projects leased to Republic Steel Corporation, DPC accepted Republic's volume-of-production rental payments without audit.[14] It seems probable, in retrospect, that the government's interest would have been better served if there had been fewer variations in the terms of rental and tighter controls over payment but, in the absence of proof of gross abuses, the lessee goodwill generated by the variations cannot be totally discounted.

The GAO found numerous other deficiencies. Some related to operational policies. GAO criticism grew out of decisions regarding railroad transportation and insurance made when the DPC program was small and no one could foresee its ultimate size. Others had to do with the quality of

DPC's record keeping, which T. Coleman Andrews, director of the audit, described as "woefully negligent."[15]

GAO was particularly critical of DPC's failure to seek preferential land-grant rates for its shipments west of the Mississippi River on certain railroads to which the government had made grants of land during the Civil War and Reconstruction eras. These preferential rates had been limited by statute in 1940 to "the transportation of military or naval property of the United States moving for military or naval and not for civil use." Because DPC believed that most of its property could not qualify for these rates, it decided against trying to use them. In view of the later huge size of its program requiring an overall outlay for rail transportation estimated at $140 million, DPC would undoubtedly have done better to have tested its rights as a defense agency. If it had been successful, its savings would have run into many millions of dollars. DPC could also have been more zealous in seeking special rates and advantageous routes on other railroads.[16]

Similarly, GAO found fault with DPC's policy requiring lessees to carry commercial insurance instead of acting as a self-insurer. The GAO auditors estimated that premium costs had outrun losses by approximately $8.4 million through March 1946. The practice of utilizing commercial insurance when the program was small seems to have been appropriate, but after the number of projects had become large, self-insurance clearly would have been the more reasonable policy.[17]

The GAO reserved its severest strictures for DPC's accounting practices, which, it said, were carried on at the level of "routine bookkeeping." It charged DPC with placing undue reliance on the lessees and management contractors both in the construction and operation of plants. DPC depended primarily on the asset property records kept at each project for knowledge of the extent of its investment. Presumably, these were maintained under the active supervision of the DPC resident engineer, but in most cases they were maintained by employees of the lessee or management contractor. These records, which were on a cash basis, took no cognizance of depreciation, loss or destruction of property, costs of administering the project, or DPC's interest burden for borrowed capital. Statements of profit and loss for projects operated directly for the account of DPC showed similar deficiencies. They were calculated free from all charges deriving from the use of the facilities.[18]

The cumulative effect of these and other deficiencies caused the GAO to report that with respect to the disposal of DPC's surplus property, it was "impossible . . . to ascertain what profits have actually been earned or losses incurred by the Company." Its overall conclusion was equally bleak: "Because of the qualifications presented in the summary . . . , we are unable to express the opinion that the financial statements accompanying this report present fairly the financial position of Defense Plant Corporation at June 30, 1945, or the results of its operations for the period ended on that date."[19]

When the GAO first made such charges in a summary way against RFC and its wartime subsidiaries in June 1946, they brought a vigorous rebuttal from the RFC chairman, Charles B. Henderson: "The GAO letter does not show that RFC has failed to carry out its responsibilities in a satisfactory manner or that the Government has suffered any loss whatsoever." Henderson wrote Senator Robert Wagner, chairman of the Banking and Currency Committee, that the report "does not contain a single statement indicating irregularities." Any deficiencies, he stated, could be attributed to hasty wartime improvisations.[20] From retirement, Jesse Jones rushed to the defense of his old agency—"the most competent government business agency that has ever operated on so vast a scale." Jones admitted that RFC's enormous wartime activities had been carried on under great pressures: "These vast operations called for many more accountants and auditors than were available, although RFC did increase the normal number from approximately 100 to more than 1,000." But he claimed that the GAO had found "nothing worthy of criticism."[21]

Although Jones and Henderson went too far in their defense, the charges made by the GAO were more procedural than substantive. As Jones indicated, RFC and its wartime subsidiaries had neither the time nor the personnel to permit practice of the generally accepted accounting standards looked for by the GAO. Their goal was the more significant one of supporting the war effort with maximum force and efficiency. Even the GAO recognized their substantial success. In discussing GAO's preliminary findings before a House committee, T. Coleman Andrews testified, "We have no desire to detract in any way from the admittedly great value of their contributions."[22]

In his defense, Jones had pointed to DPC's central wartime problem—a persistent shortage of qualified personnel. The most critical shortages were in the skilled professions of engineer and auditor. The number of engineers in RFC's Self-Liquidating Loan Division at the time of the creation of DPC was fourteen. In December 1941, at the outbreak of the war, DPC's Engineering Division had grown to 165. Meanwhile, a program that had been expected to include 150 to 200 projects had suddenly become almost limitless.[23]

In March 1942, W. L. Drager, the able chief of DPC's Engineering Division, wrote to his superior, Morton Macartney, chief of RFC's Self-Liquidating Loan Division:

> The construction and equipment of 800 armament projects (and hundreds of increases to such projects) throughout the entire country, costing

approximately $5,000,000,000, is being supervised by the Engineering Division with a force which must be doubled as fast as personnel can be obtained from Civil Service.

The Engineering Division is desperately in need of 150 engineers and 30 clerk-stenographers, while at least 100 additional engineers are also urgently needed today. At least 15 engineers and 30 clerks are required in the Washington office—the balance of the personnel is for the field since our work has been decentralized as much as possible.[24]

Drager's request was not adequately answered. During most of 1942, when construction was at flood tide, the shortage of engineers was especially trying. Most new engineers from civil service lists were over sixty years of age, and some were over seventy. Some, too, were physically handicapped. With such personnel, deaths, sickness, and retirements were all too frequent, resulting in delays on projects. As one means of spreading qualified personnel, DPC appointed a few women to projects involving solely the purchase and installation of machinery. It also made tentative efforts to recruit personnel from railroads and industries that were not engaged in war work. The response in many cases was favorable. The number was inadequate to meet the need, but it did afford a minor alleviation during the period when the shortage of engineers was most serious.[25]

Similar difficulties faced the Auditing Division. At the start of the war, RFC's Auditing Division had a total of 116 employees. This number grew, but never sufficiently to permit RFC to handle its own work and that of its subsidiaries smoothly and easily. During 1942, a few accountants and auditors were secured from civil service lists. In 1943, however, by direction of the president, all government departments and agencies were given priority numbers. The Civil Service Commission was required to recruit in accordance with those priorities. Although RFC was given a "II" priority for engineers, it was unable to gain a similar rating for auditors and accountants. RFC could not compete for such personnel on civil service rosters against departments and agencies with higher priorities. It was forced, therefore to recruit directly whatever accountants and auditors it could find.[26]

Because of the huge work load and at times the low quality of DPC engineers and auditors, DPC found it necessary to depend on the assistance and goodwill of lessees and management contractors for help in supervision and record keeping. This was not necessarily dangerous to the government's interest. Contractors who took the purchase option seriously (as most did in the defense and early war periods) had good cause to construct and operate an efficient and well-run plant. This self-interest was reinforced if their rent was determined as a percent of cost, which was the second most common form of rental. Moreover, there was too much money to be made legitimately (subject to excess profits taxes) for large corporations to put themselves at risk by shady practices at the project level.[27]

The absence of major frauds seems borne out by the findings in the GAO audit. Because it was impossible to examine carefully more than 2,000 projects, the GAO auditors chose for detailed study a sample of 175 large projects, including all 39 operated for the account of DPC. These projects ran across the spectrum of industries with which DPC was involved and represented about 60 percent of its total investment. At the conclusion of their study, the auditors singled out 17 cases as examples of "laxity and carelessness in the negotiation and administration of contracts."[28]

Ten of the cases were unlikely members of the GAO sample, for they ranged in investment from a few hundred thousand dollars to under $5 million. Only four involved investments of more than $10 million. Two of these were in the young and relatively undeveloped magnesium industry—Basic Magnesium at Las Vegas, Nevada, and Mathieson Alkali at Lake Charles, Louisiana. Both were entered into at the direction of the Office of Production Management, even though Basic was a small company of limited experience and Mathieson planned to use a process untested commercially. In both cases, it seems evident that the DPC engineers should have been more aggressive in supervising construction, but responsibility for the shortcomings was hardly limited to DPC. Two were aircraft projects. In one, the $77 million Pratt and Whitney aircraft engine plant at Kansas City, the navy, rather than DPC, appears to have been at fault. In its first production contract, the navy agreed to hold Pratt and Whitney blameless for any loss or damage to DPC property, thus freeing Pratt and Whitney from financial accountability. In the other, the widely publicized Kaiser-Hughes wooden cargo plane project, DPC was not in a position to take action because of the sturdy support given that project by President Roosevelt. The three intermediate-sized projects show substantial DPC responsibility for shortcomings with respect to investment and operation of a steel plant in Kentucky and an aircraft plant in Connecticut and lesser responsibility with respect to a pipeline investment in Texas.[29]

The shortcomings GAO revealed in these cases by no means exhaust the potential list of flawed performance on the part of DPC and its staff. Only a minority of the cases, however, came from GAO's sample of "larger plants." In only one case was a major American corporation, United Aircraft Corporation, the parent of Pratt and Whitney, directly involved. In this case, DPC had no part in drawing up the terms of contract which the GAO censured. Even though there is clear evidence in the GAO audit of defective supervision and administration by DPC engineers, auditors, and, at times, top management, the losses seem relatively minor. They were not inappropriate to a time of crisis when getting things done regardless of cost was the overriding priority. Moreover, the substantial degree of self-policing seems to have worked relatively well among the large companies where failure could have led to major scandals.

As the GAO audit makes clear, it is not possible to determine precisely the extent of recovery of the government's investment from facilities of the Defense Plant Corporation. This is true partly because of deficiencies in accounting and partly because in disposing of industrial facilities no sustained attempt was made to keep the DPC facilities that were sold or leased separate from those formerly owned by other agencies. To the War Assets Administration, surplus was surplus to be disposed of regardless of origin. The proceeds from disposal after 1946 were paid directly into the U.S. Treasury without credit to RFC.[30]

But this does not mean that a rough estimate is beyond possibility. There are several helpful sources. One is the "Report on Government Owned Industrial Plants as of September 30, 1947," put together by the War Assets Administration on recoveries made on the disposal of plants valued at more than $500,000. At that time, nearly one-fourth of the DPC investment of $6.982 billion had been sold for about 50 percent of cost.[31] Much of the remainder continued to be sold. These sales undoubtedly yielded a smaller percent of the investment, except for approximately $575 million in synthetic rubber plants that returned slightly more than cost.[32] Sales of machine tools provide another source. If DPC's machine tools were sold in the same ratio to machine tools from other former agency owners as DPC plants to other plants, the U.S. Treasury would have received approximately $210 million through December 1946, a return of slightly less than 50 percent.[33] In addition, according to an RFC financial statement, DPC had gained $817 million from rentals and other income and probably at least $100 million more from renegotiation and other sources through June 30, 1947. This does not include reimbursements made under the take-out letters amounting to $1.38 billion.[34] Offsets to these recoveries include losses for most plants operated for the account of DPC, subsidies to producers of aluminum, interest on funds borrowed to finance DPC's investment in facilities, and administrative costs aggregating approximately $218 million prior to June 30, 1945.[35] These figures are indeed exasperatingly fragmentary as the basis for an estimate. Among their more significant deficiencies are the lack of any data on cost recoveries through rentals after June 30, 1947, machine tool sales after December 31, 1946, sales of plants (except synthetic rubber) after September 30, 1947, or costs growing out of administration of the plants and interest burden on the investment after June 30, 1945, to say nothing of the appropriate share of WAA's disposal costs. Probably the

best that can be said is that the government's overall cost recovery from
the DPC facilities it sold was not more than about 35 percent.[36]

Cost recovery, while important, is only a part of the evaluation of the
DPC experience. Beyond the balancing of accounts, there is the question
of the meaning of DPC for the nation's postwar industrial balance—the
role of the DPC plants as agents of change within industries and among
regions.

For at least three industries—aluminum, synthetic rubber, and natural
gas—the DPC investment helped bring about significant change. The
DPC aluminum plants ended Alcoa's monopoly by providing the means
of entry for two strong competitors, Reynolds and Kaiser. Its synthetic
rubber facilities nurtured an industry through its infant years until the
necessary technological developments permitted the industry to stand on
its own feet. DPC's "Big Inch" and "Little Big Inch" pipelines helped the
natural gas industry to widen its markets to the mutual benefit of Texas
producers and East Coast consumers.

But DPC plants did not contribute to diminishing the extent of economic concentration in industry. The bulk of DPC's funds were invested
in large plants operated by large companies. At the direction of its sponsors, DPC concluded agreements with thirteen large companies for plants
that exceeded $100 million for each company and accounted for $3.09
billion, or about 43 percent of the total DPC investment. Another twelve
companies received contracts for plants aggregating an additional billion
dollars.[37] These large plants, some located more for strategic than economic reasons, usually proved more difficult to sell or lease after the war
than the smaller plants. In general, large surplus plants were bought by
large companies, frequently for cash, and small plants by smaller companies, often on credit. If a large company acquired a small plant, it was
likely to have been the wartime operator or, if not, to have been the only or
a substantially higher bidder than competitors. Usually the War Assets
Administration favored smaller firms in selling small plants.[38]

Although DPC's plants led to no notable change in the postwar ratio of
small to big business, they proved of more significance in accelerating
industrialization in some regions, especially the South and West. This was
in part for strategic reasons. During the defense and early war periods, it
seemed undesirable to locate much more industry in the heavily developed areas along the Atlantic Coast that could be vulnerable to enemy
attack. The presence of a larger labor pool further to the West in the more
agricultural areas was also a factor. So was the presence of natural
resources—bauxite for alumina imported chiefly from the Caribbean,
cheap electric power for aluminum reduction and fabrication in the
Pacific Northwest, magnesite for magnesium in Nevada, rich iron ore and
coal deposits in Utah, and, above all, petroleum for aviation gasoline and

for butadiene and styrene for the manufacture of synthetic rubber in Texas and Louisiana.

The Federal Reserve banks took particular note of the significance of the government-owned surplus war plants for peacetime production in their districts, though, unfortunately, they rarely distinguished DPC plants from those built by the armed services. Between 1945 and 1947, nearly all of their monthly reviews published articles on this theme. Those published in the older, more heavily industrialized regions that had been less favored areas of wartime investment took note of the phenomenon early and wrote in more general terms; the monthly reviews of the Federal Reserve banks further west and south waited until many of the war plants had been assimilated into the economy before attempting to assess this development. Based on articles written by economists of the four southern Federal Reserve banks, two executives of the St. Louis bank wrote a brief monograph in 1949 on the overall impact of war plants on the South.

During 1945, the monthly reviews of the New York, Philadelphia, and Cleveland Federal Reserve banks commented on the potential significance of war plants and equipment for their districts. DPC had been responsible for about one-third of the slightly more than $2 billion invested during the war in industrial facilities in the New York Federal Reserve district and of the $1.1 billion in the Philadelphia district. Its investment was dominantly in large plants in the aircraft and aluminum industries and in scrambled facilities in the iron and steel industry. The *Monthly Review* of the New York Federal Reserve Bank correctly pointed to the large size of the plants and inflated wartime construction costs as important deterrents in finding buyers. It also noted, "An expanding economy will require additional production capacity, so that the demand for plants built during the war will depend in part on the future level of economic activity." The Philadelphia *Business Review* was somewhat more sanguine, anticipating little difficulty, except for ordnance and shipbuilding, in absorbing war-built plants into the peacetime economy. The *Monthly Business Review* of the Cleveland Bank took a darker view. It estimated that no more than one-third of the wartime facilities were readily adaptable to peacetime use. The bank was particularly concerned over the future of the machine tool industry that was so important to the economic health of its region. It urged that a large portion of the government-owned machine tools be put on standby "so as not to hurt the industry."[39]

Further to the west, the Chicago Federal Reserve Bank published in the spring of 1947 an especially thorough survey of the outcomes in its district. More than $3.5 billion in public funds had been invested during the defense and war periods—a larger sum than in any other district. The bank found that 190 of the 251 plants declared surplus had been sold or leased. In dollar terms, two-thirds of the plants costing under $10 million had been sold, compared to only one-third of the plants costing above $25 million. The return on cost "tended to vary inversely with plant size and directly with the population of the area in which the plant [was] located." Highly urbanized Michigan, with a cost recovery of 55 percent, stood at one extreme, and rural Iowa, averaging only 24 percent, was at the other. These former war plants had 150,000 employees in 1947—5 percent of the district's industrial work force—turning out steel, agricultural machinery, aluminum, auto parts, and, it was hoped, automobiles. The remaining inventory of 61 plants, with an additional 36 in prospect, tended to be larger facilities, poorly located, and less readily adaptable to peacetime use.[40]

The Kansas City Federal Reserve Bank likewise entered a report in 1947. During the war, the government had financed 53 plants for a total investment of a little more than $1 billion in its district. Thirty of the plants, representing slightly less than half of this sum, had been declared surplus. Fifteen had been sold, frequently to their wartime operators. They usually continued to produce for a civilian market the same products they had made in wartime, such as petroleum products, glass, synthetic rubber, and iron and steel. Four plants had been transferred to municipalities. Of the remainder, nine had been leased. Several plants not yet declared surplus were large ordnance facilities of limited postwar utility. The bank soberly concluded that the transfer of government plants into private hands had "added greatly to the peacetime productive capacity of the Tenth Federal Reserve District."[41]

War plant disposal had its greatest impact across the South and West. Some years after World War II, Frank Smith, a Mississippi congressman and former editor, credited the war with bringing "a new kind of prosperity to the South" and added, "Willingly or not, knowingly or not, the South is finally entering the mainstream of American life." Reflecting on the events of World War II, an economist on the staff of the Federal Reserve Bank of Atlanta commented that the South was "no longer the nation's No. 1 economic problem."[42] These comments may have been too sanguine, but they had a basis in the wartime reality.

The government investment in war plant in the South ($4.5 billion) was roughly proportionate to the South's share (17 percent) of the national population in 1940. It was at an annual rate substantially higher than the prewar investment in industrial facilities recorded for the South in the Census of Manufactures for 1939 even when allowance is made for the inflated costs of wartime construction. This wave of new plants came to the South because of natural resources, climate, and a labor pool attractive for its size if not always for its skills. The wave was uneven, affecting some areas to a much greater degree than others. Also many of the new plants were arsenal-type facilities of limited peacetime value. But their importance outran their direct value for peacetime production. During the war, they helped train a managerial group whose entrepreneurial skills were a continuing asset to the South and acquainted many of the rural poor with an alternative way of life. Southern skills were built up and attitudes affected. After the war, numerous southern states quickened their efforts to bring about industrial development.[43]

The South Atlantic states in the domain of the Federal Reserve Bank of Richmond shared least in this great industrial expansion. This was true partly because their location made them seem more vulnerable to enemy attack and partly because of the nature of the government's investment. Forty-seven large government plants costing a total of $521 million were arsenals, mine depots, navy yards, munition plants, and shipyards that could not become important productive peacetime assets. The smaller plants, usually financed by DPC, were of greater promise. According to a Federal Reserve survey, by the end of June 1947 the War Assets Administration and its predecessors had sold thirty-nine plants in the Richmond Federal Reserve Bank District. Only a synthetic rubber facility at Institute, West Virginia, represented an investment of more than $6 million. The thirty-nine plants, costing $90,585,000, brought a return of $26,024,000. Most were sold to their wartime operators and continued to manufacture the same type of goods. An additional six plants costing $7.2 million had been leased, and seventeen more representing an investment of $63 million were in inventory.[44]

A similar survey made by the St. Louis Federal Reserve Bank had parallel outcomes. Most of the government's wartime investment in that district had been in facilities difficult to convert to peacetime use. More than two-thirds of $1.2 billion invested in publicly owned facilities was for ordnance production. Ten of the twenty-seven ordnance plants, usually the smaller in size, had been sold or leased by November 1947. Although the dollar return from the sales was not given, it quite clearly was low. The War Assets Administration was more successful in selling and leasing former DPC properties, particularly in the aircraft and aluminum industries. At the time of the survey, about one-seventh as many workers were employed in the government plants as during the wartime peak. Because of the nature of most of the remaining plants, it seemed unlikely that the extent of employment would grow much larger.[45]

Government plant financing had a greater impact on the territory served by the Atlanta Federal Reserve Bank. Approximately $1.3 billion was invested in 185 plants during the defense and war years, representing a fourfold increase over the annual rate for 1939. Many of the facilities were located in the district for military and strategic, rather than economic, reasons. For much of the production—munitions and ships, for example—the postwar outlook was bleak. But the former DPC facilities in iron and steel, synthetic rubber, chemicals, petroleum refining, aluminum, and aircraft had brighter prospects. A large portion of the $500 million in government facilities sold by the disposal agencies prior to September 30, 1947, was in these industries. In addition, in several instances civic groups had taken over large plants, like aircraft, and had sought to maintain them as operating entities through the device of multiple tenancy. In the fall of 1947, employment in the former war plants was a little more than one-quarter of its wartime peak. The shift to civilian production had deprived many war plants of their value, but those that had been used during the war for standard commercial products helped supply a powerful push toward industrialization. Partly because of these plants, postwar Atlanta became the hub of a rapidly growing industrial empire.[46]

Nowhere was this push toward industrialization more evident than in the Dallas Federal Reserve District. The district had in its favor not only strategic factors appropriate to the emergency but also natural economic advantages. These were, notably, a large labor pool and, in petroleum, a valuable natural resource with a variety of uses. Prior to World War II, Texas, the heartland of the district, had been industrialized to only a limited extent. In 1939, only 3 percent of the nation's industrial work force resided in Texas; by 1947, this proportion had grown by one-third, and Texas had become one of the ten most important industrial states.[47]

Texas would undoubtedly have become more important industrially in any case, but war sped the process. During the defense and war years, numerous synthetic rubber, chemical, oil refining, aircraft, iron and steel, magnesium, ordnance, and tin plants were built and financed, mainly with government capital. Throughout the district, which spilled over into parts of Louisiana, Oklahoma, New Mexico, and Arizona, the government invested $1.137 billion. DPC supplied approximately two-thirds of this amount, and $625 million in Texas. (Because of this heavy investment, the barbed-tongued journalists Drew Pearson and Robert S. Allen angered Jesse Jones, a favorite target, by referring to him as "Texas' last great unexploited resource!") Most of this government capital was invested in or near the burgeoning metropolitan centers: Houston, Beaumont–Port Arthur, Fort Worth–Dallas, with the lesser investments in the Panhandle and Northeast Texas. Synthetic rubber was by far the primary field of DPC investment. The usually large synthetic rubber plants—butadiene, butyl, styrene, and copolymer—absorbed approximately one-third of the government capital invested in the district. This was almost two-thirds of the total national investment in the new industry.[48]

Because natural economic advantages were more real in the location of government war plants in the Dallas Federal Reserve Bank District than in most others, the problem of postwar operation of these plants proved somewhat easier. In March 1948, of fifty-three major facilities in Texas financed with federal funds, twenty-two had been sold, seventeen were under lease, five were seeking buyers or lessees, five were on standby, and four had been dismantled or destroyed. For some of these plants, the demand was brisk. Smaller metal-product plants were being called on to support the soaring industrial growth, particularly along the Texas coast, and to manufacture oilfield and agricultural equipment for a growing world market. Chemical plants, too, were in great demand. Thirteen major new chemical projects were announced in 1947, some of which were closely related to facilities built during the war years.[49]

Next to the Southwest, no section of the nation was more affected by government financing of industrial facilities than the trans-Rocky Mountain West. DPC invested more than $900 million in these states—aluminum facilities in the Pacific Northwest and, to a lesser extent, in California; aircraft plants, particularly in southern California; aviation gasoline facilities in California; a huge magnesium facility near Las Vegas, Nevada; and a giant steel plant in Utah. The *Monthly Review* of the Federal Reserve Bank of San Francisco laconically observed in January 1947, "A number of large Government-owned war plants in steel, aluminum, aircraft and machinery and engine building industries were acquired by private concerns and placed in commercial operation."[50]

But there was more to it than that. A number of facilities, like the aluminum reduction plant at Riverbank, California, were too high-cost for peacetime operation. Other aluminum plants in the Pacific Northwest, aided by low electric power rates, proved to be highly efficient. The Geneva Steel plant and Kaiser's steel mill at Fontana in southern California (which he had financed with the aid of an RFC loan) helped double the West's share of the nation's steel capacity from 2.7 percent to 5.6 percent between 1940 and 1955. Although Basic Magnesium could not be maintained in magnesium production because of high costs and inadequate markets, other uses were gradually found for large portions of that facility, providing a minor supplement for the entertainment-based Las Vegas economy. The airframe plants in southern California and, to a lesser extent, in Washington offered aircraft companies an opportunity to expand and upgrade their manufacturing facilities, but more often than not these plants remained in government hands or were devoted to other uses.[51]

The DPC plants, it seems clear, contributed positively toward meeting national needs during the war and thereafter. During the war, by linking government capital to private know-how, they helped provide the necessary enormous flow of goods. They also helped keep down inflation, for the price of the goods produced included in no instance more than normal depreciation as a cost factor. In instances of token rentals or operation of plants under management agreement, even normal depreciation was insulated from the cost of the goods. In these cases, depreciation costs were absorbed by the whole society.

The postwar outcomes were also mainly beneficial. During the war, the DPC and other government plants were training grounds for both management and labor in areas of the nation to that time little industrialized. This was particularly true of the South. Although the number of plants and the size of employment rosters diminished after the war in lines of production of limited civilian utility and in geographic areas suffering locational disadvantages, this reservoir of skills was available to be tapped by other, more economically appropriate enterprises.

DPC's plants were never windfalls, paid for by government through excessive charges in supply contracts, so that contractors could destroy the facilities, if they chose, free from cost to themselves. The production facilities paid for by government were kept in being to serve the postwar society. Some were kept as standby facilities or for sale or lease subject to a national security clause requiring the facilities to be converted to defense or war production on demand in the event of a national emergency, but most facilities were sold without restriction on their use.

The purchase option proved unattractive to most lessees. Thus the transfer of DPC plants into private hands generally occurred through negotiated purchase on either of two bases—cost of postwar reproduction, less depreciation, to remove excess wartime construction costs, or "fair value"—a more subjective judgment of the value of the plant to the purchaser. In the latter instance, the value of parts of the plant that seemed of no use was written off.

In a sizable proportion of sales, the government failed to receive even fair value. At times there was only one, perhaps not too eager, bidder. As the disposal period ran on, there was pressure on WAA to close a deal on any even partially reasonable offer. There were other criteria, too, to be considered beyond cost recovery, like providing employment, assisting small business, and fostering competition. In instances where sales were made for less than fair value, it seems evident that purchasers received windfall gains of varying dimensions, usually minor, at the expense of government and an unfair advantage against competitors who had paid full value for their facilities.

The other major means used by the government to stimulate construction of commercial-type facilities during the defense and war years was tax amortization. Overall, tax amortization was utilized to cover nearly $6.5 billion in plant and equipment. This sum was almost as large as the amount invested by DPC. Which of these mechanisms better served the public purpose?

Behind tax amortization was the belief that private investment in additional facilities for goods useful to the defense effort was a high-risk proposition. It was based on the lively awareness that the 1930s had witnessed heavy excess capacity in most industries and the somber surmise that production for the emergency would prove only a temporary phenomenon, after which manufacturers would again suffer from limited markets. As bait, the government sought to encourage private investment in new plants and equipment by permitting companies to write off this investment for tax purposes in five years or less, depending on the length of the emergency, compared to the normal fifteen to twenty years for machinery and buildings. Thus, instead of government money flowing out of the Treasury through the armed services or DPC to finance a plant, private money would do the job. It would be recaptured later on in many instances to the extent of 80 percent or more in tax savings at the expense of the Treasury. According to statute, prime contractors benefiting from tax amortization could use no more than normal depreciation as a cost factor in determining the price of supplies sold to the government, but this proved difficult to enforce. There was no parallel prohibition for subcontractors.[52]

Beginning in the defense period, the armed services took readily to tax amortization. It protected their scanty appropriations for construction and, in their perception, took no money from the Treasury. The armed services routinely recommended certification for 100 percent of cost without always being sure that the plants would be used exclusively for defense or war production. Not until the summer of 1943 was any strong effort made to reduce the use of tax amortization. By that time the need for additional production was no longer so pressing. Moreover, it was easy to believe that the war was already far along and that full tax amortization was too lucrative a benefit for firms operating facilities that could well have substantial postwar value. Consequently, in the fall of 1943, Undersecretary of War Patterson instructed contracting officers to persuade contractors to use DPC financing, for the disposal value of DPC facilities appeared to make a DPC lease less costly. Because some contractors objected, the War Production Board came up with a formula in the spring of 1944 for certifying only a portion of the facilities for tax amortization, depending on their probable postwar value. If WPB believed the new facilities would be fully competitive, it usually certified 35 percent as representing the increased wartime costs of construction over the base period of 1937–1939. In other cases, the proportion certified might be more—or less, if not all the production was going to the armed services.[53]

The great advantage of tax amortization over DPC was that the former mechanism created no troublesome disposal problem to be dealt with following the war. But it had offsetting deficiencies. Tax amortization was used most frequently for new facilities where the risk of unprofitable postwar production was less than for facilities financed by DPC. Moreover, it was designed to appeal to the profit motive by providing a potentially lucrative tax shelter. As long as production from the facilities provided a reasonable profit, tax amortization could be used to shelter a substantial proportion of those profits from taxes. In cases of excess profits, the deductions for amortization could be vulnerable to profit renegotiation only to the extent that the facilities would have postwar value. During the war, this was impossible to determine with any degree of precision. After the war, the hurly-burly of rapid demobilization kept the attempt from being made. Tax amortization thus opened the door to windfall gains to a much greater extent than did the disposal of the DPC plants, to the disadvantage of the Treasury and the detriment of competitors.[54]

Tax amortization has suffered from the judgment of its critics. The Truman committee concluded in its final report, "Legal profiteering resulted from certificates of necessity. Many companies came out of the war with new, valuable, fully amortized facilities which they could either use, or as some have done, sell. In this way a facility actually paid for out of a contractor's war taxes was additional profit to him to the extent of its postwar value." An official responsible for issuing certificates for the War Production Board testified before the committee that if the War and Navy Departments had attempted to consider postwar value instead of granting full amortization, the cost of the war could have been reduced by $3 billion.[55]

The tax amortization incentive was obviously effective in providing facilities capable of turning out a much larger supply of war goods. Firms responded to the stimulus of tax avoidance by building and equipping a large number of usually small plants or expansions to existing facilities. The stimulus was provided by the government; the decisions as to size and location of the facilities and the source of financing remained with the private companies. The great shortcoming of tax amortization was the magnitude of the benefit received—perhaps 40 percent or more of the average cost of the facilities. The attempt at remedy, made by the War Production Board in 1944 in reducing the proportion of the facilities certified for tax amortization, if made earlier, would surely have reduced the size of the windfalls. But any reduction in the extent of tax amortization would also have diminished the number of firms seeking to use that device.

Similarly, DPC was effective in bringing about a large expansion in dominantly commercial-type facilities for the production of war goods. Private firms operated the facilities, but decisions on location and size were made by government agencies and the financing and supervision were handled by DPC. Because the decisions with respect to the location of plants were not made by their private operators and because the plants were frequently of large size, they were often placed for both economic and strategic reasons in regions hitherto lightly industrialized, even though no conscious policy was established "to exploit the war effort for region building."[56] As in the case of tax amortization, the DPC performance was flawed, though by no such single costly policy as the blanket grant of full tax amortization by the armed services during the early war years. Because many of the DPC plants were so large and because the commodities they produced had limited civilian markets, the large plants often proved difficult to sell. When maintained in standby condition, however, they could provide a cushion of diminishing utility for use in a future emergency. And the plants and equipment that were sold, like the tax-amortized facilities, contributed to the output of the postwar economy.

Tax amortization and DPC provided means to the same goal—increased war production—but there were differences in the way that goal was achieved. The former was used more for low- than high-risk investments, for small than large facilities, and tended to result in facilities concentrated in areas already highly industrialized instead of being more widely dispersed. Both means revealed operational deficiencies that in each case appear to have been in good part remediable. If the expansion in commerical-type facilities required by a war emergency is large, involving massive capital outlays and high risk, with uncertain residual value, probably the DPC alternative is better, even though a troublesome disposal problem is created. On the other hand, for a smaller conflict, primary reliance on tax amortization, more carefully policed, would seem adequate.

10
A DPC Legacy?

It is almost commonplace that modern war creates an environment especially favorable for change. The awareness that a nation's future, even its life, may be at stake brings together disparate factions and makes possible departures in institutional structure and social practice that could hardly be imagined in peacetime. The pattern of government financing of much of the industrial facilities during World War II is an example. The innovation of the Defense Plant Corporation lease is inconceivable in other than a wartime setting.

When war ends, society moves back toward its accustomed channels, but past practices and institutions are never completely restored. Some residues of change are permanently incorporated, while the bulk become a part of the reservoir of experience upon which the society can draw in meeting future catastrophes in peacetime as well as in war.[1]

The nation's history in this century provides two clear demonstrations. President Franklin Roosevelt and his associates, for one, drew heavily on their common wartime heritage in battling against the Great Depression. "There was scarcely a New Deal act or agency that did not owe something to the experience of World War I," William Leuchtenberg has written in a notable essay.[2] Although no one has yet traced out systematically the indebtedness of the emergency government of World War II to agencies established in response to the crises of the Great Depression and World War I, most of these linkages are readily apparent to even the casual student.

The differences between the emergency governments of the two wars arose primarily out of the greater magnitude of the second war and the changing nature of warfare. Production of planes, tanks, and other elements of a more sophisticated weaponry put a much heavier burden on the nation's industrial establishment, manpower, and scientific and technical personnel. World War I required no such organization of scientists as the Office of Scientific Research and Development, which developed the atomic bomb. The War Manpower Commission in World War II contemplated the possibility of a labor draft, and the Fair Employment Practices Committee (FEPC) went well beyond the limited efforts of the first war in looking after the employment interests of the nation's minorities.[3] The necessary great expansion of the nation's industries following a decade of depression depended chiefly on massive government intervention through direct appropriations to the armed services, through loans and investments by the RFC and its wartime subsidiaries, and through special tax incentives designed to stimulate private investment. The huge scope and the duration of the war required integrating agencies hitherto not seen, such as an Office of Economic Stabilization to hold in balance wages and prices and an Office of War Mobilization and Reconversion (OWMR) with ultimate responsibility over the home front.

Following V-J Day, most emergency agencies began to disappear, though because of the immensity of the war and the greater concern over reconversion, the termination process took place at a slower pace than after World War I. A number of agencies, like the Smaller War Plants Corporation, the Foreign Economic Administration, and the National War Labor Board, were folded on a diminished scale into the permanent structure of government, while others, notably OWMR, were kept in being to ease the strains of reconversion. Once again the personnel of the war agencies began to leave Washington, with those from the upper echelons generally returning to corporations and campuses. The wartime experience was over, but the memories lingered on.[4]

Since World War II, there has been no domestic crisis like the Great Depression to stimulate an important reform movement that, like the New Deal, would draw heavily on wartime precedent for new means to deal with domestic problems. But there have been continuities ranging from such important matters as the development of peacetime uses of atomic energy to new methods of teaching foreign languages in the schools. Perhaps the most notable World War II innovation thus far in its peacetime impact has been the Fair Employment Practices Committee. Although the federal FEPC ended with the war, it had a continuing effect on the evolution of the postwar civil rights movement. It has also served as the prototype for a number of state and city-based fair employment practices commissions.[5]

Memories of the World War II experience have been recurrently stirred in times of dissatisfaction with the state of the society. In 1962, the Kennedy administration, disturbed by the slow growth of the economy, briefly considered a revival of tax amortization as a business stimulant before deciding on an investment credit on the purchase of new machinery and equipment as more efficient and less costly. The National Association of Manufacturers, in particular, would have preferred the reenactment of tax amortization.[6] Vestiges of tax amortization exist today in regulations governing the depreciation of railroad rolling stock, pollution control and coal mining safety equipment, and facilities for on-the-job training and child care.[7] Special economic and social concerns can be perceived in each of these instances.

Economic distress in the 1970s has also encouraged government to look to wartime precedents. The Nixon years witnessed briefly a half-hearted revival of wage and price controls as a means of fighting inflation.[8] The recurrence of still greater inflation, along with the energy crisis and the most serious recession since World War II, have inspired more soul-searching. Not long after becoming president, Gerald Ford in his call to action against inflation made use of war imagery more than palely reminiscent of President Roosevelt's inaugural address in 1933.[9] Early in 1975, there was talk of creating a new Reconstruction Finance Corporation to supply credit to ailing enterprises. The discussion focused primarily on RFC's activities during the depression, but its wartime role was also recognized.[10] Later that year the continuing concerns over a possible recurrence of an energy crisis led to the development of a plan by the Ford administration involving massive government financing of energy facilities to help make the nation self-sufficient. The nature of this plan will be discussed later on.

Apart from the Ford administration's energy program, the idea of government financing to expand the nation's industrial facilities through loans or direct investment has twice come up for brief, abortive discussion since World War II.

The first time was in the midst of the postwar boom when the prospect of shortages in the production of basic materials, especially steel, threatened to slow the pace of economic growth. The matter of steel production was particularly alarming. In the spring of 1948, production was not far from capacity, and there was talk of gray and black markets. Leaders of big and small business made known their concern. M. E. Coyle, executive vice-president of General Motors, and Benson Ford of the Ford Motor Company attributed shortfalls in automobile production to inadequate supplies of steel. The Senate Small Business Committee reported that it was being bombarded with complaints from businessmen embittered by the shortage. There was talk of setting up a system of compulsory controls governing the distribution of steel under the Selective Service Act of 1948, but they were ruled out in favor of voluntary controls. Early in 1949, national steel production rose above nominal capacity for several weeks.[11]

These widespread expressions of concern evoked only a limited response from the steel industry. Still suffering from the grim memories of overcapacity during the depression, industry leaders were loathe to build new and expand old plants for a demand they believed to be temporary. Ben Fairless, president of U.S. Steel, said the high demand was "unrealistic"; another prominent industry official, H. G. Batcheller, claimed that a drop to 75 or 80 percent of capacity was "inevitable." They were willing to consider only minor expansions while reaping the rewards of the favorable market.[12]

Within government and labor, however, the concerns and alarms of business, big and little, received greater attention. In December 1948, C. Girard Davidson, assistant secretary of the interior, called for a ten-million-ton increase in annual capacity. He proposed that the RFC be authorized to make loans to steel companies to help expand their facilities. If the companies refused to seek loans, Davidson said the government should build the steel plants.[13]

Later that month labor leaders volunteered a similar opinion. Philip Murray, president of the CIO, and Arthur Goldberg, its general counsel, headed a delegation that told President Truman they believed the government should construct steel plants if additional capacity could be gained in no other way. Another CIO delegation led by Walter Reuther expressed the same view to the Council of Economic Advisers. Truman was sufficiently impressed that he included a slightly watered-down version of their position in what came to be the most controversial point in his "Fair Deal" State of the Union message on January 5, 1949. He urged Congress "to authorize an immediate study of the adequacy of production facilities for materials in critically short supply, such as steel." If found necessary, the president requested that government loans be authorized for the expansion of facilities. If private industry still failed to act, he proposed that the government be granted authority to build and equip plants.[14]

A few days later, without consultation with the president, a bill hailed as the Full Employment Act of 1950 was introduced into both House and Senate. Its Senate sponsors were two prominent liberals, John Sparkman of Alabama and James Murray of Montana; Wright Patman of Texas introduced the bill in the House. Murray and Patman had been the leaders in their respective houses in getting through Congress the Employment Act of 1946 setting up the Council of Economic Advisers. Both were staunch partisans of small business, and both, along with Sparkman, were strong proponents of the industrialization of the West and South. Their bill called for an enlarged and revitalized RFC with an investment loan fund of $15 billion to be used in conformity with recommendations of the Council of Economic Advisers. They envisioned loans to existing and new enterprises, to states to aid in their industrial development, and to regional authorities like the TVA. It should be noted that the bill did not provide for the construction and equipping of plants by the federal government.[15]

President Truman's proposal and the Sparkman-Murray-Patman bill brought a spirited response both within and outside Congress. The conservative Senator Homer Ferguson of Michigan denounced the Truman proposal as "another step toward socialism"; in the House, Eugene Cox of Georgia saw the nation turning into a "socialist state." Steel companies were reported to view the proposal as "a definite step toward nationalization." The *Wall Street Journal* commented dourly that the president would permit the government "to take on the function of producing wealth as well as redistributing it."[16]

World War II provided precedents for both the president's proposal and the Sparkman-Murray-Patman bill, but the peacetime crisis was not sufficient to lead to congressional action. The *New Tork Times* observed correctly, "We think the President badly misjudges the temper of the American people if he seriously believes it will quietly acquiesce in a proposal which could result in putting the Government in the steel business in peacetime, even as a 'partner' of private enterprise." The more thoughtful business journalists and industrial leaders perceived the Truman proposal as a prod—nothing more. A spokesman for the Big Three steel companies described it as a "club in the closet," a "pressure tactic." *Business Week* characterized it as an attempt at "jawbone expansion." The Sparkman-Murray-Patman bill seemed more serious in intent, but it lacked the necessary votes. Indeed, no hearings were held on the bill in either house. Whatever mild support may have existed for the bill and for Truman's proposal vanished later in 1949, when the nation slid into its first postwar recession, turning the adequacy of steel capacity for the moment into an academic question.[17]

Concern over the extent of the nation's productive powers revived the next year with the onset of the Korean War. On July 19, 1950, President Truman sent a message to Congress asking, among other things, that steps be taken "to accelerate and increase the production of essential materials, products, and resources" and that the Congress authorize "production loan guarantees and loans to increase production." The accompanying bill, H.R. 9176, listed the Reconstruction Finance Corporation as one source of funds for expanding industrial capacity, but RFC was not authorized to finance government-titled plant. Hearings were held in both houses in the last week of July. During the following month, the bill was revised and enlarged to include powers with respect to wage and price controls and the settlement of labor disputes. The final bill also took into account the national industrial reserve. It empowered the president to "install additional equipment . . . or improvements to plants, factories, and other industrial facilities owned by the United States Government, and to install Government-owned equipment in plants, factories and other industrial facilities owned by private persons."[18]

The economic climate in 1950 was markedly different from that in 1940. Except for the brief recession in 1949, the nation had enjoyed nearly a decade of prosperity. The president in his message to Congress underscored the nation's strong position: a gross national product that had grown to $270 billion; 61.5 million employed; $115 billion invested in production facilities since 1945 in a wide range of industries; an overall increase of 40 percent since 1940 in the nation's productive capacity; and less possibility of shortages in basic materials (for example, rubber, natural and synthetic) in as great magnitude as in World War II.[19]

The Defense Plant Corporation lease mechanism was not forgotten, but voices in favor of its revival were few. Americans for Democratic Action, with Francis Biddle, the former attorney general, as its chairman, and David Ginsburg, once Leon Henderson's right hand, as its secretary, was one such voice. This vigorous organization of dedicated New Dealers urged the Senate Committee on Banking and Currency to utilize the Defense Plant Corporation lease as a model in bringing about the necessary industrial expansion. Another liberal organization, the American Veterans Committee (AVC), was of similar mind. When conservative Senator Homer Capehart asked the AVC's representative, the New Deal economist Robert R. Nathan, whether tax amortization would not be a sufficient incentive to effect the necessary increase in steel production, Nathan replied, "Do not forget that the last time we had the 5-year amortization program in steel, the Defense Plant Corporation had to build some of the steel mills." But the only activity of DPC revived under the National Production Authority during the Korean War was the use of some pool orders beginning in the spring of 1951 to speed the flow of machine tools to war plants.[20]

The Senate committee was much more in sympathy with the general thrust of the testimony of a business executive like William E. Umstattd, president of the Timken Roller Bearing Company. Umstattd wanted business to be left virtually untrammeled in going about the task of meeting war needs. He was particularly wary of the possibility of the government producing goods and services. Misreading the bill, he told the committee, "I direct your attention to the provisions that authorize the President virtually without restriction to establish corporations to engage in any type of business. . . . I think we all realize that if the Government once engages in business in competition with private companies, it is extremely difficult to ever separate the Government from such activities."[21]

If the Korean War had been comparable in size to World War II, there probably would have been closer parallels between the two wars in expanding industrial facilities. The need for expansion in 1950 in such basic industries as steel, aluminum, electric power, magnesium, transportation, and machine tools was substantial, but, except for electric power, considerably less than a decade earlier. Moreover, in 1950, there was a stockpile of plants and equipment in the national industrial reserve that could be brought into use to produce larger quantities of munitions and aircraft and some basic materials like magnesium and synthetic rubber. These plants numbered about 450. Half were idle; the rest had been sold or leased to private firms subject to a provision permitting their conversion to the production of war goods within ninety days in the event of a national emergency. In addition, the national industrial reserve encompassed 150,000 machine tools. During the Korean War, the government built few plants—and these were of arsenal type.[22]

Private financing took care of virtually all the increase in war-related commercial-type facilities. The postwar years of prosperity and rising prices had helped swell corporate coffers and had contributed to a feeling of optimism concerning the nation's economic future. This time, too, a larger proportion of the expansion was for goods with a likely continuing peacetime demand.

Business sought a revival of tax amortization, which was written into the Revenue Act of 1950. This legislation differed from that of World War II in three important respects. The new law expressly provided for tax amortization at less than 100 percent of the investment by declaring that the certificates of necessity should cover "only such portions . . . as [were] attributable to defense purposes." Second, the duration of tax amortization for Korean War facilities was fixed at five years; accelerated depreciation could be taken over no briefer period, regardless of the length of the emergency. Finally, profits from the sale of amortized facilities were made taxable as ordinary income instead of at the lower rates for capital gains allowed under the World War II legislation. In each instance, the intent was to protect the government by reducing the extent of possible benefit from tax amortization. The National Security Resources Board (NSRB) within the Department of Defense was briefly the certifying agency before the Defense Production Administration (DPA) took over in January 1951.[23]

The lineup of firms seeking certificates was both swift and long. Within the first three months, the NSRB and DPA granted certificates for facilities requiring an estimated investment of more than $1.5 billion. By June 8, 1,776 projects costing $6.2 billion had been approved. Nearly two years later, on March 25, 1953, the number of approved applications had grown to 16,191 for facilities costing $26.7 billion. Tax amortization did not end with the armistice in July 1953. By April 18, 1956, when the use of tax amortization was virtually over, 20,971 certificates had been issued for projects representing an investment of $36.2 billion. Although the number of certificates issued during the Korean War was less than half that during World War II, the average investment per certificate was more than ten times as large.[24]

Steel was early and prominent among the industries seeking amortization. The first eight certificates were submitted by Jones and Laughlin late in November 1950 for facilities already in process of construction. Within the first month, forty-eight certificates had been issued to steel companies for facilities costing nearly $500 million. Within seven months, five big companies—Armco, Jones and Laughlin, Bethlehem, U.S. Steel, and Republic—had received certificates covering the bulk of an investment of approximately $1 billion. Spurred on by tax amortization, the steel industry willingly undertook a large-scale expansion of facilities on which it had been unwilling to embark on its own initiative in 1949. During the first three months, steel accounted for over 80 percent of the total investment covered by the certificates. This ratio declined to approximately 37 percent by June 1951 because of increasing certification of projects in other industries, notably transportation, electric power, chemicals, petroleum refining, aluminum, paper, lumber, and machine tools. By October 1952, the ratio had declined further to little more than 16 percent, but the amount of iron and steel facilities covered by tax amortization ($3.771 billion) was second only to transportation ($4.321 billion). Tax amortization had brought about an expansion in the nation's annual steel capacity from 100 million to 113 million tons.[25]

Because tax amortization in World War II had been "the source of considerable war profiteering" and because the language of the tax amortization provision during the Korean War explicitly called for certification at less than 100 percent in particular circumstances, facilities under the Revenue Act of 1950 almost without exception were certified for less than total cost. The degree of improvement over World War II practice, however, was minor. The agencies issuing the certificates had neither the manpower, the expertise, nor the time to evaluate each project presented to them. Consequently, the National Security Resources Board and the Defense Production Administration sought to develop formulas for use on an industrywide basis. These rates were based on the dubious assumption that the degree of risk and of postwar utility was virtually the same throughout the industry regardless of the company or the location of the facilities.[26]

The steel industry can serve as an example. The formula provided for 60 percent certification for finishing facilities, 75 percent for ingot-producing facilities, and 85 percent for blast furnaces. For integrated facilities, big companies were usually allowed 75 percent. In the case of small companies, the extent of certification was 10 percent higher.[27]

Such percentages seemed much too high to many officials. Secretary of the Interior Oscar Chapman, still an ardent New Dealer, believed that most expansions in industrial facilities did not require a tax incentive. The new steel facilities of Jones and Laughlin, for example, were already being built in December 1950 at the time certification took place. He argued that the high percentages granted for facilities of assured postwar value mocked the central purpose of tax amortization, which was to shield from loss the investor in facilities of little or no postwar value.[28]

Late in the spring of 1951, the House Subcommittee on Government Operations, chaired by Porter Hardy, Jr., a Virginia Democrat and graduate of Harvard's Graduate School of Business Administration, came down hard on the tax amortization program. It denounced the program as "the biggest bonanza that ever came down the Government pike." The committee severely criticized the generous certification granted companies for facilities of obvious postwar utility, but reserved its heaviest fire for a few cases where companies of limited or no financial strength had sought to combine RFC loans with the benefits of accelerated depreciation. Because of excessively high certification, the committee also questioned a Defense Department policy that permitted companies to use accelerated depreciation as a cost factor in determining the price of supplies and in sheltering from renegotiation the extra profits thus derived. Only by this means, the Defense Department maintained, could a contractor with a certificate authorizing 100 percent amortization hope to recover the full cost of the facilities at the going tax rates.[29]

The Hardy Committee's report helped force a shutdown in authorizations for certificates for sixty days except in the most urgent cases. When the certification process again began to operate at full blast, the average percent of the cost of the facilities certified declined from 65.4 to 51.2 during the subsequent six months. Over the full period from November 1950 to April 1956, however, the average rate of certification was 58.6 percent.[30] Thus the enduring impact of the report was slight.

The Hardy Committee briefly considered "providing authority for Government construction of defense plants" as an alternative but concluded that "such a program [had] many undesirable features." The committee said that such authority "could be used mainly for standby purposes and exercised only in rare, last resort instances." Congress took no action.[31]

Tax amortization accounted for nearly 90 percent of the expansion in commercial-type facilities for war production during the Korean War, compared to approximately 40 percent during World War II. Approximately 8 percent was financed through private loans guaranteed by government agencies, chiefly the armed forces. The balance consisted in approximately equal amounts of loans authorized by the Defense Production Administration, which drew on the resources of the Reconstruction Finance Corporation, or of loans made directly by the RFC. The latter means, combined, accounted for less than $400 million in facilities prior to the end of May 1952.[32]

Unlike during World War II, RFC was little involved during the Korean War in financing facilities for war production. Nor was the national industrial reserve—that residue of plants and tools set up primarily from DPC's activities in the earlier war—drawn upon to the extent it might have been. Numerous idle plants from the reserve, notably aircraft, synthetic rubber, magnesium, aluminum, and nickel, were restored to service, but virtually none of the plants sold to private owners under the national reserve clause were diverted to war production. Even more strangely, despite the earnest efforts of Eugene M. Zuckert, assistant secretary of the air force, the armed services moved very slowly in their use of the machine tool reserve.[33]

During the Korean War, the production of machine tools was the one notable area of revival of a significant Defense Plant Corporation innovation. The National Production Authority initiated a machine tool pool in February 1951 that became more attractive in August, when pool orders began to be accompanied by advances of up to 30 percent of the amount of the contract. By the end of the year, a total of 127 pool orders had been made, covering 74,295 tools valued at $1.165 billion. Once again, the national government was underwriting the production of machine tools. The National Production Authority recommended the size, type, and quantity, but this time the General Services Administration, rather than an RFC subsidiary, was the contracting agency. A small fraction of the tools, 2,925 valued at $9 million, were leased to government contractors by the General Services Administration during the year ending August 31, 1952.[34]

The Joint Committee of the Congress on Defense Production commented in its *Second Annual Report,* "It is national policy to hold Government lending and Government ownership of defense facilities to a minimum." Clearly, that policy was carried out. It had benefits. Most important, disposal of government-owned defense plants and equipment was not a significant problem after the Korean War. But it also had costs. In September 1955, Secretary of the Treasury George Humphrey estimated the loss in taxes from tax amortization at $4.472 billion during the 1950s. Not only was there the loss in dollars because of the lower rates of taxation prevailing after the five-year tax amortization period, but the purchasing power of the tax dollars after the period of amortization was less because of inflation. As in World War II, the use of tax amortization was not joined to any social goal, such as a greater dispersion of industry or stimulating competition.[35]

In the conduct of war, the nation has been and inevitably will continue to be influenced to a very large extent by business. Business cooperation is essential. The experience of the Korean War suggests that business influence is likely to be greater in smaller wars with their lesser impact on the life of the society. Business influence is also likely to be greater in prosperous times, when there is less pressure for change, and in special cases where unusual circumstances may ease the pressure for increased war production. The economic pressures of the Korean War were undoubtedly reduced to some extent because that conflict followed so closely upon the major expansion in industrial facilities during World War II.

Thus there were marked differences in the ways the expansion in industrial facilities was achieved in the two wars. Unlike tax amortization, which business desired, the Defense Plant Corporation mechanism, responsible for much of the expansion in industrial capacity in World War II and feared by industry, was not revived in the Korean War. But the Defense Plant Corporation mechanism is a part of the record. It is more likely to be called upon in the event of a major war, particularly in times of limited prosperity when business influence is less.

Can the DPC experience have significant peacetime applications? Can a mechanism created to further the production of war supplies by bringing government capital into conjunction with private initiative be used to achieve peacetime economic and social goals? We have noted that talk of using the wartime mechanism, with whatever serious intent, to bring about expansion of steel capacity got nowhere in 1949 at a time of relatively high prosperity. Could effective programs be initiated with respect to goals such as the alleviation of poverty or of sustained high unemployment, the decentralization of industry for environmental or other reasons, or moderating the energy crisis? As suggestive examples, let us look at two of these possibilities, the reduction of poverty and easing the energy crisis.

State governments in the nation's most poverty-ridden region, the South (and, more recently, in other states), for many years have sought to improve their economic condition by encouraging new industry to locate within their borders. Nearly all southern states have a development office, or some office with a similar title. These offices cooperate with municipalities, or agencies tied to municipalities, in attracting industry to the state. They propagandize, trumpeting advantages in labor supply, resources, climate, and so on. But they also have offered direct economic incentives, like tax exemption for a period of years, training a work force at taxpayers' expense through programs administered by state boards of education, and financing and leasing a plant to an industrial firm by a municipality or a government-related agency. Such efforts appear to have been almost universally beneficial to the sponsoring communities.

At least one of these programs, Mississippi's "Balance Agriculture with Industry" (BAWI), predates World War II. Enacted in 1936, it provided for a State Agricultural and Industrial Board that would consider proposals to bring industries into the state and, if satisfied, authorize municipalities, districts, or counties to issue bonds to finance the construction of facilities. These facilities were either leased to the new firm at a rental sufficiently high to cover maintenance of the plant and payment of the bonds, principal and interest, or a contract was written providing for annual payments leading to the eventual purchase of the plant. In 1947, fifteen plants with an annual payroll in excess of $25 million were in operation, and fourteen more were under construction. "The BAWI plan was socialistic in tendency," said a Mississippi banker, "but it worked."[36]

Similar programs came into being elsewhere. They drew part of their stimulus from southern experience with wartime industrialization. In Alabama, for example, the Cater Act, passed in 1949, authorized municipalities to establish industrial development corporations with power to sell tax-exempt bonds for the purpose of financing the construction and equipment of plants. Two years later, another statute, the Wallace Act, granted these powers directly to municipalities. Partly because of these measures linking public capital and private enterprise, Alabama has been unusually successful in attracting new industry. During 1973, the State Development Office reported $1.65 billion in new and expanded industrial facilities—more than any other state in the Deep South. But, during the same year, four other states—South Carolina, Georgia, North Carolina, and Mississippi—added facilities costing in excess of $500 million.[37]

Since the early 1960s, poverty has been viewed as a national, not a regional problem, particularly because of its urban dimension. During these years the federal government has become directly involved with helping the urban poor. Could it, by extension, become directly concerned with poverty on a much larger scale, and, through careful planning, utilize the DPC mechanism to advantage?

There is some evidence that it could. All DPC plants, large and small, that were transferred into private hands contributed to the continuing high employment of the postwar years. Among large plants, probably this was nowhere more evident than in the synthetic rubber and aluminum industries. Synthetic rubber was a major new industry forced into being by war needs that soon became self-sustaining in the peacetime economy. During World War II, the aluminum industry expanded nearly sixfold. After the war, the industry became more competitive because of the entry of Kaiser through the acquisition of DPC plants and the strengthening of Reynolds through the same means. Both companies, along with Alcoa, continued to grow.[38]

The new entrant, Kaiser, started out as a strong western regional company based upon DPC's former alumina facility at Baton Rouge and former DPC aluminum plants located in the Pacific Northwest primarily because of cheap electric power. But Kaiser wanted a national market. First, it built a large reduction plant at Chalmette, Louisiana, in 1951, to which it added fabricating plants in the Midwest and East to help it invade those regions. Using the same kind of careful economic analysis that had caused the government to locate most of its DPC reduction plants in the Pacific Northwest, Kaiser built a huge new mill and smelter complex in the mid-1950s on the Ohio River near Ravenswood, West Virginia, for still greater competitive strength.[39]

Kaiser chose the site for its $216 million facility near Ravenswood for sound economic reasons, but it was also contributing to the revitalization of a long-depressed economic region. Ravenswood and its surrounding countryside had been in economic decline for decades, a sleepy area that could not hold its young people. Most of the schools in the county were old one-room buildings without running water.

When a *New York Times* reporter visited Ravenswood in the spring of 1957, he noted the revolution Kaiser had wrought in the life of the town. Young people were again to be seen on its streets. Cash registers in the stores were ringing briskly. Urban planners were helping the town council plan for four thousand new homes. And Kaiser had built a twenty-room modern school that it leased to Ravenswood for one dollar per year. The quickening effect on the economic and social life of the town was also felt in lesser measure throughout Jackson County and beyond.[40]

Behind Ravenswood lay wise choices by government agencies during the war years for efficient aluminum plants in the Pacific Northwest and elsewhere that supplied Kaiser with its base for growth. Kaiser's decision to build its mill and smelter complex in an impoverished area could also have been made by a government agency, for the economic factors were favorable. Other examples could be given from the experience of the synthetic rubber industry, which grew to an even greater extent from government decisions and stimulated the economic pulse of numerous communities in the Gulf Southwest. Similar sound judgments in peacetime, backed with government capital, utilizing either leases at real rentals or, in some cases, management contracts, could enhance competitiveness in industry, add to the nation's product, and improve the material condition of many lower-income Americans.

Plants financed by government need not be large, nor need they be financed solely by the national government. If poverty existing anywhere on a substantial basis was viewed as a threat to national well-being and an appropriate matter for national concern, national and local interest could well be joined through the joint provision of capital for industrial facilities under programs administered at the state level after the patterns currently in use in many states. Because the national government today uses more than one-fifth of the nation's goods and services, it could possibly also supply a market for some of the products of the companies it had helped finance.

A government called upon to bail out mismanaged companies like Lockheed and Penn Central could surely afford to experiment with the use of government capital to strive more imaginatively for new answers to the problem of poverty.[41] A revived RFC could assist ailing areas as well as ailing companies. Such a possibility could become real, however, only if it were supported by public opinion and only if the resulting programs were skillfully planned and administered.

Currently, the energy crisis commands a higher level of public consciousness than the alleviation of poverty. Since the Arab oil embargo in the winter of 1973–1974, much public discussion has been heard concerning the need for greater self-sufficiency in energy. Impressive studies have been made, like the *Project Independence Report* prepared in 1974 by the newly established Federal Energy Administration without, however, moving the nation closer toward that goal.[42] In 1976, after two years of a modest decline, the use of all forms of energy jumped 4.8 percent over 1975. It has continued to move upward. In 1976, instead of a diminished use of oil, petroleum supplied 47.2 percent of the nation's energy needs compared to 46.3 percent in the preceding year. Because of increasing demand and inadequate production, more and more of our oil supply must come from abroad. Between 1970 and 1976, domestic oil production declined from approximately 10 million to 8 million barrels daily. In 1978, oil imports accounted for more than 42 percent of our supply.[43]

The energy crisis differs from a wartime crisis in being episodic. The public feels the shortage when the Arabs turn off the oil spigot or when the eastern United States shiver because of an exceptionally cold winter. After the moment of acute discomfort passes, however, public concern falls off. A large section of the public can be lulled into a belief that there is no crisis. Proponents of various plans and interests have room for maneuver and, in so doing, check each other. Politicians can fear wasteful or scandal-ridden public expenditures and subsequent accountability damaging to the party in power. Ideological strife can arise between those who favor a large role for government and those who fear government intervention as a threat to private enterprise. In the absence of a widespread, deep, and sustained concern over the seriousness of the crisis, the danger exists that the nation may settle for superficial attempts at solution that can cost it dearly later on because of steadily rising oil prices and attendant problems associated with the international balance of payments. The contribution of oil imports to the nation's trade deficit has been projected at from $55 to $60 billion for 1979, compared to $45 billion in 1977.[44]

Three ways exist to bring the supply and demand for energy into better balance. Conservation of energy is one obvious means. Forcing owners to provide better insulation for buildings, stimulating industrialists to switch from scarce oil and gas to more plentiful coal for fuel, pressuring the public to purchase smaller cars through tax incentives, and requiring more efficient engines providing higher gas mileage are among the methods that can be used.[45]

A second way is to stimulate domestic production of additional oil and gas. Price policies by the government that speed the search for new sources can contribute toward this goal. So can offshore leases by the states and by the federal government carefully monitored to avoid oil spills. Improved methods of oil recovery may be found to renew or increase production from older oil fields.[46]

The third way, development of other less conventional forms of energy, is also a matter of high priority. These forms include nuclear energy, synthetic fuels (oil produced from oil shale deposits and oil and gas from coal), solar energy, and geothermal energy. Thus far only nuclear energy has proved its commercial worth.[47]

The utilization of these forms of energy involve, in various degrees, high risk, the need for development of new or more efficient technologies, and, in some instances, very large capital expenditures. A study by the Congressional Budget Office in 1976 concluded that a large-scale increase in nuclear energy, for example, would require investments in plants costing more than $1 billion each to provide enriched uranium as fuel through the as yet commercially unproved centrifuge process. Or plants costing $3.5 billion each could be built for the same purpose using the older diffusion process pioneered by the Atomic Energy Commission. The CBO reported that a single commercial-scale plant producing synthetic crude oil or gas at prices too high to be competitive would cost from $300 million to over $1 billion. At that time, some estimates of investment requirements to make the nation self-sufficient in energy, utilizing all sources, old and new, were running from $500 to $600 billion for the decade ending in 1985. These huge sums reveal clearly both inflation and the enormous growth of the economy since World War II.[48]

Few private firms can contemplate investing large sums in new sources of energy that could well wind up as commercial disasters. In 1975 only 160 industrial corporations had assets greater than $1 billion. Only 29 (including 10 oil companies) had assets running above $4 billion. Except for laboratory experiments and, possibly, demonstration plants, even large corporations are unlikely to put private capital at risk in financially hazardous ventures unless government supplies substantial offsetting incentives.[49]

Even apart from the huge investment likely to be required, it is appropriate that the federal government be deeply involved. The energy crisis is national in scope, affecting the welfare of the whole society. As before and during World War II, private investors can be timid, even though this time they need not fear excess capacity after the crisis has ended. But this time they must reckon with environmental laws and concerns as a significant cost factor.

The situation in some ways is similar to the potentially crippling rubber and magnesium shortages the nation faced during World War II. The technology for producing synthetic rubber was known, but it was by no means certain that after the war synthetic rubber could be competitive with natural rubber in either price or quality. The magnesium story was a little different. Instead of one proven technology, five different technologies were used in an effort to bring about the giant increase required by the war. Virtually all of the new capacity in both industries was financed and owned by DPC. Thus the government shouldered most of the risk in helping solve national problems. It also controlled the disposal of its plants following the war. In the case of synthetic rubber, DPC contracted with sixteen oil, gas, and chemical companies to produce the basic raw materials. Six rubber companies turned out the finished product. When the development of cold rubber after the war made synthetic preferable to natural rubber for manufacturing automobile tires, among other uses, the future of the synthetic product was assured. So was competition in the new industry when the government sold its plants. The government's experience with magnesium had a different outcome. Because the peacetime economy could not provide sufficient demand and because no other technology matched that of the Dow Chemical Company, most of the war-built magnesium plants were placed on standby, dismantled, or sold at a heavy loss. The losses in this case were shared by the whole society for whose protection the plants had been built.[50]

After the Arab oil embargo, the Nixon and Ford administrations made finding new sources and supplies of energy their primary goal. They wanted to restore the nation's energy independence, if possible, by 1985. In June 1974, the Federal Energy Administration was set up as a planning agency with special authority over the oil industry. A few months later the Energy Research and Development Administration was established. An "umbrella" agency, it was designed to plan and administer federal energy and development programs in accordance with the prescriptions and limitations written into its budget by Congress. A Naval Petroleum Reserves Production Act became law opening up the naval reserves for development, and two more broadly based measures were enacted, the Energy Policy and Conservation Act of 1975 and the Energy Conservation and Production Act of 1976.[51]

The most dramatic effort of the Ford Administration was embodied in a bill calling for an energy independence authority. It provided for an authority directed by a bipartisan five-member board with a life of ten years. In structure, the proposed energy independence authority resembled a more narrowly focused joint Reconstruction Finance and Defense Plant Corporation. The plans provided for giving the authority $25 billion in capital and the additional power to borrow $75 billion.

This huge fund was intended to support the construction of high-risk energy facilities that could not be financed solely from private sources. Loans and loan guarantees were favored over investments and price guarantees in helping finance this giant "crash" program. The bill would also have permitted the purchase and leaseback of facilities to private operators, similar to the Defense Plant Corporation pattern, but the Ford administration expressly stated, "No permanent ownership, control and operation of energy production by the Federal Government will be authorized."[52]

Because large sums would inevitably be put at risk in the hands of major oil companies and other big private contractors, the bill received heavy criticism. Henry Reuss, chairman of the House Banking Committee, denounced it as "way out of line . . . piling incentive on incentive" and "putting the agency beyond the normal budget process." Brock Adams, chairman of the House Budget Committee, denied that the energy industries required such massive support and feared that the $75 billion borrowing authority could have an unsettling effect on money markets. The Ford administration was itself split over the measure. It had originated with Vice-President Nelson Rockefeller and the Domestic Council, but it was opposed by Secretary of the Treasury William Simon and the chairman of the Council of Economic Advisers, Alan Greenspan.[53] The avalanche of criticism from both conservatives and liberals doomed the bill. It was conspicuously dead well before the end of the Ford administration.

President Jimmy Carter and his advisors inherited an energy problem still far from solution. Their options remained the same—conservation, finding additional domestic supplies of oil and natural gas, and developing other efficient sources of energy to help reduce dependence on oil and natural gas as the nation's primary fuels. The dilemma they faced was how to blend the options in such a way as to command the support of a majority of the public and of Congress and to power the options so that they might make an effective program. Shortly after the middle of April 1977 Carter presented a carefully contrived, complex program designed to reduce the nation's dangerous dependence on imported oil by bringing about a saving in the use of oil and natural gas by 1985 of approximately 4.5 million barrels daily.

Carter's program differed from those of his predecessors in making conservation of oil and gas his overriding priority. If Americans consumed two to three times as much energy per capita as citizens of nations with comparable living standards—for example, Switzerland, Sweden, and West Germany—surely, he believed, there was ample room to reduce wasteful use of oil and gas.[54] But Carter failed to reckon adequately with the degree of public disbelief in the existence of an energy shortage, the power of special interests, and the wariness of politicians concerned with the outcomes of the next election.

In August 1977, a *New York Times*/CBS national poll showed that a larger proportion of the public believed there was no energy shortage (49 to 39 percent), and 33 percent believed that domestic oil production was sufficient to meet the nation's needs.[55] This extent of misunderstanding hardly supplied a solid base from which to ask for sacrifices. In the House, the program was speedily stripped of a politically dangerous standby gasoline tax. It would have required an increase in the tax on gasoline of as much as five cents a gallon in any year in which consumption exceeded a predetermined consumption target. The House also removed a provision for a rebate of up to $500 on the purchase of fuel-efficient small cars and weakened a provision imposing heavy taxes on gas-guzzlers. The fact that many small cars were foreign-built and that gas-guzzlers were almost wholly American-made undoubtedly entered in this decision.[56]

In the Senate, the president's energy program fared even less well. The Senate was less oriented to conservation and more sympathetic to special interests. When the energy bill passed the Senate in mid-October, it lacked four major provisions desired by the president: an equalization tax designed to increase gradually the price of domestic oil from old fields to that of foreign oil and thus discourage consumption; a tax on industrial and utility users of oil and natural gas designed to encourage them to convert to coal; a tax on gas-guzzling automobiles; and repeal of the federal income tax deduction for state and local gasoline taxes.[57]

Reconciliation of the differences between the House and Senate bills took a full year. Senate members on the House-Senate conference committee agreed to a tax on gas-guzzling cars and to regulations designed to force some industrial plants to switch from oil and natural gas to coal, but they refused to accept the equalization tax on domestic crude oil so ardently sought by the president. On another matter of controversy, natural gas pricing, a compromise notable for its complexity was worked out only toward the close of the congressional session. The energy bill passed in October 1978 was a far cry from what the president had hoped. Indeed, it was conceded that the volume of oil imports would continue to increase.[58]

The 1978 National Energy Act quite clearly fell short of the nation's need. If oil imports are to decrease, it will be necessary to enact more stringent conservation legislation. It will also be desirable to pay more attention to the "supply" side of the energy equation. If sufficient additional supplies of oil and gas are not found, it may then become necessary to step up the pace of development of alternate forms of energy. In such an instance, the problem of how to finance these larger-scale efforts will take on greater urgency.

Proponents of more energy have been by no means mute. One such voice has been that of Thornton Bradshaw, president of Atlantic Richfield and a member of Carter's campaign task force on energy. Early in 1977, in an article in *Fortune,* Bradshaw called for "goal setting" on the part of government, in addition to having it carry the lion's share of the risk associated with the development of a greater range of energy sources. In suggesting that government take the lead, he was running against dominant business sentiment. But he argued that goal setting was "not a new role for our government" and offered the national experience in World War II as an example: "The government quickly set the goal— victory—and the sub-goals: so many aircraft, so many tanks, trucks, guns, etc. Government also defined the means necessary to achieve these goals.

Our people, our industry responded. Our plants produced, and the war was won."[59]

The Defense Plant Corporation was responsible for financing nearly half of the increase in commercial-type facilities "necessary to achieve these goals."

Developing efficient alternate sources of energy is akin to the World War II problem of developing increased production capacity. At this time, however, as the fate of Ford's bill for an Energy Independence Authority showed, there is by no means the same sense of urgency. There may never be. But frustration and fear may work a change in the public mind, especially if more rigorous conservation measures prove unacceptable or inadequate.

In that case, government capital will necessarily be involved. The question is how? One means is to forego tax revenue by offering tax amortization benefits or investment tax credits to private contractors. Ventures in which government shares the risk by putting up most of the capital (as is being done in at least one solar energy project), makes loans backed solely by the facilities being built, guarantees private loans to contractors (as is being sought for some synthetic gas projects), or guarantees a price and a market for high-cost energy, are other means.[60] Or government can build and own the plants.

In the latter instance, the DPC experience should become relevant, both in its lease and management-fee contract forms. Something closely similar already exists with respect to the three government-owned uranium enrichment plants, each of which is operated for the Department of Energy by a private contractor for a management fee.[61] In such cases, the government assumes the risk while availing itself of the expertise of the contractor. This pattern has the advantage of simplicity. Standard contracts can be drawn offering the same deal to all contractors. If significant discoveries are made, government can make them available to other corporations on terms that would help the government recover its investment. If government owns the plants, it can also consider carefully a larger range of factors in determining the locations of the plants—for example, poverty, unemployment, and the physical environment.

A prolonged and intense energy crisis may not yet be upon us, but such a crisis remains a likely reality.[62] If it does occur, the judicious use of government capital will have much to do with determining the speed and extent of success in surmounting the crisis. The DPC experience deserves to be recaptured. It could help shape a useful option.

ABBREVIATIONS

CBO	Congressional Budget Office
CPA	Civilian Production Administration (successor agency to WPB)
DPC	Defense Plant Corporation
DSC	Defense Supplies Corporation
FEA	Federal Energy Administration
FLA	Federal Loan Agency
NDAC	Advisory Commission to the Council of National Defense
NDP	National Defense Planning
NPA	National Production Authority
OCDM	Office of Civil and Defense Mobilization
OCMH	Office, Chief of Military History
ODP	Office of Defense Plants
ODS	Office of Defense Supplies
OTA	Office of Technology Assessment
OWMR	Office of War Mobilization and Reconversion
RFC	Reconstruction Finance Corporation
SPA	Surplus Property Administration
Stat.	*United States Statutes at Large*
SWPB	Surplus War Property Board
SWPC	Smaller War Plants Corporation
WAA	War Assets Administration
WNRC	Washington National Records Center
WPB	War Production Board

Notes

Chapter 1

1. U.S., Congress, House, *Congressional Record,* 76th Cong., 3d sess., May 16, 1940, pp. 6243–44.

2. Table, "Military Forces of Nations of the World, Nov., 1939," *World Almanac, 1940* (New York, 1940), p. 849; William G. Cunningham, *The Aircraft Industry: A Study in Industrial Location* (Los Angeles, 1951), pp. 47–48; Tom Lilley et al., *Problems of Accelerating Aircraft Production during World War II* (Boston, 1947), p. 7; *New York Times,* Jan. 17, 1961, p. 22.

3. On interwar planning, see particularly Harry B. Yoshpe, "Economic Mobilization Planning between Two World Wars," *Military Affairs* 15 (Winter 1951):200–02, and "Planning between Two World Wars," ibid. 16 (Summer 1952):77–81; "Industrial Mobilization Plans," 1930, 1933, 1936, 1939, Library, Industrial College of the Armed Forces, Washington, D.C.; R. Elberton Smith, *The Army and Economic Mobilization* (Washington, 1959), pp. 73–103; Robert H. Connery, *The Navy and Industrial Mobilization in World War II* (Princeton, 1951), pp. 31–53. On plant investment during World War I, see Lowell J. Chawner, "Factory Plant and Equipment Expenditures over a Quarter Century," *Dun's Review,* Oct. 1942, pp. 12–13; A. D. H. Kaplan, *The Liquidation of War Production* (New York, 1944), p. 87; Robert R. Russel, "Expansion of Industrial Facilities under Army Air Force Auspices, 1940–1945," p. 16, Office, Chief of Military History files, Department of the Army, henceforth cited as OCMH; *New York Times,* Apr. 7, 1940, p. 39.

4. *New York Times,* May 18, 1940, p. 6.

5. Ibid., May 27, 1940, p. 12.

6. On the isolationists, see Wayne Cole, *America First: The Battle against Intervention* (Madison, 1953), pp. 93–103. On business attitudes, see Roland N. Sternberg, "American Business and the Approach of War, 1935–1941," *Journal of Economic History* 13 (Winter 1953):58–78; Hadley Cantril, ed., *Public Opinion, 1935–1946* (Princeton, 1951), p. 346; Thomas C. Cochran, *American Business in the Twentieth Century* (Cambridge, 1972), pp. 139–44; Russel, "Expansion of Industrial Facilities," p. 28; Troyer Anderson, "Introduction to the History of the Under Secretary of War's Office," chap. 5, pp. 12–17, OCMH.

7. James R. Mock and Evangeline Thurber, *Report on Demobilization* (Norman, Okla., 1944), pp. 145–53; J. Donald Edwards, "Termination of Ordnance Contracts, 1918," History Study No. 57, Bureau of Labor Statistics (Washington, 1944), p. 32; U.S., Congress, Senate, Subcommittee on Contract Termination, Special Committee on Post-War Economic Policy and Planning, *Problems of Contract Termination,* 78th Cong., 1st sess., 1943, pp. 13, 54.

8. U.S., Congress, Senate, *Report on Government Manufacture of Munitions by the Special Committee on Investigation of the Munitions Industry*, 74th Cong., 2d sess., 1936, S. Rept. 944, pt. 7; John Wiltz, *In Search of Peace: The Senate Munitions Inquiry* (Baton Rouge, 1963), pp. 145–46; Yoshpe, "Planning between Two Wars," pp. 79–80; "Report of the War Resources Board," Oct. 12, 1939, Library of the Industrial College of the Armed Forces; Civilian Production Administration, *Industrial Mobilization for War: History of the War Production Board and Predecessor Agencies, 1940–1945* (Washington, 1947), pp. 6–11; Eliot Janeway, *The Struggle for Survival* (New Haven, 1951), pp. 53–68; testimony of Leon Henderson, U.S. Congress, Senate, *Hearings before the Committee on Finance, Second Revenue Act of 1940,* 76th Cong., 3d sess., Sep. 4, 1940, p. 178.

9. Chart, "Total Value of Facilities Put in Place during Designated Periods . . . Third Quarter 1940–Second Quarter 1945," in Civilian Production Administration, *Facilities Expansion, July 1940–June 1945* (Washington, 1946), p. 9; Glen E. McLaughlin, "Wartime Expansion in Industrial Capacities," *Papers and Proceedings of the 55th Annual Meeting of the American Economic Association, American Economic Review* 33 (Mar. 1943):108. This comparison, however, is flawed. Most wartime plant was built pell-mell, with little attention to keeping costs down or to other factors that would make the plants more attractive for postwar operation; moreover, a rising price level understates prewar values in comparison with those of wartime.

10. Civilian Production Administration, *Industrial Mobilization,* pp. 18–36; Janeway, *Struggle for Survival,* pp. 121–24.

11. *New York Times,* June 20, 1940, p. 10; Harold L. Ickes, *The Secret Diary of Harold L. Ickes,* (New York, 1954) 3:195.

12. Ethan P. Allen, *Policies Governing Plant Financing of Emergency Facilities, May 1940 to June 1942* (Washington, 1944), p. 13; I. F. Stone, *Business as Usual* (New York, 1941), pp. 134–35; Donald Nelson, *Arsenal of Democracy* (New York, 1946), pp. 97-98; Margaret Coit, *Mr. Baruch* (Boston, 1951), pp. 482–83.

13. Smith, *The Army and Economic Mobilization,* pp. 448–55; Connery, *The Navy and Industrial Mobilization,* pp. 350–65.

14. Interviews with Hans Kundlich, Service, Supply and Procurement, War Department, General Staff, Apr. 10, 1947, Hudson Cox, general counsel, Navy Department, Apr. 16, 1947, and Frederic C. Lane, historian, Maritime Commission, Apr. 30, 1947; Smith, *The Army and Economic Mobilization,* pp. 496–502; Connery, *The Navy and Industrial Mobilization,* p. 351. The navy plants, perhaps influenced by the DPC lease agreements, frequently included purchase options to the wartime contractor in their management-fee contracts.

15. *New York Times,* June 5, 1940, p. 41; also Emmet F. Connely, president of Investment Bankers Association, ibid., June 18, 1940, p. 42; Frank A. Bonner, chairman, National Association of Securities Dealers, ibid., June 21, 1940, p. 33; on industry, see statement of National Association of Manufacturers, ibid., June 23, 1940, p. 10, Irving S. Olds, U.S. Steel Corporation, ibid., Nov. 16, 1940, p. 20.

16. Mark S. Watson, *Chief of Staff: Prewar Plans and Preparations* (Washington, 1950), p. 170; Lenore Fine and Jesse Remington, *The Corps of Engineers: Construction in the United States* (Washington, 1972), pp. 151, 309.

17. 40 Stat. 1078 (1919); E. C. Brown and Gardner Patterson, "A Neglected Chapter in War Taxation," *Quarterly Journal of Economics* 57 (Aug. 1943):632–36.

18. Senate, *Hearings before the Committee on Finance, Second Revenue Act of 1940,* pp. 160–76; "Minutes of the Tax and Finance Committee of NDAC," Aug. 1, 1940, War Production Board records, Record Group 179, National Archives.

19. 54 Stat. 999–1005 (1940); 55 Stat. 849 (1941); Senate, *Hearings before the Committee on Finance, Second Revenue Act of 1940,* pp. 168–69.

20. Senate, *Hearings before the Committee on Finance, Second Revenue Act of 1940,* pp. 169, 176.

21. Anderson, "Introduction," chap. 5, pp. 183–92; Russel, "Expansion of Industrial Facilities," pp. 229–31; *Business Week,* Aug. 10, 1940, p. 7; 55 Stat. 757–58 (1941). The Couzens Committee of the Senate concluded in 1926 that $210 million of the $597 million allowed for tax amortization had been improperly granted (Smith, *The Army and Economic Mobilization,* p. 459).

22. 56 Stat. 50 (1942); Smith, *The Army and Economic Mobilization,* p. 460; WPB Press Release 4699, Dec. 18, 1943, War Production Board records.

23. "Tax Amortization, Loans and Procurement in the Office of the Construction and Resources Expansion, Defense Production Administration and Predecessor Agencies" [1953], chap. 5, National Production Authority records, Record Group 277, National Archives; U.S., Congress, Senate, *Hearings before a Special Committee Investigating the National Defense Program Pursuant to S. Res. 46,* 80th Cong., 1st sess., 1947, pt. 42, pp. 25932–34; Smith, *The Army and Economic Mobilization,* p. 473; M. D. Ketchum, "Plant Financing in a War Economy," *Journal of Business of the University of Chicago* 16 (Jan. 1943):41.

24. Harold Stein, ed., *Public Administration and Policy Development* (New York, 1952), p. 289.

25. Table 7, chapter 6; Smith, *The Army and Economic Mobilization,* pp. 484–96; Connery, *The Navy and Industrial Mobilization,* pp. 348–50; Frederic C. Lane, *Ships for Victory: A History of Shipbuilding under the U.S. Maritime Commission in World War II* (Baltimore, 1951), pp. 400–01; *Preliminary Inventory of the Records of the Reconstruction Finance Corporation, 1932–1964* (Washington, 1973), p. 31; Comptroller General of the United States, *Report on Audit of Reconstruction Finance Corporation and Affiliated Corporations as of June 30, 1945: Defense Plant Corporation,* 80th Cong., 1st sess., 1947, H. Doc. 474, 4:4. (The figure on DPC disbursements [$7.3 billion] given in Table 7 and in the DPC description in the *Preliminary Inventory* is higher than the $6.982 billion arrived at in 1946 by the General Accounting Office after its audit of DPC's wartime operations. I have chosen to use the latter figure as probably more accurate.)

Chapter 2

1. The capital of the corporation was reduced to $325 million during the second quarter of 1941 *(Report of the RFC, Second Quarter, 1941,* p. 76) under the amendment to the RFC Act of June 25, 1940. The life of the corporation was extended an additional five years by the amendment to the RFC Act of June 10, 1941.

2. The statistical data are derived from *Reconstruction Finance Corporation-Seven-Year Report* (February 2, 1939), and from various *Quarterly Reports* of RFC.

3. 48 Stat. 1108–09 (1934).

4. Even after Emil Schram, former chairman of RFC, became chairman of the

New York Stock Exchange and John W. Snyder, former executive vice-president of DPC, became secretary of the treasury, both men began their letters, "Dear Mr. Jones." The letters from Jones to them began, "Dear Emil," "Dear John" (Box 131, "D," General Correspondence, Jesse H. Jones papers, Mss. Division, Library of Congress).

5. Interviews with Clifford Durr, Aug. 4, 1971, Hans Klagsbrunn, Aug. 31, 1971, John W. Snyder, Sept. 2, 1971; Harold L. Ickes, *The Secret Diary of Harold L. Ickes* (New York, 1955), 3:314, 597–98; Francis Biddle, *In Brief Authority* (New York, 1962), p. 136; John M. Blum, ed., *From the Morgenthau Diaries: Years of Crisis, 1928–38* (Boston, 1959), p. 58, *From the Morgenthau Diaries: Years of Urgency, 1938–41* (Boston, 1965), p. 41; Rexford G. Tugwell, *The Democratic Roosevelt* (New York, 1957), pp. 378–79; Eliot Janeway, *The Struggle for Survival* (New Haven, 1951), p. 83; James M. Burns, *Roosevelt: The Soldier of Freedom* (New York, 1970), pp. 39, 431; Arthur Schlesinger, Jr., *The Age of Roosevelt: The Politics of Upheaval, 1935–36* (Boston, 1960), p. 411; Pendleton Herring, "Executive-Legislative Responsibilities," *American Political Science Review* 38 (Dec. 1944):1159–60; Richard C. Fenno, Jr., "President-Cabinet Relations: A Pattern and a Case Study," *American Political Science Review* 52 (June 1958):388–405.

6. Interviews with Hans Klagsbrunn, Aug. 20, 1948, Emil Schram, Aug. 23, 1948; Jesse H. Jones and Edward Angly, *Fifty Billion Dollars: Thirteen Years with the RFC, 1932–1945* (New York, 1951), pp. 529, 531, 533–34.

7. Husbands obituary, *New York Times,* Nov. 3, 1955, p. 31; interviews with Clifford Durr, Aug. 4, 1971, Hans Klagsbrunn, Aug. 31, 1971, John W. Snyder, Sept. 2, 1971; Jones and Angly, *Fifty Billion Dollars,* pp. 529, 534.

8. Jones and Angly, *Fifty Billion Dollars,* p. 541; Schlesinger, *Age of Roosevelt,* p. 228.

9. Interviews with Emil Schram, Aug. 23, 1948, Clifford Durr, Aug. 4, 5, 1971, Hans Klagsbrunn, Aug. 31, 1971, and standard biographical sources.

10. Durr Ms., undated, Durr files, in the possession of Mrs. Clifford J. Durr, Wetumpka, Alabama.

11. Ibid.; interview with Hans Klagsbrunn, Aug. 31, 1971; *New York Times,* May 18, 1940, p. 6; memo, FDR to Jesse Jones, May 20, 1940, 643 RFC, Franklin D. Roosevelt Library, Hyde Park, New York.

12. Clifford Durr, "The Defense Plant Corporation," in Harold Stein, ed., *Public Administration and Policy Development* (New York, 1952), p. 294.

13. U.S., Congress, Senate, *Hearings before the Committee on Banking and Currency on S. 3939,* 76th Cong., 3d. sess., 1940, pt. 2, p. 31.

14. Ibid., pp. 42–46.

15. Ibid., p. 39. See also *New York Times,* June 2, 1940, p. 12.

16. Ibid., p. 65.

17. U.S., Congress, House, *Congressional Record,* 76th Cong., 3d sess., June 14, 1940, pp. 8274, 8386–88, 8292.

18. 54 Stat. 573–74 (1940).

19. See Chapter 6.

20. J. H. Jones to Franklin D. Roosevelt, Apr. 21, 1942, the President file, Secretary of Commerce files, Record Group 234, National Archives. Some of the text in the latter part of this chapter and in the following chapter draws on my article, "Financing Industrial Expansion for War: The Origin of the Defense Plant Corporation Leases," *Journal of Economic History* 9 (Nov. 1949):156–83.

Chapter 3

Much of the research on which Chapters 3 through 7 are based was done during 1946–1947 at the RFC building, 811 Vermont Avenue, N.W., in Washington, D.C., when the DPC records were still in the custody of the parent agency. After RFC ceased to be an independent agency on June 30, 1954, these records, along with others from RFC and its subsidiary and allied corporations, were transferred to the National Archives. The RFC records have been classified as Record Group 234, and a published *Preliminary Inventory of the Records of the Reconstruction Finance Corporation, 1932–1964* (Washington, 1973) serves as a guide for scholars and other researchers. These records are housed in the National Archives and in the Washington National Records Center a few miles away in Suitland, Maryland. The DPC records, listed in thirteen series on pages 37–41 of the *Preliminary Inventory*, bulk large—approximately 803 of 4,159 cubic feet for the RFC group. In addition, 20 cubic feet of records of the Federal Loan Agency (hereafter FLA) and the secretary of commerce relating to the activities of the RFC and its wartime subsidiaries are listed in five series on pages 30–32. Many of my notes in Chapters 3 through 7 could be extended to indicate the series in which the document is likely to be found, but because I lack absolute certainty as to the survival and location of all documents, I have not done so. I believe the likely locations will be apparent to anyone who uses the *Preliminary Inventory*.

1. Tom Lilley et al., *Problems of Accelerating Aircraft Production during World War II* (Boston, 1947), p. 36; G. R. Simonson, ed., *The History of the American Aviation Industry* (Cambridge, 1967), pp. 121–33.

2. Draft form of agreement and memo, E. H. Foley, Jr., general counsel of the Treasury, to Henry Morgenthau, June 18, 1940, DPC file, pt. 1, FLA files, Record Group 234, National Archives.

3. Memo, Jan. 20, 1944, DPC file 14, Secretary of Commerce files, lists a number of contracts containing this restrictive clause; also, Troyer Anderson, "Introduction to the History of the Under Secretary of War's Office," chap. 5, pp. 12–17, 140, OCMH; Bruce Catton, *The War Lords of Washington* (New York, 1948), pp. 61–62; interview with David Ginsburg, Aug. 20, 1948.

4. Interview with Claude Hamilton, Aug. 23, 1948; Clifford J. Durr, "The Defense Plant Corporation," in Harold Stein, ed., *Public Administration and Policy Development* (New York, 1952), p. 294.

5. W. S. Knudsen to Jesse H. Jones, June 20, 1940, NDP, Council of National Defense, John W. Snyder files, DPC files.

6. J. H. Jones to M. B. Gordon, June 20, 1940, DPC–Wright Aeronautical Corporation file, FLA files.

7. Memo, C. J. Durr to Jesse Jones, June 29, 1940, Organization, By-laws file, DPC files.

8. Durr, "The Defense Plant Corporation," p. 295.

9. Memo for Jesse H. Jones, July 25, 1940, DPC–Wright Aeronautical Corporation file, FLA files.

10. J. H. Jones to M. B. Gordon, July 26, 1940, DPC–Wright Aeronautical Corporation file, FLA files.

11. RFC Minutes, Aug. 7, 1940, pp. 392–99.

12. Durr, "The Defense Plant Corporation," p. 296.

13. Ibid., pp. 297–98.

14. Ibid., p. 298.

15. Interview with Emil Schram, Aug. 23, 1948.

16. Durr, "The Defense Plant Corporation," p. 298; interviews with Durr, Aug. 5, 1971, and John W. Snyder, Sep. 2, 1971.

17. Norman Beasley, *Knudsen* (New York, 1947), pp. 264–67.

18. Durr, "The Defense Plant Corporation," p. 299. Durr quoted Bodman (from memory): "Investigations are unpleasant and indictments are still more unpleasant whether or not there are convictions, and I do not propose to let my clients place themselves in a position where they may have to defend themselves before a Congressional committee or even possibly an indictment. Packard expects to make a profit, but it wants to make that profit above the table and not in a concealed bonus on the side in the form of a hand-out of plant or machinery. If this Government and the British will put up the money for the plant [?] and machinery, we are ready to go ahead and do the job."

19. There is a more extended discussion of the Packard negotiations in Durr, "The History of the Defense Plant Corporation," pp. 22–24, from which the printed version is taken. The manuscript is in the possession of Mrs. Clifford Durr, Wetumpka, Ala.

20. DPC Minutes, Sep. 6, 1940, pp. 16–24.

21. Ibid., Sep. 12, Oct. 14, 1940, pp. 36–44, 76–83; interview with Durr, Aug. 5, 1971.

22. DPC Minutes, Oct. 5, 1940, pp. 50–57; Durr, "The Defense Plant Corporation," p. 300.

23. Interview with Durr, Aug. 5, 1971; Minutes of the Tax and Finance Committee, NDAC, Aug. 1, 1940, War Production Board records, Record Group 179, National Archives.

24. *New York Times,* Aug. 9, 1940 p. 21; "Weekly Progress Report of the Advisory Commission to the Council of National Defense, Report No. 3, Aug. 7, 1940," p. 114, NDAC reports, file 813A, FDR Library, Hyde Park, New York.

25. *Minutes of the Advisory Commission to the Council of National Defense* (Washington, 1946), pp. 71–73.

26. As originally drafted, the contract provided for repayment by the government in five annual installments. This was soon changed to monthly payments to conform to the amortization provisions of the Second Revenue Act of 1940 to which the payments were linked. On the emergency plant facilities contract, see R. C. McGrane, *The Facilities and Construction Program of the War Production Board and Predecessor Agencies, May 1940 to May 1945* (Washington, 1946), pp. 5–7; E. P. Allen, *Policies Governing Private Financing of Emergency Facilities, May, 1940 to June, 1942* (Washington, 1946), pp. 28–41.

27. 54 Stat. 1029 (1940).

28. Memo, C. J. Durr, Aug. 24, 1940, Council of National Defense, RFC files; U.S., Congress, House, *Congressional Record,* 77th Cong., 1st sess., Jan. 21, 1941, p. 219. See also Allen, *Policies Governing Private Financing of Emergency Facilities,* pp. 37–39.

29. Emergency Plant Facilities Contract between War Department and Ford Motor Company, Nov. 23, 1940, p. 9, RFC files. (This contract was subsequently canceled.) See also *Business Week,* Oct. 5, 1940, p. 17.

30. DPC Minutes, Sep. 12, 1940, pp. 31–35.

31. C. J. Durr, "The Defense Plant Corporation," pp. 305–06.

32. Ibid., p. 306.

33. Ibid., pp. 307–08.

34. Ibid., pp. 309–10; interview with Hans Klagsbrunn, Aug. 31, 1971.

35. Durr, "The Defense Plant Corporation," p. 309. On the ultimate outcome from the "take-outs," see Chapter 5.

36. DPC Minutes, Oct. 18, 1940 [sic], pp. 91–99. An early statement of these two forms of lease agreement, dated Oct. 15, 1940, is to be found in Lease Agreements, General file, pt. 1, DPC files.

37. DPC Minutes, Oct. 14, 1940, pp. 66–75.

38. Durr, "The Defense Plant Corporation," p. 306. A third type of rental arrangement, "depreciation rental," in contrast to full rental, later came into use in many cases. This arrangement was used to equalize competition between suppliers manufacturing goods in government plants and those supplying similar goods from their own plants.

39. DPC Minutes, Oct. 25, 31, and Nov. 14, 1940, pp. 131–58, 179–89, 248–58.

40. Schram to Knudsen, Jan. 4, 1941, NDP, John W. Snyder files, DPC files. On the operation of the machine tool pool, see Chapter 7.

41. Business Week, Oct. 5, 1940, p. 17; letters, Proctor to Schram, in DPC Minutes, Oct. 23, 1940, pp. 125–27, Schram to Proctor, Oct. 25, 1940, Durr files, Wetumpka, Ala.; memo, Proctor to judge advocate general, Oct. 29, 1940, Troyer Anderson notes, OCMH; Myron Cramer, chief of section, judge advocate general, to Proctor, Nov. 5, 1940, in the possession of Hans Klagsbrunn, Washington, D.C.

42. Wall Street Journal, Nov. 19, 1940, pp. 1, 7; Nov. 20, 1940, pp. 1, 4; Business Week, Nov. 23, 1940, p. 7; interview with Hans Klagsbrunn, May 23, 1947.

43. Interviews with Warren S. Ege, Apr. 23, 1947, and R. S. Whittlesey, May 8, 1947. For these and other criticisms, see R. Elberton Smith, The Army and Economic Mobilization (Washington, 1959), pp. 480–84; memo, C. J. Durr, Aug. 24, 1940, Council of National Defense, RFC files; memo, Durr to Emil Schram, Sep. 30, 1940, NDP, Snyder files; memo [no author named], Oct. 16, 1940, and testimony prepared for Undersecretary of War Robert P. Patterson for submission to the Appropriations Committee, House of Representatives, July 1941, DPC file, both in FLA files; Hans A. Klagsbrunn, "Some Aspects of War Plant Financing," American Economic Reveiew 33, supplement (Mar. 1943):121–22.

44. Wall Street Journal, Jan. 11, 1941, p. 11, Jan. 14, 1941, p. 4; New York Times, Feb. 13, 1941, p. 31.

45. Wall Street Journal, Dec. 6, 1940, p. 7, Jan. 21, 1940, pp. 1, 9; Banking, Jan. 1941, p. 81.

46. New York Times, Feb. 1, 1941, p. 1.

47. Industrial College of Armed Forces, Construction of New Facilities (Washington, 1947), p. 122.

48. Business Week, Sep. 28, 1940, p. 8, Oct. 5, 1940, p. 17; New York Times, Nov. 10, 1940, p. 26; Wall Street Journal, Nov. 20, 1940, p. 7, Dec. 9, 1940, p. 3; New York Times, Jan. 7, 1941, p. 7.

49. Washington Post, Jan. 13, 1941; interviews with Hans Klagsbrunn, Aug. 20, 1948, and Clifford Durr, Aug. 4, 1971; Durr, "The History of the Defense Plant Corporation," pp. 58–59.

50. Durr, "The History of the Defense Plant Corporation," pp. 60–61; interview with Emil Schram, Aug. 23, 1948; Jesse H. Jones to the president and Congress, Jan. 16, 1941, FLA Press Release 76, RFC Information Division files.

51. FLA Press Release 85, Mar. 15, 1941, RFC Information Division files; President F. D. Roosevelt to Jesse Jones, June 3, 1941, "R," Snyder files, DPC files; U.S., Congress, Senate, *Congressional Record*, 77th Cong., 1st sess., Oct. 13, 1941, p. 7867.

52. Interviews with Durr, Aug. 5, 1971, and John W. Snyder, Sep. 2, 1971; By-law 5, DPC By-laws, Durr files, Wetumpka, Ala.

53. Memo, president to the secretary of war, May 4, 1941, 4245 C file, FDR Library; I. F. Stone, *Business as Usual* (New York, 1941), pp. 42, 45.

54. James N. Ravlin to C. H. Hamilton, Jr., May 6, 1941, RFC file 4, FLA files.

55. U.S., Congress, Senate, *Congressional Record*, 77th Cong., 1st sess., May 16, 1941, p. 4161.

56. Ibid., May 28, 1941, p. 4510.

57. *New York Times*, May 30, 1941, p. 14.

58. *Congressional Record*, May 16, 1941, p. 4161.

59. Ibid., May 16, 1941, p. 4167.

60. 55 Stat. 249–50 (1941).

61. The five proscribed projects were concerned either with water transportation or public power: Great Lakes–St. Lawrence Seaway, Passamaquoddy, Florida, ship canal, Tombigbee River projects, and the Nicaragua canal.

62. *Statistical Abstract of the United States, 1946*, p. 207; interview with Frank M. Eliot, Personnel Division, RFC, Apr. 15, 1947. Figures of amounts billed DPC for salaries were from the Treasurer's Office, RFC, and RFC payroll figures from the Budget Office, RFC.

Chapter 4

1. Minutes of conferences of War Department and DPC officials, June 3 and 10, 1941, Undersecretary of War Patterson to DPC, June 13, 1941, Ordnance Expansion Program, Snyder files, DPC files; interview with Hans Klagsbrunn, Aug. 20, 1947; Lenore Fine and Jesse Remington, *The Corps of Engineers: Construction in the United States* (Washington, 1972). pp. 412–13; U.S., Congress, Senate, *Congressional Record*, 77th Cong., 1st sess., June 28, 1941, p. 5666; U.S., Congress, Senate, *Hearings before the Committee on Appropriations on H. J. Res. 194* (TVA Appropriation Act, 1941), 77th Cong., 1st sess., pp. 50–53.

2. MS of testimony is in DPC files, FLA files; U.S., Congress, House, *Congressional Record*, 77th Cong., 1st sess., July 10, 1941, pp. 5937, 5986–87. For an earlier favorable judgment, see Patterson to Emil Schram, Feb. 20, 1941, "P," Snyder files, DPC files.

3. Eliot Janeway, *The Struggle for Survival* (New Haven, 1951), 168–70; Clifford J. Durr, "The History of the Defense Plant Corporation," p. 55, manuscript in the possession of Mrs. Clifford J. Durr, Wetumpka, Ala.; interviews with Durr, Aug. 4, 1971, Hans Klagsbrunn, Aug. 31, 1971, and John W. Snyder, Sep. 2, 1971; "The War Goes to Mr. Jesse Jones," *Fortune* 24 (Dec. 1941):189–90; Jesse H. Jones and Edward Angly, *Fifty Billion Dollars: Thirteen Years with the RFC, 1932–1945* (New York, 1951), pp. 533–34.

4. Durr, "The History of the Defense Plant Corporation," pp. 66–70; memo of discussion with Emil Schram, signed by C. C. Monrad, NDAC, Aug. 23, 1940, War Production Board records, Record Group 179, National Archives; "Trouble in Synthetic Rubber," *Fortune* 35 (June 1947):157; Frank A. Howard, *Buna Rubber: The Birth of an Industry* (New York, 1947), pp. 116–20, 133, 274–80; interview with Durr, Aug. 4, 1971.

5. Jones and Angly, *Fifty Billion Dollars,* pp. 405–06; I. F. Stone, *Business as Usual* (New York, 1941), pp. 34–35; interview with John W. Snyder, Sep. 2, 1971; E. B. Alderfer and H. E. Michl, *The Economics of American Industry* (New York, 1957), p. 316.

6. FLA Press Release, May 16, 1941, FLA file 3720, Franklin D. Roosevelt Library, Hyde Park, New York; Durr, "This History of the Defense Plant Corporation," pp. 70–72; Frank A. Howard to R. R. Deupree, Apr. 4, 1941, in Howard, *Buna Rubber,* p. 150.

7. Jones and Angly, *Fifty Billion Dollars,* pp. 403–05; Bruce Catton, *The War Lords of Washington* (New York, 1948), pp. 152–53; Harold L. Ickes, *The Secret Diary of Harold L. Ickes,* (New York, 1954), 3:315; Bascom N. Timmons, *Jesse H. Jones: The Man and the Statesman* (New York, 1956), p. 311.

8. Janeway, *Struggle for Survival,* pp. 81–82; Jones and Angly, *Fifty Billion Dollars,* p. 406.

9. Civilian Production Administration, *Industrial Mobilization for War: History of the War Production Board and Predecessor Agencies, 1940–1945* (Washington, 1947), pp. 93–95.

10. *Wartime Production Achievements and the Reconversion Outlook: Report of the Chairman, War Production Board, October 9, 1945* (Washington, 1945), pp. 62–63; Jones and Angly, *Fifty Billion Dollars,* pp. 331–33; U.S., Congress, Senate, *Additional Report of the Special Committee Investigating the National Defense Program Pursuant to S. Res. 6,* 78th Cong., 2d sess., 1944, Rept. 10, pt. 17, pp. 12–14.

11. Knudsen to Patterson, June 6, 1941, War Department, pt. 16, RFC records, Record Group 234, National Archives; *Wartime Production Achievements,* pp. 63–64; memo, F. D. Roosevelt to Jones, Knudsen, and Sidney Hillman, July 16, 1941, FLA file 3720, FDR Library.

12. "The War Goes to Mr. Jesse Jones," *Fortune* 24 (Dec. 1941):192.

13. Harold Stein, "The Disposal of the Aluminum Plants," in Harold Stein, ed., *Public Administration and Policy Development* (New York, 1952), p. 319.

14. *Wartime Production Achievements,* p. 57; Stone, *Business as Usual,* pp. 53–54, 83–113; memo, "Tax Amortization Certificates of Necessity and the Connection with Subcontracting," Oct. 18, 1941, Sen. 79A–F30, National Defense Committee records, Record Group 46, National Archives; Janeway, *Struggle for Survival,* p. 181.

15. Knudsen to Jones, May 24, 1941, Alcoa—226 General file, DPC files.

16. Memo re terms of proposed DPC contract with Alcoa, July 22, 1941, Durr files, Wetumpka, Ala.

17. Durr, memo to Jones, July 26, 1941, Durr files.

18. Interview with Durr, Aug. 7, 1971; Knudsen to Jones, Aug. 4, 1941, Durr files; Stein, "Disposal of Aluminum Plants," pp. 318, 329–30 ff.

19. FLA Press Release re Alcoa contract Aug. 20, 1941, RFC Information Division files; *New York Times,* Nov. 1, 1941, p. 9; "The War Goes to Mr. Jesse

Jones," pp. 194–97; U.S., Congress, Senate, *Report of the Special Committee Investigating the National Defense Program Pursuant to S. Res. 71*, 77th Cong., 2d sess., 1942, Rept. 480, pt. 5.

20. Charles M. Wiltse, *Aluminum Policies of the War Production Board and Predecessor Agencies, May 1940 to November 1945* (Washington, 1946), pp. 55–75; memo on Reynolds Aluminum Company, Sep. 19, 1943, DPC file, Secretary of Commerce files; *Wartime Production Achievements*, p. 58.

21. Stein, "Disposal of Aluminum Plants," pp. 318–19.

22. U.S., Congress, Senate, *Report of the Special Committee Investigating the National Defense Program Pursuant to S. Res. 6*, 78th Cong., 1st sess., 1943, Rept. 10, pt. 3, p. 196.

23. *New York Times*, July 26, 1940, p. 1.

24. *Business Week*, Dec. 14, 1940, p. 15; Jan. 25, 1941, p. 8, Mar. 3, 1941, p. 15; Janeway, *Struggle for Survival*, pp. 246–47; *Wartime Production Achievements*, p. 43; Civilian Production Administration, *Industrial Mobilization*, pp. 137, 153–54; W. A. Hauck, *Steel Expansion for War*, (Cleveland, 1945), pp. 17–19.

25. J. H. Jones to DPC, July 11, 1941, DPC file, FLA files; "The War Goes to Jesse Jones," p. 197; Hauck, *Steel Expansion*, pp. 40–44.

26. R. E. McMath, Bethlehem Steel Corporation, to J. H. Jones, July 31, 1941; Knudsen to Jones, Aug. 27, 1941; H. A. Klagsbrunn, "Analysis of Projected Bethlehem Contract," Dec. 11, 1941, all in Bethlehem No. 287 file, pt. 1, DPC files; Jones to Knudsen, Oct. 16, 1941, RFC file 5, FLA files.

27. J. H. Jones [Sam H. Husbands] to Knudsen, Oct. 16, 1941, RFC file 5, FLA files; memo, J. H. Jones, on Bethlehem Plancors, Jan. 26, 1942, DPC file, FLA files.

28. Memos, W. L. Allen, DPC, on Bethlehem lease terms, Sep. 30 and Oct. 3, 1941, DPC–Bethlehem Steel Corporation file, FLA files; "The War Goes to Mr. Jesse Jones," p. 197.

29. Memo criticizing Bethlehem Lease Draft, Oct. 27, 1941, Durr files, Wetumpka, Ala.; *Report of the Special Committee Pursuant to S. Res. 71*, pp. 28–29, Appendix, pp. 224–31.

30. Interviews with Durr, Aug. 4, 1971, and Klagsbrunn, Aug. 31, 1971; Jones and Angly, *Fifty Billion Dollars*, p. 340. Durr's career was marked by his ability and his devotion to principle. For him, values and beliefs were meaningful only if fused with action. While a federal communications commissioner, he had a major part in setting aside certain radio frequencies for nonprofit educational broadcasting—an important precedent for today's National Educational Television. In 1948, he refused reappointment to the commission because of his dissatisfaction with Truman's loyalty order, Executive Order 9835 (Mar. 22, 1947). Durr became a founder of the National Lawyers' Guild and was a battler for civil rights during the McCarthy era and after. In 1955, he defended Rosemary Parks at the time of the Montgomery bus boycott. Because of his bright mind, sharp wit, gentle manner, and idealism, he was much sought as a visitor by faculty and students alike on campuses of major universities in the United States and England. A review by Geoffrey Cowan of a popular book on the Washington legal scene, Joseph C. Goulden's *The Super-Lawyers* (New York, 1972), effectively contrasts Durr's career with those of many other New Deal lawyers who later went on to "make their pile" in private practice (*New York Times Book Review*, May 28, 1972, p.

1). Principle, not power or money, was always Durr's controlling motivation. He died at his home in Wetumpka, Alabama, on May 12, 1975 (*New York Times,* May 13, 1975, p. 42; *Washington Post,* May 13, 1975, p. 26).

31. Interview with Hans Klagsbrunn, Aug. 31, 1971; memo, Klagsbrunn to Jones, Dec. 18, 1943, DPC file 14, Secretary of Commerce files; *Iron Age,* Feb. 3, 1941, p. 91.

32. Memo, S. M. Thrift to Gerald White, July 15, 1947, RFC Information Division files; "RFC Authorizations in Connection with Construction and Equipping of Defense and War Facilities, June 25, 1940–December 31, 1945," RFC Research and Statistics Division files.

33. Comptroller General of the United States, *Report on Audit of Reconstruction Finance Corporation and Affiliated Corporations for the Fiscal Year Ended June 30, 1945: Defense Plant Corporation,* 80th Cong., 1st sess., 1947, H. Doc. 474, 4:43.

34. 56 Stat. 351 (1942); "Statistical Report," Plants Division, DPC, June 30, 1945, Rentals—General file, DPC files; "Closing Report of SWPC," Feb. 1, 1946, Frank Prince files, RFC files.

35. Undersecretary of war to DPC, May 27, 1943, War Department, Miscellaneous, Snyder files; Admiral Ralph Davidson to DPC, July 19, 1943, Navy Department, Miscellaneous, Snyder files; memo, Dec. 15, 1944, Rentra General file, pt. 2, all in DPC files; interviews with H. R. Rutland, Apr. 23, 1947, and James G. Boss, May 6, 1947.

Chapter 5

1. RFC Minutes, Aug. 22, 1940. Jesse Jones was DPC's chairman and Emil Schram its president. Jones was replaced in March 1945 by Fred M. Vinson, his successor as federal loan administrator. When Schram resigned in June 1941, he was succeeded by another RFC and DPC director, Sam H. Husbands. Husbands continued as president until the dissolution of DPC at the end of June 1945. The other three directors of RFC, C. B. Merriam, C. B. Henderson, and H. J. Klossner, were also original directors of DPC, as were Claude E. Hamilton, Jr., general counsel of RFC, John W. Snyder, vice-president of DPC, and R. J. Lindquist, chief auditor of RFC. Clifford Durr, the first general counsel of DPC, was later made a director. When Durr resigned at the end of October 1941, he was succeeded as general counsel by Hans Klagsbrunn. Subsequently, Klagsbrunn became a director. While retaining his title as general counsel, Klagsbrunn also succeeded John W. Snyder as executive vice-president following Snyder's resignation from that office on August 15, 1943. Klagsbrunn continued as executive vice-president for the balance of the life of the corporation. (Data on DPC directors and other officers have been gathered from RFC Minutes, DPC Minutes, and the files of DPC Bulletins and RFC Press Releases.)

2. Resolution on Quorum, DPC Board of Directors, Feb. 15, 1941, Organization, By-laws file, DPC files.

3. DPC Minutes, Aug. 22, 1940, p. 10.

4. Interview with S. W. Livingston, former assistant general counsel, DPC, Apr. 10, 1947.

5. Interview with G. H. Connerat, former assistant treasurer, DPC, Apr. 7, 1947.

6. DPC Minutes, Jan. 18, 1941, pp. 242–43.

7. Interview with G. H. Connerat, Apr. 7, 1947. See also Chapter 9.

8. Interview with W. W. Wiley, former principal head auditor, DPC, Apr. 8, 1947. Also "List of Auditing Division Personnel," Jan. 1, 1943, Auditing Procedure, Miscellaneous, Snyder files, DPC files.

9. Memo, Nathaniel Royall, chief auditor, DPC, to W. L. Drager, chief engineer, DPC, Nov. 10, 1941, Auditing Procedure, Miscellaneous, Snyder files; "List of Auditing Division Personnel," Jan. 15, 1941, Administrative file, both in DPC files.

10. Interview with Major. A. W. Greely, former chief engineer, DPC, Apr. 7, 1947.

11. DPC Minutes, Apr. 1, 1941, p. 86; DPC Engineering Section Circular No. 100, June 6, 1942, Engineering Circulars file; memo, W. D. Wrightson, chief, Construction Equipment Section, to W. E. Joyce, Sep. 2, 1943, Policy and Procedure file, both in DPC files.

12. Interview with Major A. W. Greely and R. H. Dietz, Apr. 7, 1947. See also "Historical Report, Engineering Section, Self-Liquidating Division," 1946, RFC Information Division files.

13. Special memo, W. L. Drager to division engineers, June 3, 1942, Engineering Circulars file, DPC files.

14. Ibid.

15. DPC Minutes, Jan. 12, 1942, pp. 349–50; memo, Albert E. Bassett, Jan. 12, 1942, Organization, By-laws file, DPC files.

16. Interview with Bryan Mack, formerly of Credit Division, DPC, Apr. 24, 1947.

17. Interview with H. R. Rutland, deputy director, Office of Defense Plants (ODP), Apr. 23, 1947.

18. Ibid.

19. Interview with S. M. Thrift, Apr. 28, 1947.

20. "Meetings," Weekly Conferences, Snyder files, DPC files.

21. Memo, John W. Snyder, July 24, 1940, War Department, Snyder files, DPC files.

22. Between July 1940 and June 1945, the War Department financed industrial facilities directly in the amount of $5,416,286,000; through DPC, $3,879,938,000; through EPF, $172,052,000. Parallel figures for the Navy Department are direct financing, $2,849,095,000; through DPC, $656,403,000; through EPF, $179,252,000. The Maritime Commission financed directly industrial facilities in the amount of $507,527,000 and through DPC, $101,804,000 (Program and Statistics Bureau, WPB, *Facilities Financed with Public Funds* [Washington, 1945], p. 3).

23. Harry Hopkins to Jesse Jones, May 31, 1941, Maritime Commission, Miscellaneous, Snyder files, DPC files.

24. Table IV, "Defense Plant Corporation Authorizations in Connection with Construction and Equipping of Defense and War Facilities, August 22, 1940–December 31, 1945," in C. B. Henderson, "War Construction Activities of the RFC," article prepared for use by the Associated General Contractors of America, Incorporated, in a projected History of Defense and War Construction Activities of the United States Government, which apparently was never published.

25. Ibid.

26. Chart, "Procedural Steps for Negotiating a Defense Plant Corporation Agreement . . ." [1941], DPC Projects, CPA file 221.224, War Production Board records, Record Group 179, National Archives; interview with Warren S. Ege, former special legal assistant, Office of the Undersecretary of War, Apr. 23, 1947.

27. "Memorandum re DPC Procedure, July 3, 1943," Stansfield file, RFC files; memo, R. J. O'Hara to all attorneys negotiating leases, May 8, 1942, Administrative file, DPC files.

28. "Memorandum re DPC Procedure, July 3, 1943."

29. Draft of an article with accompanying charts, Oct. 23, 1941; memo, F. T. Ronan to H. Klagsbrunn, Apr. 15, 1942, Administrative file, both in DPC files.

30. Husbands was president of DPC.

31. Office memo, Jesse Burkhead to Pendleton Herring, Oct. 23, 1942, DPC, War Records Section, Bureau of the Budget file, FLA files.

32. "Memorandum re DPC Procedure, July 3, 1943."

33. Donald Nelson, WPB, to Jesse Jones, Jan. 29, 1943, 221.22 Plant Expansion Projects—Financing, CPA file, War Production Board records; S. H. Husbands to W. L. Drager, Feb. 13, 1943, Administrative file, DPC files.

34. For an early example of Form 1, see the Wright Aeronautical Corporation lease already cited, DPC Minutes, Oct. 18, 1940, pp. 91–99. For an early example of Form 2, see the Bendix Aviation Corporation lease already cited, DPC Minutes, Oct. 14, 1940, pp. 66–75.

35. For an example of Form 3, see the Crown Central Petroleum Corporation lease, Plancor 1068, Apr. 30, 1942, Crown Central Petroleum Corporation file, Document, pt. 1, DPC files.

36. For an example of Form 4, see the Standard Oil Company of Louisiana lease, Plancor 1572, Apr. 20, 1942, Standard Oil Company of Louisiana file, Document, pt. 1, DPC files.

37. For an example of Form 5, see the agreement with Basic Magnesium, Incorporated, Plancor 201, Aug. 1, 1941, Basic Magnesium, Incorporated file, Document, pt. 1, DPC files.

38. Memo on Options [no name], Sep. 9, 1943, DPC file 10, Secretary of Commerce files; H. L. Ickes to the president, July 14, 1941; memo, Franklin D. Roosevelt to Jesse Jones, William S. Knudsen, and Sidney Hillman, July 16, 1941, The President, FLA files.

39. Interview with T. A. Martin, RFC Treasurer's Office, Apr. 3, 1947.

40. *Minutes of the Advisory Commission to the Council of National Defense* (Washington, 1946), p. 88.

41. C. J. Durr to Colonel Greenbaum, Dec. 26, 1940; memo, "Defense Plant Corporation—Method of Operation," July 14, 1941, Organization, By-laws file, both in DPC files; "Memorandum re DPC Procedure," July 3, 1943, Stansfield file, RFC files.

42. "Statistical Report," Plants Division, DPC, June 30, 1945, Rentals—General file, DPC files.

43. Interview with S. W. Livingston, former assistant general counsel, DPC, Apr. 10, 1947.

44. "Statistical Report," Plants Division, DPC, June 30, 1945.

45. "Statistical Report," Plant Servicing Division, ODP, Sep. 10, 1945, Rentals—General file, DPC files.

46. R. P. Patterson to Jesse Jones, Nov. 19, 1940; Jesse Jones to R. P. Patterson, Dec. 12, 1940, DPC files, FLA files.

47. Interview with Frank H. Rivers, Administrative Section, ODP, July 8, 1947.

48. Interview with S. W. Livingston, July 8, 1947.

Chapter 6

1. Quoted in Seymour Harris, *The Economics of America at War* (New York, 1943), p. 105.

2. Surplus Property Administration, *Aircraft Plants and Facilities: Report of the Surplus Property Administration to the Congress, Jan. 14, 1946* (Washington, 1946), p. 7.

3. See Chapter 3; Norman Beasley, *Knudsen* (New York, 1947), p. 267.

4. Defense Plant Corporation, *Advance Listing of Industrial Plants and Plant Sites to be Disposed of by Defense Plant Corporation, Oct. 14, 1944* (Washington, 1944), p. 102; Beasley, *Knudsen*, p. 361.

5. *Aircraft Plants and Facilities*, p. 9.

6. R. O. Palstine, assistant division engineer, Office of Defense Plants (ODP), "Report on Construction of Plancor 20 . . . ," Aug. 7, 1946, Publicity, Engineering Division files, DPC files.

7. Comptroller General of the United States, *Report on Audit of Reconstruction Finance Corporation and Affiliated Corporations for the Fiscal Year Ended June 30, 1945: Defense Plant Corporation*, 80th Cong., 1st sess., 1947, H. Doc. 474, 4:76–77.

8. *Wartime Production Achievements and the Reconversion Outlook: Report of the Chairman, War Production Board, Oct. 9, 1945* (Washington, 1945), p. 106.

9. Surplus Property Administration, *Aviation-Gasoline Plants and Facilities: Report of the Surplus Property Administration to the Congress, Jan. 14, 1946* (Washington, 1946), pp. 1, 5.

10. Chart, "100 Octane Aviation Gasoline Program . . ." [May 27, 1947]; chart, "Statement of Production and Estimated Cost of New Facilities of 100 Octane Gasoline Program" [ca. 1944], both in Office of Defense Supplies (ODS) files, RFC files.

11. Report, "Aviation Gasoline and Related Projects," Jan. 3, 1946, RFC Statistical and Economic Division files.

12. Interview with S. W. Livingston, Legal Division, ODP, Apr. 11, 1947; interview with H. R. Rutland, deputy director, ODP, Apr. 23, 1947.

13. Historical Report, Engineering Section, Self-Liquidating Division, 1946, RFC Information Division files; interview with H. R. Rutland, Apr. 23, 1947.

14. DPC Bulletin No. 41 to Loan Agencies, May 14, 1943, DPC Bulletin file.

15. Charles M. Wiltse, *Aluminum Policies of the War Production Board and Predecessor Agencies, May 1940 to November 1945* (Washington, 1946), pp. 173–75; J. H. Jones to Donald Nelson, Oct. 2, 1942, DPC-Alcoa file, Secretary of Commerce files.

16. *Wartime Production Achievements*, p. 58.

17. Surplus Property Board, *Aluminum Plants and Facilities: Report of the Surplus Board to the Congress, Sep. 21, 1945* (Washington, 1945) 1, p. 91.

18. J. H. Jones to W. S. Knudsen, Oct. 13, 1941, DPC file 3, Secretary of Commerce files.

19. Interview with M. M. Repass, Engineering Division, ODP, June 12, 1947.

20. *Wartime Production Achievements*, p. 64.

21. Surplus Property Administration, *Report to Congress on Disposal of Government Iron and Steel Plants and Facilities, Oct. 8, 1945* (Washington, 1945), pp. 7–8; "Steel; Report on the War Years," *Fortune* 31 (May 1945):121–23; Report on DPC steel and pig iron projects, Jan. 30, 1946, RFC Statistical and Economic Division files.

22. *Advance Listing of Industrial Plants,* p. 131; Sam H. Husbands to J. H. Jones, Nov. 13, 1944, DPC file 20, Secretary of Commerce files.

23. Jesse H. Jones to the president, Feb. 10, 1944, The President file, Secretary of Commerce files.

24. Copy prepared for a brochure on RFC's war activities, Jan. 1947, RFC Information Division files, based on data supplied by RFC Statistical and Economic Division. See also memo, Sam H. Husbands to Jesse H. Jones, Dec. 9, 1944, DPC file 20, Secretary of Commerce files.

25. FLA Press Release 82, Feb. 26, 1941, RFC Information Division files; *Wartime Production Achievements*, p. 72.

26. Report on DPC Metals and Minerals projects, Jan. 14, 1946, RFC Statistical and Economic Division files.

27. Report on DPC Machine Tool projects, Dec. 6, 1945, RFC Statistical and Economic Division files.

28. FLA Press Release 85, Mar. 15, 1941, RFC Information Division files; J. H. Jones to Tennessee Powder Company, Memphis, Tennessee, Mar. 19, 1941, NDP–Defense Plant Corporation, Snyder files, DPC files.

29. The president to J. H. Jones, June 3, 1941, "H," Snyder files.

30. Report on DPC Ordnance projects, Jan. 4, 1946, RFC Statistical and Economic Division files.

31. *Wartime Production Achievements,* p. 89.

32. War Production Board, *Alcohol Policies of the WPB and Predecessor Agencies May 1940 to January 1945* (Washington, 1946), pp. 44–45, 48–49; Report on DPC Chemical projects, Jan. 16, 1946, RFC Statistical and Economic Division files.

33. Report on DPC Chemical projects, Jan. 16, 1946.

34. U.S., Congress, Senate, *Additional Report of the Special Committee Investigating the National Defense Program Pursuant to S. Res. 6,* 78th Cong., 1st sess., 1943, S. Rept. 10, pt. 4, *Second Annual Report,* App., p. 71.

35. Report of DPC Rubber projects, Jan. 14, 1946, RFC Statistical and Economic Division files.

36. Surplus Property Administration, *Interim Report of the Surplus Property Administration to the Congress: Radio and Electrical Equipment, Jan. 31, 1946* (Washington, 1946), p. 31.

37. Report on DPC Radio, Communication, and Field Equipment projects, Dec. 12, 1945, RFC Statistical and Economic Division files.

38. Report on DPC Ships and Parts projects, Dec. 12, 1945, RFC Statistical and Economic Division files.

39. Report on DPC Miscellaneous Plant projects, Dec. 12, 1945, RFC Statistical and Economic Division files.

40. A. I. Henderson, WPB, to Jesse H. Jones, Oct. 5, 1942; J. H. Jones to A. I. Henderson, Oct. 5, 1942, DPC file 3, Secretary of Commerce files.

41. "Two Pipelines for Sale," *Fortune* 31 (Jan. 1945):125–28.

42. RFC Press Release 1630, July 7, 1942; RFC Press Release 1793, Apr. 21, 1943, RFC Information Division files.

43. RFC Press Release 1650, Sep. 14, 1942; RFC Press Release 1791, Apr. 20, 1943, RFC Information Division files.

44. RFC Press Release 1759, Feb. 24, 1943, RFC Information Division files.

45. Surplus Property Administration, *Government-Owned Pipe Lines: Report of the Surplus Property Administration to the Congress, Jan. 4, 1946* (Washington, 1946), p. 1.

46. Ibid., p. 6; "Two Pipelines for Sale," *Fortune* 31 (Jan. 1945):125–28.

47. *War Emergency-Pipelines, Incorporated* [brochure] (1946), p. 2, RFC Information Division files.

48. Report on DPC Transportation projects, Jan. 4, 1946, RFC Statistical and Economic Division files; Senate, *Additional Report Pursuant to S. Res. 6,* pt. 13, *Transportation,* p. 33.

49. W. S. Knudsen to R. P. Patterson, Jan. 14, 1942, 610.424 Power projects; Donald Nelson to J. H. Jones, Oct. 13, 1942, 610.42 Power Facilities, both in Civilian Production Administration files, Record Group 179, National Archives.

50. Joseph B. Eastman, Office of Defense Transportation, to Jesse H. Jones, Apr. 11, 1942; J. H. Jones to J. B. Eastman, Apr. 16, 1942, Snyder files, DPC files.

51. Report on DPC Transportation projects, Jan. 4, 1946, RFC Statistical and Economic Division files.

52. Report on DPC Housing projects, Jan. 8, 1946, RFC Statistical and Economic Division files.

53. See the remarks of Abe Fortas at the memorial service for Clifford Durr, held in Washington, D.C., June 12, 1975, Lyndon B. Johnson Library, Austin, Texas; also *New York Times,* June 13, 1975, p. 42.

Chapter 7

1. Norman Beasley, *Knudsen,* (New York, 1947), pp. 293, 315–16.

2. Memo, H. J. Klossner for files, July 4, 1940, Council of National Defense, RFC files; RFC Minutes, July 22, 1940, pp. 1157–58; interview with John W. Snyder, May 8, 1947.

3. "Machine Tool Maker's Dilemma," *Fortune* 26 (Oct. 1942):106; James R. Mock and Evangeline Thurber, *Report on Demobilization* (Norman, Okla., 1944), pp. 145–53.

4. Henry F. Pringle, "Biggest Big Shot: Uncle Sam," *Saturday Evening Post* 216 (Dec. 18, 1943):61.

5. H. A. Klagsbrunn, "Some Aspects of War Plant Financing," *Papers and Proceedings of the 55th Annual Meeting of the American Economic Association, American Economic Review* 33, supplement (Mar. 1943):126; interview with H. A. Klagsbrunn, May 23, 1947. See also "Analysis of War Department Procurement, World War II," pp. 102–03, War Department files.

6. Emil Schram to W. S. Knudsen, Jan. 4, 1941, Machine Tool Pool files, pt. 1, DPC files; War Production Board, *Aircraft Production Policies under National Defense Advisory Commission and Office of Production Management: May 1940 to December 1941* (Washington, 1946), pp. 111–15; A. T. Hobson to H. L. Sullivan, July 28, 1941, Machine Tool Pool files, pt. 1.

7. G. C. Brainerd, chief, Tools Branch, OPM, to John W. Snyder, Jan. 16, 1942, Machine Tool file, pt. 1; R. P. Patterson, undersecretary of war, to DPC, Jan. 19, 1942, Organization, By-laws file, DPC files.

8. R. P. Patterson to DPC, Feb. 2, 1942; A. T. Hobson to R. P. Patterson, Feb. 13, 1942, both in Organization, By-laws file.

9. Frank T. Ronan, Nov. 1, 1942, Machine Tool Pool files, pt. 2.

10. "Cutting Tool and Industrial Equipment Pool—Plancor 615," Report as of Feb. 28, 1947, S. M. Thrift files, RFC files.

11. S. M. Thrift to Gerald T. White, July 14, 1947, RFC Information Division files.

12. Machine Tool Pool meeting, Dec. 1, 1941, DPC file 20, Secretary of Commerce files; Geoffrey Smith, assistant general counsel, OPM, to John W. Snyder, Dec. 8, 1941, Machine Tool Pool files, pt. 1.

13. Frank T. Ronan to DPC board, Jan. 23, 1942, Policy and Procedure files, DPC files.

14. R. P. Patterson to DPC, June 25, 1943, Machine Tool Pool files, pt. 3.

15. Interview with S. M. Thrift, Apr. 28, 1947.

16. John S. Chaffee, director, Tools Division, WPB, to all machinery builders, Dec. 12, 1944, Machine Tool Pool files, pt. 4.

17. Frank T. Ronan to Peyton Stapp, Clearance Office, Bureau of the Budget, Dec. 28, 1944, Machine Tool Pool files, pt. 4, "Machine Tools—Plancor #51," Report as of Feb. 28, 1947, S. M. Thrift files, RFC files.

18. Memo forms, Frank Ronan to Roger A. Wilson, Machine Tool Pool files, pt. 4.

19. Wire message, Jesse Jones to all DPC lessees, Dec. 26, 1944, RFC Release 2132, Dec. 27, 1944, RFC Information Division files.

20. RFC Release 2204, Mar. 26, 1945, RFC Information Division files.

21. Brigadier General G. H. Drewry, deputy director, Production Division, War Department, to ODP, RFC, Aug. 23, 1945, Machine Tool Pool file, pt. 5.

22. "Machine Tools—Plancor #51," Report as of Feb. 28, 1947, S. M. Thrift files.

23. Comptroller General of the United States, *Report on Audit of Reconstruction Finance Corporation and Affiliated Corporations for the Fiscal Year Ended June 30, 1945: Defense Plant Corporation,* 80th Cong., 1st sess., 1947, H. Doc. 474, 4:50.

24. Robert P. Patterson, secretary of war, to Samuel M. Thrift, June 10, 1946, Machine Tool Pool file, pt. 5. On its use during the Korean War, see Chapter 10.

Chapter 8

1. On the Jones-Wallace feud, see Russell H. Lord, *The Wallaces of Iowa* (Boston, 1947), pp. 499–512; Edward L. Schapsmeier and Frederick H. Schapsmeier, *Prophet in Politics: Henry A. Wallace and the War Years, 1940–1945* (Ames, Iowa, 1970), pp. 57–68; Bascom M. Timmons, *Jesse H. Jones: The Man and the Statesman* (New York, 1956), pp. 317–28. On the Roosevelt appointment of Wallace and the ensuing storm, see Lord, *The Wallaces of Iowa,* pp. 543–51; Schapsmeier and Schapsmeier, *Prophet in Politics,* pp. 119–24; U.S., Congress, Senate, *Hearings before the Committee on S. 375,* 79th Cong., 1st sess., 1945. On Byrd's statement, *New York Times,* Jan. 24, 1945, p. 12.

2. *New York Times,* Mar. 6, 1945, p. 1, Apr. 3, 1945, p. 1.

3. Ibid., Apr. 5, 1945, p. 1; Patton to President Roosevelt, Apr. 3, 1945, James M. Barnes to William D. Hassett, Apr. 6, 1945, file 3720-A, FDR Library, Hyde Park, New York.

4. *New York Times,* Apr. 18, 1945, p. 14, May 11, 1945, p. 20, May 16, 1945, p. 11.

5. A. D. H. Kaplan, *The Liquidation of War Production* (New York, 1944), p. 89; War Assets Administration, "Report on Government-Owned Industrial Plants as of September 30, 1947," p. 1, Library, National Archives; Surplus Property Board Press Release 69, July 4, 1945, War Assets Administration (WAA) files, Washington National Records Center, Suitland, Md. (hereafter cited WNRC); James A. Cook, *The Marketing of War Surplus Property* (Washington, 1948), pp. 15–19; William Haber, "The American Road from War to Peace," *American Political Science Review* 38 (Dec. 1944):119–20; "Surplus War Property Disposal under the Surplus War Property Administration," p. 78, WAA files, WNRC.

6. Surplus Property Board Press Release 69. DPC's share was given as 96 percent of the nation's capacity in synthetic rubber, 90 percent in magnesium, 71 percent in aircraft and aircraft engines, 58 percent in aluminum metals, and 50 percent in aluminum fabrication in Comptroller General of the United States, *Report on Audit of Reconstruction Finance Corporation and Affiliated Corporations for the Fiscal Year Ended June 30, 1945: Defense Plant Corporation,* 80th Cong., 1st sess., 1947, H. Doc. 474, 4:36.

7. U.S., Congress, House, *Report of the Special Committee on Post-War Economic Policy and Planning,* 78th Cong., 2d sess., 1944, H. Rept. 1796, p. 4.

8. Jerome Bruner, *Mandate from the People* (New York, 1944), pp. 199–200, 268.

9. Clifford J. Durr, "The Postwar Relationship between Government and Business," *Papers and Proceedings of the 55th Annual Meeting of the American Economic Association, American Economic Review* 33, supplement (Mar. 1943):50; James G. Patton, "The Federal Government's Role in the Postwar Economy," *American Political Science Review* 38 (Dec. 1944):1130–33; U.S., Congress, Senate, *Hearings before the Special Committee on Post-War Economic Policy and Planning Pursuant to S. Res. 102,* 78th Cong., 1st sess., 1943, pp. 532–33.

10. American Enterprise Association, *Disposal of Government-Owned Industrial War Properties* (New York, 1944), p. 16; *New York Times,* Apr. 15, 1944, p. 2, Apr. 27, 1944, p. 36.

11. Senate, *Hearings on Post-War Economic Policy and Planning,* pp. 471–72, 509–11; U.S., Congress, Senate, *Report of the Special Committee on Post-War Economic Policy and Planning,* 78th Cong., 2d sess., 1944, S. Rept. 539, pt. 2, pp. 3–8.

12. U.S., Congress, Senate, *Additional Report of the Special Committee Investigating the National Defense Program Pursuant to S. Res. 6,* 78th Cong., 2d sess., 1944, S. Rept. 10, pt. 16, *Third Annual Report,* pp. 33, 36–39, 389–90, 400.

13. Bernard Baruch and John M. Hancock, *Report on War and Post-War Adjustment Policies, Feb. 15, 1944* (Washington, 1944); Herman Somers, *Presidential Agency: OWMR* (Cambridge, 1950), pp. 176–78.

14. Baruch and Hancock, *Report,* pp. 13–14.

15. Ibid., pp. 24, 23, 62. Italics in original.

16. Hadley Cantril, ed., *Public Opinion, 1935–1946* (Princeton, 1951), p. 350.

In the earlier *Fortune* survey, 2.5 percent of the executives either failed to reply or replied "don't know."

17. This information has been drawn from various standard biographical sources, particularly *Current Biography, 1944* (New York, 1945), pp. 95–99.

18. "Background and Passage of the Surplus Property Act"; "WAA and Predecessors Chronology, 1944–1948"; Minutes, Surplus War Property Policy Board, Mar. 2, 1944; Surplus War Property Administrator Press Releases, June 5 and July 19, 1944, all in WAA files, WNRC.

19. "The War Inventory," *Fortune* 30 (Sept. 1944):254; "Surplus Disposal under the Surplus War Property Administration," pp. 58–74, WAA files, WNRC.

20. "Draft of a Proposed Final Report of the Surplus War Property Administrator," Oct. 12, 1944, SWPA file, Bureau of the Budget, Record Group 51, National Archives.

21. Jones to Smith, Aug. 12, 1943, Durr files, Wetumpka, Ala.; Senate, *Hearings on Post-War Economic Policy and Planning*, Nov. 5, 1943, p. 435; "Surplus Disposal under the Surplus War Property Administration," pp. 91–92; "Draft of a Proposed Final Report of the Surplus War Property Administrator," Oct. 12, 1944.

22. Minutes, Surplus War Property Policy Board, Apr. 25, 1944; "Background and Passage of the Surplus Property Act"; "Summary of Recommendations Submitted on Surplus Property Legislation," U.S., Congress, Senate, *Report of War Contracts Subcommittee of Committee on Military Affairs*, 78th Cong., 2d sess., 1944, Senate Subcommittee Print No. 5.

23. 58 Stat. 765 (1944).

24. "War Surplus," *Fortune* 33 (Mar. 1946):105; "WAA and Predecessors Chronology, 1944–1948," WAA files, WNRC; "William L. Clayton," *Current Biography*, 1944, pp. 98–99; Clayton to James F. Byrnes, Sep. 14, 1944, in Frederick J. Dobney, ed., *Selected Papers of Will Clayton* (Baltimore, 1971), pp. 85–86.

25. Surplus Property Board Press Release 48, May 12, 1945, WAA files, WNRC; Harold Stein, ed., *Public Administration and Policy Development* (New York, 1952), p. 321; 59 Stat. 245.

26. Biographical data have been drawn from various standard sources, particularly *Current Biography, 1945* (New York, 1946), pp. 585–87; also, "A Yaleman and a Communist," *Fortune* 27 (Nov. 1943):148.

27. Surplus Property Board Press Release, July 25, 1945, Surplus Property Administration Press Release, Oct. 15, 1945; "The Disposal of the Aluminum Plants," in Stein, ed., *Public Administration*, pp. 321–57.

28. Surplus Property Administration Press Release, Jan. 20, 1946.

29. Surplus Property Board Press Release, Sep. 9, 1945; Special Order 19, Jan. 6, 1946, WAA files, WNRC.

30. "War Surplus," *Fortune*, p. 190; Minutes, Nov. 15, 1945–Mar. 25, 1946, War Assets Corporation, WAA files; memo, Harold D. Smith, director, Bureau of the Budget, to chairmen, War Assets Corporation and RFC, Mar. 25, 1946, WAA file, Bureau of the Budget records; "WAA and Predecessors Chronology, 1944–1948"; Harry K. Stanford, *Disposal of Surplus Property: Experiment in Organization, 1944–46* (New York, 1951), p. 7.

31. U.S., Congress, Senate, *Report of Hon. Joseph C. O'Mahoney to the Special*

Committee on Post-War Economic Policy and Planning Pursuant to S. Res. 102, 78th
Cong., 1st sess., 1943, S. Doc. 106, p. 52; "Preliminary Report on Demobilization
Planning Activities," Nov. 1943, Bureau of the Budget records.

32. F. T. Ronan to lessees, Mar. 28, 1944, RFC Agency Division files; memo,
S. H. Husbands, Oct. 17, 1944, DPC file 20, Secretary of Commerce files.

33. RFC Press Release 2075, Sep. 6, 1944, RFC Information Division files;
memo, J. A. Rhodes to J. H. Jones, Sep. 25, 1944, DPC Surplus War Property,
Secretary of Commerce files.

34. Memo, W. H. Dorsey, ODP, Apr. 2, 1947, RFC Information Division files;
SWPA Regulation Number 3, Aug. 9, 1944; interview with T. A. Martin, RFC
Treasurer's Office, June 24, 1947.

35. *Report by the Director of Contract Settlement to the Congress, Oct. 1944* (Washington, 1944), pp. 67–70.

36. Interview with Henry Greene, former assistant chief engineer, DPC, June
9, 1947; Sections 17.00–17.138, *Memoranda to Supervising Engineers*, DPC files.

37. Interview with Henry Greene, June 9, 1947; F. T. Ronan and J. L. Kelehan,
"Progress Report to the Board of Directors," Aug. 21, 1946, p. 8; J. L. Kelehan,
"Second Progress Report to the Board of Directors," Nov. 1946, Kelehan files,
RFC files.

38. Ronan and Kelehan, "Progress Report to the Board of Directors," pp. 8–9;
interview with J. D. Paul, Engineering Division, ODP, July 24, 1947.

39. RFC Press Release 2051, July 27, 1944, RFC Information Division files;
U.S., Congress, Senate, *Hearings of the Special Committee Investigating the National
Defense Program, Pursuant to S. Res. 6*, 78th Cong., 2d sess., 1944, p. 10992; Defense
Plant Corporation, *Advance Listing of Industrial Plants and Plant Sites to be Disposed of
by Defense Plant Corporation, Oct. 14, 1944* (Washington, 1944), RFC Information
Division files; H. A. Klagsbrunn, "Defense Plant Corporation," Jan. 15, 1945,
Organization, By-laws file, DPC files.

40. Memo, Sam H. Husbands to Will Clayton, June 27, 1944, WAA files,
WNRC; "Draft of a Proposed Final Report of Surplus War Property Administrator," Oct. 12, 1944.

41. Resolution, DPC Board of Directors, Apr. 2, 1945, Organization, By-laws
file.

42. Memo, J. P. Bonner to A. W. Greely, Mar. 23, 1945, Organization, By-laws
file.

43. Interviews with J. P. Bonner, June 6, 1947, and M. M. Repass, June 9, 1947.

44. Comptroller General of the United States, *Report on Audit of Reconstruction
Finance Corporation* 4:65.

45. A. L. Gates, acting secretary of navy, to RFC, July 28, 1945; R. P. Patterson,
undersecretary of war, to RFC, Aug. 20, 1945; J. A. Krug, WPB, to C. B. Henderson, Aug. 29, 1945, all in Administrative file, DPC files.

46. Sam Husbands left RFC early in 1946 to become executive vice-president,
and later president, of Transamerica Corporation; Hans Klagsbrunn resigned in
July 1946 to serve briefly as deputy director of OWMR before entering the private
practice of law. On salaries, see Franklin Kilpatrick, *The Image of the Federal Service*
(Washington, 1964), p. 44.

47. Biographical information is from standard sources, particularly *Current
Biography, 1945* (New York, 1946), for both Murray and O'Mahoney; also U.S.,

Congress, Senate, Committee on Military Affairs, *S. Res. 129,* 70th Cong., 1st sess., June 29, 1945.

48. U.S., Congress, Senate, *Progress of Plant Disposal: Report of the Surplus Property Subcommittee of the Committee on Military Affairs Pursuant to S. Res. 129,* 79th Cong., 2d sess., 1946, Subcommittee Print No. 5, p. 5.

49. "Statement to the Congress on the Findings of the Congressional Committees Dealing with Surplus Property Activities of the War Assets Administration," Mar. 17, 1947, WAA files, WNRC.

50. U.S., Congress, Senate, Committee on Expenditures in Executive Departments, *S. Res. 75,* 80th Cong., 1st sess., Feb. 17, 1947; U.S., Congress, Senate, *Investigation of Surplus Property and Its Disposal: Report of Committee on Expenditures in Executive Departments Pursuant to S. Res. 75,* 80th Cong., 2d sess., 1948, S. Rept. 1365, pp. 23–24; James A. Cook, *The Marketing of War Surplus Property* (Washington, 1948), p. v.

51. "Statement by the War Assets Administrator to the Armed Forces Committee of the House of Representatives in regard to H. R. 6098," Bureau of the Budget records.

52. Surplus Property Board Press Release 48, May 12, 1945, WAA files, WNRC.

53. Senate, *Investigation of Surplus Property,* Appendix, pp. 7–12.

54. War Assets Administration, "Report on Government-Owned Industrial Plants as of September 30, 1947," pp. 1–11, Library, National Archives.

55. War Assets Administration, *Quarterly Report to the Congress, 4th Quarter, 1948* (Washington, 1949), Appendix D, pp. 52–74. Records relating to the disposal of each plant are in WAA files, WNRC.

56. War Assets Administration, *Quarterly Report to the Congress, 1st Quarter, 1949* (Washington, 1949), Appendix B, pp. 27–31.

57. Comptroller General of the United States, *Report on Audit of Reconstruction Finance Corporation,* 4:75–78; Cook, *Marketing of War Surplus,* p. 19.

58. William G. Cunningham, *The Aircraft Industry: A Study in Industrial Location* (Los Angeles, 1951), p. 179; E. B. Alderfer and H. E. Michl, *The Economics of American Industry* (New York, 1957), p. 171; Surplus Property Administration Press Release 191, Jan. 14, 1946, WAA files, WNRC; U.S., Congress, Senate, *Special Committee Investigating the National Defense Program Pursuant to S. Res. 55,* 79th Cong., 2d sess., 1946, S. Rept. 110, pt. 7, *Fifth Annual Report,* pp. 136–37.

59. See, for example, files on Plancor 10 (aircraft engines, Lockland, Ohio) to Electric Auto-lite; Plancor 16 (aircraft assembly, Cheektowaga, New York) to Westinghouse; Plancor 39 (aircraft engines, Melrose, Illinois) to International Harvester; Plancor 40 (aircraft engines, Chicago, Illinois) to Western Electric; Plancor 55 (aircraft engines, Buffalo, New York) to General Motors, and others, all in WAA files, WNRC.

60. On Playboy, see *New York Times,* Apr. 4, 1947, p. 7, Nov. 23, 1947, sec. 3, p. 5, May 28, 1948, p. 38, Aug. 29, 1948, sec. 3, p. 3.

61. Ibid., July 4, 1946, p. 17, July 6, 1946, p. 21, Aug. 14, 1947, p. 36, Dec. 18, 1948, p. 23, Jan. 23, 1950, p. 1, Feb. 21, 1950, p. 32; brief on Dodge-Chrysler plant transaction, Robert Burns to General R. M. Littlejohn, WAA administrator, June 12, 1947, Plancor 792 file, WAA files, WNRC; Senate, *Investigation of Surplus Property,* pp. 15–18.

62. S. H. Husbands to Stuart Symington, Dec. 20, 1945, Exhibit 287, SPC Minutes, WAA files, WNRC; "Adventures of Henry and Joe in Autoland," *Fortune* 33 (Mar. 1946):91 ff.; *New York Times,* Nov. 11, 1953, p. 1.

63. Comptroller General of the United States, *Report on Audit of Reconstruction Finance Corporation,* 4:78; Surplus Property Administration Press Release 195, Jan. 15, 1946; H. A. Williamson et al., *The American Petroleum Industry: The age of energy, 1899–1959* (Evanston, 1963), pp. 798–801; "R. F. C. Aviation Gasoline Plants, as of Sept. 30, 1947," in WAA, "Report on Government-Owned Industrial Plants as of September 30, 1947."

64. Comptroller General of the United States, *Report on Audit of Reconstruction Finance Corporation,* 4:80; "Disposal of Aluminum Plants," in Stein, ed., *Public Administration,* pp. 319–20; Surplus Property Administration Press Release 193, Jan. 10, 1946; War Assets Corporation Press Release C-247, Feb. 21, 1946, WAA files, WNRC; Alderfer and Michl, *Economics,* pp. 109–15; Robert Sheehan, "Kaiser Aluminum—Henry J's Marvelous Mistake," *Fortune* 54 (July 1956):79 ff; "R. F. C. Aluminum Plants as of September 30, 1947," in WAA, "Report on Government-Owned Industrial Plants as of September 30, 1947."

65. Comptroller General of the United States, *Report on Audit of Reconstruction Finance Corporation,* 4:81; Surplus Property Administration Press Release 148, Dec. 7, 1945; memo, Curtis A. Ross to commissioner, Utilization and Disposal Service, General Services Administration, Nov. 3, 1961, Basic Magnesium file, WAA files, WNRC.

66. Comptroller General of the United States, *Report on Audit of Reconstruction Finance Corporation,* 4:80; W. A. Hauck, *Steel Expansion for War* (Cleveland, 1945), pp. 14, 18–19, 37–39, 41–44, 92–116.

67. U.S., Congress, Senate, War Contracts Subcommittee of the Committee on Military Affairs, *War Plants Disposal: Iron and Steel Plants,* 79th Cong., 1st sess., 1945, S. Rept. 199, pp. 4–11; Surplus Property Administration Press Release 110, Oct. 11, 1945; memorandum to Price Review Board on proposed sale of Geneva Steel plant, May 22, 1946, Plancor 301 (Geneva) files, WAA files, WNRC; also Plancor files 186 and 302 (Carnegie-Illinois), 266 (Inland), and 284 (Republic), WAA files, WNRC.

68. Comptroller General of the United States, *Report on Audit of Reconstruction Finance Corporation,* 4:82; Office of Rubber Reserve, RFC, *Report on the Rubber Program, Supplement No. 1, Year 1945* (Washington, 1946); "Trouble in Synthetic Rubber," *Fortune* 35 (June 1947):116–17; 62 Stat. 100 (1948); Harold Stein, "Notes on Economic Mobilization," *Public Administration Review* 10 (Autumn 1950):238.

69. Comptroller General of the United States, *Report on Audit of Reconstruction Finance Corporation,* 4:68; "R. F. C. Synthetic Rubber Plants as of September 30, 1947," in WAA, "Report on Government-Owned Industrial Plants as of September 30, 1947"; 67 Stat. 408 (1953); Alderfer and Michl, *Economics,* pp. 317–20; White House file, Rubber Producing Facilities Disposal Commission, RFC records, Record Group 234, National Archives; Dero Saunders, "The New Bounce in Rubber," *Fortune* 54 (Aug. 1956):97 ff.; *Fifth Report of the Attorney General on Competition in the Synthetic Rubber Industry* (Washington, 1960), pp. 2–3.

70. Comptroller General of the United States, *Report on Audit of Reconstruction Finance Corporation,* 4:68, 83; "Two Pipelines for Sale," *Fortune* 31 (Jan. 1945):125

ff.; Surplus Property Administration Press Release 167, Jan. 4, 1946; Williamson et al., *American Petroleum Industry,* p. 801; "Statement to the Congress on the Findings of the Congressional Committees Dealing with Surplus Property Activities by the War Assets Administration," Mar. 1, 1947, WAA files, WNRC.

71. "Disposition Status of Industrial Plants Owned by the Reconstruction Finance Corporation," in WAA, "Report on Government-Owned Industrial Plants as of September 30, 1947."

72. Comptroller General of the United States, *Report on Audit of Reconstruction Finance Corporation,* 4:49–50; Surplus Property Administration Press Release 124, Nov. 6, 1945; U.S., Congress, Senate, War Contracts Subcommittee, Committee on Military Affairs, *War Plants Disposal: Aircraft Plants,* 79th Cong., 1st sess., 1945, S. Rept. 199, pt. 2, pp. 21–22; "Statement of Surplus Property Board Regarding the Disposition of Surplus Machine Tools for the Hearings of the Subcommittee, Apr. 25, 1945," Exhibit 119, Surplus Property Board, WAA files, WNRC.

73. American Enterprise Association, *Disposal of Government-Owned Industrial War Properties,* p. 17; Federal Reserve Bank of Chicago, "Machine Tools—Bottleneck to Reconversion," *Business Conditions,* July 1945, pp. 1, 6–8; Surplus Property Administration Press Releases 115, Jan. 15, 1946, and 203, Jan. 16, 1946.

74. "Draft of a Proposed Final Report of Surplus War Property Administrator," Oct. 12, 1944, SWPA file, Bureau of the Budget records; "Disposal of World War II Surplus under War Assets Corporation," pp. 144–45, WAA files, WNRC.

75. "Surplus Disposal under the Surplus War Property Administration," p. 75, WAA files, WNRC; U.S., Congress, Senate, *Surplus Disposal: Selling through Agents, Report of the Surplus Property Subcommittee of the Committee on Military Affairs Pursuant to S. Res. 129,* 79th Cong., 2d sess., 1946, Subcommittee Print No. 12, pp. 7–8; "Disposal of Surplus War Material World War II through September 30, 1947," pp. 54, 57, WAA files, WNRC; War Assets Administration, *Quarterly Report to the Congress by the War Assets Administration, First Quarter, 1947* (Washington, 1947), p. 18; War Assets Administration, *War Surplus in the Peacetime Economy: Quarterly Progress Report to the Congress by the War Assets Administration* (Washington, 1947), pp. 8–9.

76. *Quarterly Report by War Assets Administration, First Quarter, 1947,* pp. 18–20; Cook, *Marketing of War Surplus,* p. 180.

77. 61 Stat. 774 (1947).

78. U.S., Congress, Senate, *Mobilization and Demobilization Problems: Hearings before a Subcommittee of the Committee on Military Affairs on S. 1730 and S. 1893,* 78th Cong., 2d sess., 1946, p. 527; Colonel Earl S. Greever to RFC, Jan. 18, 1946, War Department file, pt. 16, RFC records, Record Group 234, National Archives; *Quarterly Report by War Assets Administration, First Quarter, 1947,* p. 19; 62 Stat. 1225 (1948); Senate, *Additional Report Pursuant to S. Res. 6,* pt. 16, *Third Annual Report,* pp. 36, 389.

79. "History of Disposal Policy Division," WAA files, WNRC; "Report on Rearmament," *Fortune* 43 (Apr. 1951):93; Federal Reserve Bank of Chicago, "New Goals for Industrial Expansion," *Business Conditions,* Dec. 1950, p. 1.

80. 62 Stat. 1225 (1948); Elmer Staats, Bureau of the Budget, to W. J. Hopkins, White House, July 1, 1948, Public Law 833 file, Bureau of the Budget records; memo, Spencer C. Shannon, director, Materials Office, National Security Re-

sources Board, to W. T. Hack, Chemicals, Nov. 16, 1949, Records of the Office of Civil and Defense Mobilization, Record Group 304, National Archives; "New Goals for Industrial Expansion," *Business Conditions,* Dec. 1950, p. 1; "National Industrial Reserve, Jan. 1, 1952," 319.1 Status, WAA files, WNRC.

Chapter 9

1. The comprehensive audit of RFC and its subsidiaries was made by the GAO under the act of February 24, 1945 (59 Stat. 6) which split the Federal Loan Agency from the Department of Commerce. The audit consists of ten volumes, of which portions of the first, an overview of all RFC activities (80th Cong., 1st sess., H. Doc. 316), and the fourth, devoted exclusively to DPC (80th Cong., 1st sess., H. Doc. 474), are particularly useful: Comptroller General of the United States, *Report on Audit of Reconstruction Finance Corporation and Affiliated Corporations for the Fiscal Year Ended June 30, 1945,* 10 vols. (Washington, 1947–1948).

2. Memo, Office of Bureau of Aeronautics, Navy Department, to Procurement Legal Division, Nov. 26, 1943, DPC file, Office of the General Counsel, Navy Department files; interview with W. S. Ege, former special legal assistant, Office of the Undersecretary of War, Apr. 23, 1947.

3. Interviews with John W. Snyder, May 8, 1947, and H. A. Klagsbrunn, Apr. 29, 1947, June 28, 1948.

4. Memo, Office of Bureau of Aeronautics, Navy Department, to Procurement Legal Division, Nov. 26, 1943, DPC file, Office of the General Counsel, Navy Department files.

5. Interview with H. A. Klagsbrunn, Apr. 29, and John W. Snyder, May 8, 1947.

6. Interviews with W. S. Ege and H. R. Rutland, deputy director, ODP, both on Apr. 23, 1947.

7. WPB Directive 13, Feb. 6, 1943, WPB records, Record Group 179, National Archives; interview with James G. Boss, former general counsel, ODP, May 6, and John W. Snyder, May 8, 1947.

8. Undersecretary of War Robert P. Patterson to DPC, May 27, 1943, War Department, Miscellaneous, Snyder files; Admiral Ralph Davidson, Bureau of Aeronautics, Navy Department, to DPC, July 19, 1943, Navy Department, Miscellaneous, Snyder files; R. P. Patterson to DPC, Jan. 17, 1944, and J. V. Forrestal, undersecretary of navy, to DPC, Feb. 28, 1944, Rentra General File, pt. 1, all in DPC files.

9. Comptroller General of the United States, *Report on Audit of Reconstruction Finance Corporation,* 4:27, 44; memo, Dec. 15, 1944, Rentra General file, pt. 2, DPC files; interviews with H. R. Rutland, Apr. 23, and James G. Boss, May 6, 1947.

10. Interview with James G. Boss, May 6, 1947; RFC Press Release 2204, Mar. 26, 1945, RFC Information Division files.

11. Interview with H. A. Klagsbrunn, Apr. 29, 1947.

12. "Classification of Lessees Serviced according to Basis of Rental," Statistical Report, June 30, 1945, Rentals—General file, DPC files.

13. Interview with H. R. Rutland, Apr. 23, 1947.

14. Comptroller General of the United States, *Report on Audit of Reconstruction Finance Corporation,* 4:27–29.

15. *New York Times,* July 3, 1946, p. 41.

16. Comptroller General of the United States, *Report on Audit of Reconstruction Finance Corporation,* 4:29–31; interviews with H. A. Klagsbrunn, June 28 and Aug. 20, 1948.

17. Comptroller General of the United States, *Report on Audit of Reconstruction Finance Corporation,* 4:33–34; interview with H. A. Klagsbrunn, June 28, 1948.

18. Comptroller General of the United States, *Report on Audit of Reconstruction Finance Corporation,* 4:17–22, 38.

19. Ibid., pp. 22, 61.

20. *New York Times,* June 22, 1946, pp. 1, 14; July 3, 1946, p. 41.

21. Ibid., July 5, 1946, p. 23.

22. U.S., Congress, House, *Hearings before the Committee on Expenditures in the Executive Departments on H. Doc. 674,* 79th Cong., 2d sess., July 2, 1946, p. 39.

23. Historical Report, Engineering Section, Self-Liquidating Division, RFC, [1946], RFC Information Division files.

24. Memo, W. L. Drager to Morton Macartney, Mar. 16, 1942, Engineering, Miscellaneous, Snyder files, DPC files.

25. Historical Report, Engineering Section, Self-Liquidating Division, RFC, RFC Information Division files; J. H. Jones to various railroads and other companies, Aug. 29, 1942, and summary of replies, Jesse H. Jones, Snyder files, DPC files.

26. Report on the War Time Experiences, Auditing Division, RFC and Affiliates [1946], by Nathaniel Royall, chief auditor, RFC, RFC Information Division files.

27. Interviews with H. A. Klagsbrunn, Aug. 31, and Clifford Durr, Aug. 5, 1971.

28. Comptroller General of the United States, *Report on Audit of Reconstruction Finance Corporation,* 4:14–15.

29. Ibid., pp. 15–16, 98–136. The Kaiser-Hughes project had an interesting origin. According to John W. Snyder, that versatile entrepreneur Henry Kaiser viewed the war as an opportunity to invade the aircraft industry. He discussed his plans with Howard Hughes and considered how he might get government financing. Prior to an interview with the president in the summer of 1942, Kaiser had a craftsman from the toy department of the Washington department store of Woodward and Lothrop make a model plane which he took with him to the White House. The toy excited the president's curiosity, as Kaiser had hoped. Only haltingly and with seeming reluctance did he explain his plans. The president took the bait and arranged for DPC to supply financing. The project was not a success. Only one of the huge planes was built. Known as the "Spruce Goose," it was flown once briefly by Howard Hughes. Thereafter for many years this government-owned white elephant has been kept in a hangar at Long Beach, Cal. (interview with Snyder, Sep. 2, 1971).

30. Ibid., p. 22.

31. The WAA report shows a return of $832 million on an original investment of $1.663 billion.

32. On June 30, 1947, the ODP investment in synthetic rubber plants amounted to $575,125,000. By this time, RFC was making deductions for depreciation and interest *(Annual Report and Financial Statement, Reconstruction Finance*

Corporation, 1952). The government received $25,885,000 more than the remaining net investment when it sold twenty-six of the twenty-seven synthetic rubber facilities in 1955 (White House file, Rubber Producing Facilities Disposal Commission, RFC files).

33. "Surplus Disposal under the Surplus War Property Administration," p. 75, WAA files, WNRC; U.S., Congress, Senate, *Surplus Disposal: Selling through Agents,* Property Subcommittee of the Committee on Military Affairs Pursuant to S. Res. 129, 79th Cong., 2d sess., 1946, Subcommittee Print No. 12, pp. 7–8; War Assets Administration, *War Surplus in the Peacetime Economy: Quarterly Progress Report to the Congress by the War Assets Administration,* 2d Quarter, 1947 (Washington, 1947), p. 9.

34. Reconstruction Finance Corporation and Subsidiaries, *Annual Report and Financial Statements, June 30, 1948,* p. 27. For the GAO's statement of cost recoveries through June 20, 1945, see Comptroller General of the United States, *Report on Audit of Reconstruction Finance Corporation,* 4:38.

35. Comptroller General of the United States, *Report on Audit of Reconstruction Finance Corporation,* 4:53. The GAO pointed out (p. 8) that the 1 percent per annum at which RFC borrowed from the Treasury was about half the average rate paid by the Treasury when it borrowed, thus understating the actual cost of DPC's investments to the government.

36. If funds received under the take-outs are included, DPC's recoveries would be higher, but since these funds were merely being transferred between government agencies, they could not contribute to the extent of recovery by the government. Of course, there was also a residual of former DPC property either in the machine tool reserve or the custodial reserve under the National Industrial Reserve Act of 1948 which were of some value to the government. On the residual plants, see War Assets Administration, *Quarterly Report to the Congress, 4th Quarter, 1948* (Washington, 1949), Appendix C. Cost figures for administration and interest expense through June 30, 1947, are in the RFC *Annual Report and Financial Statements,* June 30, 1948, p. 27, but the costs are not broken down and charged to the various wartime subsidiaries.

37. Comptroller General of the United States, *Report on Audit of Reconstruction Finance Corporation,* 4:43.

38. "Sales of Industrial Plants and Sites," *Report of the Surplus Property Subcommittee of the Committee on Military Affairs Pursuant to S. Res. 129,* 79th Cong., 2d sess., 1946, Subcommittee Print No. 5, pp. 7–8; "Disposal of World War II Surplus Property under War Assets Corporation," and "Statement to the Congress on the Findings of the Congressional Committees Dealing with Surplus Property Activities of the War Assets Administration," Mar. 17, 1947, pp. 33–33a, both in WAA files, WNRC; "List of Real Property Sales with Credit of Terms Extending 10 or More Years, as of Jan. 31, 1947," *Independent Offices Appropriation Bill, 1948,* pp. 24–27; James A. Cook, *The Marketing of War Surplus Property* (Washington, 1948), pp. 34–37.

39. Federal Reserve Bank of New York, *Monthly Review of Credit and Business Conditions,* Nov. 1945, pp. 86–87; Federal Reserve Bank of Philadelphia, *Business Review,* Nov. 1, 1945, pp. 2, 5; Federal Reserve Bank of Cleveland, "Plant Facilities," *Monthly Business Review,* July 31, 1945, pp. 7–8.

40. Federal Reserve Bank of Chicago, "Surplus Manufacturing Plant Disposals," *Business Conditions,* May 1947, pp. 1–4.

41. Federal Reserve Bank of Kansas City, "War Plant Disposals," *Monthly Review,* Oct. 31, 1947, pp. 1–3.

42. Frank E. Smith, "The Changing South," *Virginia Quarterly Review* 31 (1955):279–80; Federal Reserve Bank of Atlanta, "Economic Appraisal of the Postwar South," *Monthly Review,* Jan. 31, 1946, p. 1.

43. Frederic L. Deming and Weldon A. Stein, *Disposal of Southern War Plants* (Washington, 1949), pp. 6, 17–18, 43; U.S. Department of Commerce, Bureau of the Census, "Expenditures for Plant and Equipment, by Geographic Divisions and by States: 1939," *Census of Manufactures, 1939* (Washington, 1942), 1:373; Federal Reserve Bank of Richmond, "Capital Augmentation in the War Period in the Fifth Federal Reserve District," *Monthly Review,* July 31, 1947, p. 4.

44. Federal Reserve Bank of Richmond, "Capital Augmentation," pp. 3–6.

45. Federal Reserve Bank of St. Louis, "Surplus War Plant Disposal," *Monthly Review,* Nov. 1, 1947, pp. 121–28.

46. Federal Reserve Bank of Atlanta, "Sixth District War Plants," *Monthly Review,* Aug. 31, 1947, pp. 93–99; ibid., Sep. 30, 1947, pp. 105–11.

47. Federal Reserve Bank of Dallas, "Disposal and Utilization of War Manufacturing Facilities in the Southwest," *Monthly Business Review,* Mar. 1, 1948, pp. 37, 47.

48. Ibid., pp. 37–42; Federal Reserve Bank of Dallas, "The Synthetic Rubber Industry in the Southwest," *Monthly Business Review,* June 1, 1948, pp. 91–100; Fletcher H. Etheridge and Stanley A. Arbingast, *Disposal of Surplus War Plants in Texas* (Austin, 1950).

49. Federal Reserve Bank of Dallas, "Disposal and Utilization of War Manufacturing Facilities," pp. 42–47; Deming and Stein, *Disposal of Southern War Plants,* pp. 41–42.

50. Federal Reserve Bank of San Francisco, "Industry and Trade in 1946," *Monthly Review,* Jan. 1947, p. 5; Table 7, Chapter 6.

51. War Assets Administration, *Quarterly Report, 4th Quarter, 1948,* p. 50; E. B. Alderfer and H. E. Michl, *The Economics of American Industry* (New York, 1957), pp. 64, 67–69, 109–12; memo, Curtis A. Ross to commissioner, Utilization and Disposal Service, General Services Administration, Nov. 3, 1961, Basic Magnesium file, WAA files, WNRC.

52. See Chapter 1. Interview with David Ginsburg, Aug. 20, 1948.

53. Civilian Production Administration, *Industrial Mobilization for War: History of the War Production Board and Predecessor Agencies, 1940–1945* (Washington, 1947), p. 657; Robert R. Russel, "Expansion of Industrial Facilities under Army Air Force Auspices, 1940–1945," pp. 229–38, OCMH files; R. Elberton Smith, *The Army and Economic Mobilization* (Washington, 1959), pp. 465–72.

54. Smith, *The Army and Economic Mobilization,* pp. 373–75; "History of the Purchasing Division, Army Service Forces," p. 606, OCMH files.

55. U.S., Congress, Senate, *Additional Report of the Special Committee Investigating the National Defense Program Pursuant to S. Res. 46,* 80th Cong., 2d sess., 1948, S. Rept. 440, pt. 6, pp. 233–34. Also U.S., Congress, Senate, *Hearings before a Special Committee Investigating the National Defense Program Pursuant to S. Res. 46,* 80th Cong., 1st sess., 1947, pt. 42. pp. 25518–21, 25554–58, 25562. For an extreme example of a windfall, see Robert Schlaifer et al., "Accelerated Amortization," *Harvard Business Review* 29 (May 1951):117.

56. George B. Tindall, *The Emergence of the New South, 1913–1945* (Baton Rouge, 1967), p. 696.

Chapter 10

1. Arthur Marwick, "The Impact of the First World War on British Society," *Journal of Contemporary History* 3 (Jan. 1968):55, 61–62; Arthur Marwick, *Britain in the Century of Total War* (Boston, 1968), pp. 12, 13; Jonathon Hughes, *Industrialization and Economic History* (New York, 1970), p. 110.

2. William Leuchtenberg, "The New Deal and the Analogue of War," in *Change and Continuity in 20th Century America,* eds. John Braeman, Robert Bremner, and Everett Walters (Columbus, 1964), pp. 99, 107–23. On the World War I emergency government, see W. F. Willoughby, *Government Organization in Wartime and After* (New York, 1919), and F. L. Paxson, *American Democracy and the World War,* 3 vols. (Boston and Berkeley, 1936–1948).

3. *Report of the Department of Labor, 1919* (Washington, 1919), pp. 133–35.

4. On the emergency government of World War II, see War Records Section, Bureau of the Budget, *The United States at War* (Washington, 1946); Civilian Production Administration, *Industrial Mobilization for War* (Washington, 1947).

5. Pauli Murray, *State Laws on Race and Color* (Cincinnati, 1955).

6. U.S., Congress, Senate, Committee on Finance, *Hearings on H. R. 10650,* 87th Cong., 2d sess., 1962, pt. 1, pp. 79–80, 85, 295.

7. U.S. *Internal Revenue Code of 1954,* secs. 168, 169, 184, 187, 188.

8. *New York Times,* Aug. 16, 1971, p. 1, Oct. 8, 1971, p. 1, Mar. 12, 1972, p. 1, Aug. 11, 1972, p. 1, Jan. 12, 1973, p. 1, May 1, 1973, p. 1.

9. Ibid., Oct. 9, 1974, p. 1.

10. Ibid., Dec. 1, 1974, sec. 3, p. 1, Dec. 22, 1974, sec. 3, p. 12; *Newsweek,* Jan. 6, 1975, pp. 50–51; *New Republic,* Apr. 5, 1975, pp. 7–8; *Los Angeles Times,* Aug. 14, 1975, sec. 3, p. 24.

11. Marvin Barloon, "The Question of Steel Capacity," *Harvard Business Review* 27 (Mar. 1949):211; *New York Times,* Feb. 28, 1948, p. 19, May 29, 1948, p. 19, July 2, 1948, p. 27, Feb. 1, 1949, p. 37, Mar. 15, 1948, p. 41.

12. *New York Times,* Dec. 17, 1948, p. 45, Dec. 22, 1948, p. 37; Federal Reserve Bank of Philadelphia, "Should Our Steel Capacity be Expanded?" *Business Review,* Mar. 1948, pp. 28–32.

13. Barloon, "The Question of Steel Capacity," pp. 210–11.

14. Stewart Alsop, "The CIO and the White House," *Washington Post,* Jan. 20, 1949, p. 11; *New York Times,* Jan. 6, 1949, p. 4.

15. *San Francisco Chronicle,* Jan. 10, 1949, p. 2, Jan. 11, 1949, p. 5, Jan. 12, 1949, p. 14; *Wall Street Journal,* Jan. 11, 1949, p. 9; *New York Times,* Jan. 12, 1949, p. 23.

16. *New York Times,* Jan. 6, 1949, p. 3; *Wall Street Journal,* Jan. 6, 1949, p. 4.

17. *New York Times,* Jan. 7, 1949, p. 20, Jan. 6, 1949, p. 3, Mar. 2, 1949, p. 2, Mar. 25, 1949, p. 3, June 28, 1949, p. 39; *Business Week,* Jan. 15, 1949, p. 15, Jan. 22, 1949, p. 15.

18. *New York Times,* July 20, 1950, p. 14; U.S., Congress, House, *Defense Production Act of 1950,* 81st Cong., 2d sess., 1950, H. Rept. 2759, pp. 8–9; U.S., Congress, Senate, *Defense Production Act of 1950,* 81st Cong., 2d sess., 1950, S. Rept. 3042, pp. 4–5.

19. House, *Defense Production Act,* H. Rept. 2759, pp. 2–3.

20. U.S., Congress, Senate, Committee on Banking and Currency, *Defense Production Act of 1950, Hearings,* 81st Cong., 2d sess., 1950, on S. 3936, pp. 263, 250; "Report on Rearmament," *Fortune* 43 (Apr. 1951):204. For another voice in support of a DPC revival, see Public Affairs Institute, *Big Business Grabs Defense Plants* (Washington, 1951).

21. Senate, *Defense Production Act, Hearings on S. 3936,* p. 253.

22. Federal Reserve Bank of Chicago, "New Goals for Industrial Expansion," *Business Conditions,* Dec. 1950, pp. 1–2.

23. Ibid., pp. 2–4; 64 Stat. 939–40 (1950); "Tax Amortization, Loans, and Procurement in the Office of Construction and Resources Expansion, Defense Production Administration and Predecessor Agencies" (1953), chaps. 1 and 5, pp. 36–40, National Production Authority records, Record Group 277, National Archives.

24. Robert Schlaifer, J. Keith Butters, and Pearson Hunt, "Accelerated Depreciation," *Harvard Business Review* 29 (May 1951):113, 116; Federal Reserve Bank of Chicago, "Quick Write-Offs Aid Expansion," *Business Conditions,* July 1951, pp. 9–10; U.S., Congress, Senate, *Review of Tax-Amortization Program by the Joint Committee on Defense Production,* 83d Cong., 1st sess., 1953, S. Rept. 154, p. 9; memo, "Implications of Recent Expansion of Special Amortization Program," Senator Paul H. Douglas to members of the Joint Economic Committee, Apr. 29, 1956, Treasury Department files. Schlaifer, Butters, and Hunt, who were members of the faculty of the Harvard Graduate School of Business Administration, argued against the use of tax amortization. They considered it a crude instrument, costly to government in lost revenues and unfair to competitors of firms that benefited from windfall gains from excessively high tax amortization rates. They proposed as fairer to all parties a simple system of guarantees against loss for war contractors who had financed the construction of new facilities. The terms of the supply contract would specify the amount of depreciation that could be charged against income during the emergency and would offer the contractor the option at its conclusion of either retaining the facility for peacetime use or surrendering it to the government in return for payment of the depreciated book value. The authors also considered their proposal superior to government financing and ownership because the latter pattern would be more inflationary and, based on the DPC experience, less likely to permit the government to achieve a maximum recovery of costs at the conclusion of the emergency. The authors believed that because of political pressures, the DPC facilities were sold too rapidly and, consequently, at too low prices.

The dollar-value comparison of certificates in the two wars requires some correction; for example, the price level in 1952 was nearly 60 percent higher than it had been in 1945 (Bureau of the Census, *Historical Statistics of the United States to 1957* [Washington, 1960], p. 117).

25. U.S., Congress, House, *Fifth Intermediate Report Submitted by the Government Operations Subcommittee, Certificates of Necessity and Government Plant Expansion Loans,* 82d Cong., 1st sess., 1951, H. Rept. 504, pp. 19–20; Federal Reserve Bank of Chicago, "Quick Write-Offs Aid Expansion," pp. 9–10; "Tax Amortization," chap. 5, Table 3; "Economic Statistics in Defense Mobilization: History of the Central Statistical Operations of the National Production Authority and Defense Production Administration," (1953), p. 47, NPA records.

26. *Fifth Intermediate Report,* pp. 23–27; "Five Year Gravy," *Fortune* 44 (Oct.

1951):214; "Facilities and Construction: History of the Facilities and Construction Bureau and Its Divisions of the National Production Authority" (1953), pp. 59–69, NPA records.

27. *Fifth Intermediate Report,* p. 27.

28. Ibid., pp. 25–26, 32; Federal Reserve Bank of Chicago, "Quick Write-Offs Aid Expansion," pp. 9–10.

29. *Fifth Intermediate Report,* pp. 1, 4, 9–16, 21–34.

30. "Five Year Gravy," p. 85; *New York Times,* Aug. 14, 1951, p. 33, Aug. 17, 1951, p. 16, Oct. 19, 1951, p. 37; Press Release DPA-355, "Facilities Expansion Program: Industry-by-Industry Summary," June 5, 1952, Office of Civil and Defense Mobilization records, Record Group 304, National Archives; memo, "Implications of Recent Expansion of Special Amortization Program," Senator Paul H. Douglas to members of the Joint Economic Committee, Apr. 29, 1956, Treasury Department files.

31. *Fifth Intermediate Report,* p. 38.

32. Defense Production Administration, "Expansion under the Mobilization Program," F20-1, May 1952, OCDM records.

33. Roger Seybold, acting chairman, Munitions Board, to W. Stuart Symington, chairman, National Security Resources Board, Oct. 10, 1950, OCDM records; William G. Cunningham, *The Aircraft Industry: A Study in Industrial Location* (Los Angeles, 1951), pp. 186–87; "Report on Rearmament," *Fortune* 43 (Apr. 1951):93, 202; Federal Reserve Bank of Chicago, "New Goals for Industrial Expansion," *Business Conditions,* Dec. 1950, p. 1; interview with Dr. Elliott Cassady, former historian, Munitions Board, Mar. 5, 1975. The reasons for the limited use of the national industrial and machine tool reserves could stand further exploration. At the time of my last research trip to Washington early in 1975, Munitions Board files that might have shed light on this subject were still classified. My subsequent request for clearance, made to the Office of the Secretary of Defense, received no response. It is possible that some of the tools, in particular, may have been poorly maintained or outmoded.

34. Memo, Swen E. Bergstrom, director, Metalworking Division, to Frank M. Shields, deputy assistant administrator, NPA, Nov. 30, 1951, OCDM records, Record Group 304, National Archives; U.S., Congress, Senate, *Second Annual Report of the Joint Committee on Defense Production,* 83d Cong., 1st sess., 1953, S. Rept. 3, pp. 6–8, 139.

35. *Second Annual Report,* p. 279; Secretary of the Treasury George Humphrey to Government Operations Committee, House of Representatives, July 18, 1955, and memo, Walter Heller to Lazlo Ecker-Racz, Mar. 20, 1951, both in Amortization of Emergency Facilities files, Treasury Department.

36. Albert Lepawsky, *State Planning and Economic Development in the South* (Washington, 1949), pp. 70–75; James R. Rinehart, "Rates of Return on Municipal Subsidies to Industry," in M. L. Greenhut and W. T. Whitman, eds., *Essays in Southern Economic Development* (Chapel Hill, 1964), pp. 473–87.

37. Alabama Bond Counsel, "Memorandum with Respect to Alabama Statutes Authorizing the Public Financing of Industrial and Commercial Facilities" (Montgomery, Ala., n.d.); *Christian Science Monitor,* May 20, 1974, p. 2.

38. E. B. Alderfer and H. E. Michl, *The Economics of American Industry* (New York, 1957), pp. 109–10.

39. Robert Sheehan, "Kaiser Aluminum—Henry J's Marvelous Mistake," *Fortune* 54 (July 1956):79.

40. Kaiser Aluminum and Chemical Corporation, *Kaiser Aluminum News* (Summer 1958); *New York Times,* May 26, 1957, sec. 3, p. 1.

41. Internationally, the possibility of alleviating poverty in less developed countries by bringing foreign managerial expertise into conjunction with government-owned facilities through the device of the management contract has been explored positively by Peter P. Gabriel in *The International Transfer of Corporate Skills* (Boston, 1967).

42. Federal Energy Administration, *Project Independence Report* (Washington, 1974), and associated Task Force Reports, especially *Finance* and *An Historical Perspective.*

43. *Christian Science Monitor,* Mar. 16, 1977, pp. 1, 11, Dec. 16, 1977, p. 31, Jan. 16, 1979, p. 3; *Los Angeles Times,* Oct. 11, 1977, sec. 2, p. 6. In 1977 there was a turnaround in domestic oil production—an increase of 35 million barrels, or approximately 1 percent, due largely to Alaskan oil (U.S. Bureau of Mines, *Minerals and Materials,* Apr. 1978, p. 11).

44. For an evidence of alarm, see Robert W. Tucker, "Oil and American Power—3 Years Later," *Commentary* 63 (Jan. 1977):29–35; also *Los Angeles Times,* Outlook Section, Nov. 20, 1977, p. 1; Executive Office of the President, *The National Energy Plan* (Washington, 1977), p. 21; *Christian Science Monitor,* Aug. 24, 1977, p. 3; Mar. 2, 1979, p. 7. On fear of "pork barrel" politics, see *Christian Science Monitor,* June 7, 1978, p. 22.

45. FEA, *Project Independence Report,* pp. 153–98; *Business Week,* Feb. 28, 1977. p. 30.

46. FEA, *Project Independence Report,* pp. 81–82, 92–96; *Newsweek,* Feb. 28, 1977, p. 69.

47. The accident at Three Mile Island late in March 1979 has cast a dark shadow over nuclear power. However, I believe it unlikely that this accident of itself will for long impede further nuclear power development because of the overriding need for more energy. If there are accidents with heavy fatalities, the outcome would surely be different.

48. Congressional Budget Office, *Uranium Enrichment,* Background Paper No. 7, May 18, 1976, pp. 10, 45–46; CBO, *Commercialization of Synthetic Fuels,* Background Paper No. 3, Jan. 16, 1976, p. 17; CBO, *Financing Energy Development,* Background Paper No. 12, July 26, 1976, pp. 63–64; *Business Week,* Sep. 23, 1975, pp. 50–53, Nov. 17, 1975, pp. 98–106, *Christian Science Monitor,* Oct. 25, 1977, p. 88.

49. CBO, *Financing Energy Development,* p. 9; "The 500 Largest Industrial Corporations," *Fortune* 91 (May 1975):210–18.

50. See discussions of synthetic rubber and magnesium in Chapters 4 and 8. Also Comptroller General of the United States, *Report on Audit of Reconstruction Finance Corporation and Affiliated Corporations for the Fiscal Year Ended June 30, 1945: Defense Plant Corporation,* 80th Cong., 1st sess., 1947, H. Doc. 474, 4:82.

51. *Business Week,* July 5, 1976, pp. 58–59; *U.S. Government Manual, 1976–77* (Washington, 1977), pp. 476, 505; CBO, *Energy Policy Alternatives,* Budget Issue Paper, Jan. 1977, pp. 3–4.

52. Ibid., pp. 63–72; U.S., Congress, *Energy Independence Authority,* 94th Cong.,

1st sess., 1974, S. 2532, H. R. 10267; Office of White House Press Secretary, "Fact Sheet, Energy Independence Authority," Oct. 10, 1975, p. 4.

53. The proposed energy independence authority was announced by President Ford on September 22 in a speech in San Francisco. The bill was introduced into Congress on October 10. For criticisms of the proposal, see Los Angeles Times, Sep. 25, 1975, sec. 2, p. 6; Christian Science Monitor, Sep. 30, 1975, p. 1; New York Times, Oct. 11, 1975, p. 62; Congressional Quarterly 32 (Oct. 18, 1975):2237–38; Business Week, Oct. 20, 1975, pp. 45–46. The well-known economic historian Walt Rostow, in arguing for "greatly enlarged levels of cooperative public-private investment" in the battle against "stagflation," was one partisan who strongly endorsed the proposal as "certainly a step in the right direction." In addition to having the federal government write annual investment allotments into the federal budget, he would have it "create a federal bank like the old Reconstruction Finance Corporation" to provide capital to help achieve a wide variety of social goals, including developing new sources of energy, promoting energy conservation, improving mass transit, combating air and water pollution, and radically expanding research and development (Los Angeles Times, Apr. 1, 1976, sec. 2, p. 12).

54. New York Times, Apr. 19, 1977, p. 24; Los Angeles Times, Apr. 21, 1977, pp. 7, 9–10; Executive Office of the President, The National Energy Plan; Business Week, Apr. 18, 1977, pp. 142–43, Apr. 25, 1977, pp. 66–80, June 27, 1977, p. 544.

55. New York Times, Sep. 1, 1977, pp. 1, 58.

56. Business Week, May 2, 1977, p. 24; Christian Science Monitor, June 16, 1977, pp. 1, 9.

57. Los Angeles Times, Sep. 21, 1977, p. 22, Oct. 15, 1977, pp. 1, 10; Christian Science Monitor, Sep. 22, 1977, p. 28, Sep. 28, 1977, p. 1.

58. Christian Science Monitor, Dec. 8, 1977, p. 5, Oct. 11, 1978, pp. 1, 8, Oct. 18, 1978, p. 14; Los Angeles Times, Dec. 23, 1977, pp. 1, 22, Sep. 28, 1978, pp. 1, 10, Oct. 12, 1978, pp. 1, 10; Wall Street Journal, Oct. 16, 1978, p. 2.

59. Thornton Bradshaw, "My Case for National Planning," Fortune 95 (Feb. 1977):100–01. A few months later, an agency of Congress, the Office of Technology Assessment, was also calling for more attention to the development of new and less conventional forms of energy. The OTA was evaluating the Carter program, which it found highly inadequate. It urged, especially, a more speedy development of plants for manufacturing pipeline-quality synthetic gas and greater incentives to use solar energy, along with more adequate funding for research and development of all new energy forms (Office of Technology Assessment, U.S., Congress, Analysis of the Proposed Energy Plan, Aug. 1977). For similar sentiments of Senators Abraham Ribicoff, Floyd Haskell, and Russell Long, see Los Angeles Times, Sep. 21, 1977, pp. 8, 22, Oct. 15, 1977, p. 10.

60. On solar energy, see Business Week, Jan. 24, 1977, p. 23; on synthetic gas, Los Angeles Times, Mar. 13, 1977, sec. 5, p. 3, Mar. 17, 1977, sec. 3, p. 23; El Paso Company, 1976 Annual Report (Houston, 1977), p. 34.

61. CBO, Uranium Enrichment, p. 2. According to Alan Brown, a DPC attorney from its inception and an RFC attorney thereafter, members of the legal staff of the Atomic Energy Commission came to RFC in the later 1940s prior to the building of these plants to discuss DPC's management-fee contracts (interview, Feb. 1, 1972). AEC representatives must also have sought advice from the Defense

Department because of the long experience of the armed services with management-fee contracts in operating arsenal-type facilities.

62. Long queues of motorists at gas pumps in service stations in California in May 1979, and the next month in other sections of the nation, notably in the Northeast, at last spurred Congress to action. Evidence of change can be seen in the passage on June 26, 1979 of the Moorhead bill in the House by a lopsided vote of 368 to 25 to stimulate the manufacture of snythetic fuels from coal, oil shale, corn, and other resources. The bill, supported by the Carter administration, has moved on to the Senate. A modest measure, it is designed to facilitate the construction of plants turning out 500,000 barrels of snythetic fuel daily by 1985 and 2 million barrels daily by 1990. The proposed plan, by itself, is not likely to do more than offset declining oil production in the United States, if that. It provides for guaranteed purchases of synthetic fuel by the Defense Department and for loan guarantees and direct loans to companies that construct synthetic fuel plants. If private enterprise proves reluctant to build the plants, the bill authorizes the government to build and lease plants after the pattern of the Defense Plant Corporation during World War II. The bill has been drafted as an amendment to the Defense Production Act of 1950. If it becomes law, it may well prove to be only the first of a series of progressively more ambitious measures, especially if OPEC prices continue to rise. (U.S., Congress, House of Representatives, *H. R. 3930,* 96th Cong., 1st sess., May 15, 1979; *Los Angeles Times,* May 31, 1979, II, p. 17, June 16, 1979, p. 26, June 19, 1979, II, p. 10, June 27, 1979, 1, 15; *Christian Science Monitor,* June 28, 1979, p. 10).

Bibliography

UNPUBLISHED MATERIALS
Archival Records

This book draws heavily on the records of the Defense Plant Corporation and related agencies located in the National Archives in Washington and in the Washington National Records Center, Suitland, Maryland. An excellent finding aid, which also includes relevant records from the Federal Loan Agency and the office of the Secretary of Commerce, is the *Preliminary Inventory of the Records of the Reconstruction Finance Corporation, 1932–1964* (Washington, 1973).

A second important body of records are those of the War Assets Administration and predecessor agencies. They are chiefly in the WNRC.

Other useful records housed in the National Archives are to be found in the following record groups: Record Group 51, Bureau of the Budget; Record Group 179, War Production Board; Record Group 277, National Production Authority; Record Group 304, Office of Civil and Defense Mobilization.

Finally, mention should be made of records in the Franklin D. Roosevelt Library, Hyde Park, New York, and in the files of Clifford J. Durr in the Durr home, Wetumpka, Alabama.

Manuscripts

Anderson, Troyer. "Introduction to the History of the Under Secretary of War's Office." Office, Chief of Military History, Department of the Army.
Durr, Clifford J. "The History of the Defense Plant Corporation." [1942.] In the possession of Mrs. Clifford J. Durr, Wetumpka, Alabama.
Russel, Robert R. "Expansion of Industrial Facilities under Army Air Force Auspices, 1940–1945." OCMH.

Documents

"Minutes of the Tax and Finance Committee of NDAC," August 1940. WPB records, Record Group 179, National Archives.
"Tax Amortization, Loans and Procurement in the Office of Construction and Resources Expansion, Defense Production Administration and Predecessor Agencies." [1953.] NPA records, Record Group 277, National Archives.
War Assets Administration. "Report on Government-Owned Industrial Plants as of September 30, 1947." Library, National Archives.

GOVERNMENT PUBLICATIONS
Congressional Publications

U.S., Congress. *Congressional Record.* 1940–1946.

U.S., Congress, House. *Report of the Special Committee on Post-War Economic Policy and Planning.* 78th Cong., 2d sess., 1944. H. Rept. 1796.

———. *Fifth Intermediate Report Submitted by the Government Operations Subcommittee, Certificates of Necessity and Government Plant Expansion Loans.* 82d Cong., 1st sess., 1951. H. Rept. 504.

U.S., Congress, Senate. *Hearings before the Committee on Banking and Currency on S. 3939.* 76th Cong., 3d sess., 1940.

———. *Hearings before the Committee on Finance, Second Revenue Act of 1940.* 76th Cong., 3d sess., 1940.

———. *Hearings before the Special [Truman] Committee Investigating the National Defense Program.* 1941–1946.

———. *Hearings before the Special Committee on Post-War Economic Policy and Planning Pursuant to S. Res. 102.* 78th Cong., 1st sess., 1943.

———. *Reports of the Special [Truman] Committee Investigating the National Defense Program.* 1941–1946.

———. *Report of Hon. Joseph C. O'Mahoney to the Special Committee on Post-War Economic Policy and Planning Pursuant to S. Res. 102.* 78th Cong., 1st sess., 1943. S. Doc. 106.

———. *Report of the Special Committee on Post-War Economic Policy and Planning.* 78th Cong., 2d sess., 1944. S. Rept. 539.

———. *Report of War Contracts Subcommittee of Committee on Military Affairs.* 78th Cong., 2d sess., 1944. Subcommittee Print No. 5.

———. *Progress of Plant Disposal: Report of the Surplus Property Subcommittee of the Committee on Military Affairs Pursuant to S. Res. 129.* 79th Cong., 2d sess., 1946. Subcommittee Print No. 5.

———. *Investigation of Surplus Property and Its Disposal: Report of Committee on Expenditures in Executive Departments Pursuant to S. Res. 75.* 80th Cong., 2d sess., 1948. S. Rept. 1365.

———. *Review of Tax-Amortization Program by the Joint Committee on Defense Production.* 83d Cong., 1st sess., 1953. S. Rept. 154.

Comptroller General of the United States. *Report on Audit of Reconstruction Finance Corporation and Affiliated Corporations for the Fiscal Year Ended June 30, 1945: Defense Plant Corporation.* 80th Cong., 1st sess., 1947. H. Doc. 474, vol. 4.

RFC Publications

Seven-Year Report. February 2, 1939.

Quarterly Reports. 1940–1946.

Defense Plant Corporation. *Advance Listing of Industrial Plants and Plant Sites to be Disposed of by Defense Plant Corporation, October 14, 1944.*

Office of Rubber Reserve. *Report on the Rubber Program, Supplement No. 1, Year 1945.* 1946.

Annual Report and Financial Statements. 1946–1952.

War Production Board Publications

Allen, E. P. *Policies Governing Private Financing of Emergency Facilities, May 1940 to June 1942.* Washington, 1944.

Civilian Production Administration. *Industrial Mobilization for War: History of the War Production Board and Predecessor Agencies, 1940–1945.* Washington, 1947.

McGrane, R. C. *The Facilities and Construction Program of the War Production Board and Predecessor Agencies, May 1940 to May 1945.* Washington, 1946.

Minutes of the Advisory Commission to the Council of National Defense. Washington, 1946.

Wartime Production Achievements and the Reconversion Outlook: Report of the Chairman, War Production Board, October 9, 1945. Washington, 1945.

Wiltse, Charles M. *Aluminum Policies of the War Production Board and Predecessor Agencies, May 1940 to November 1945.* Washington, 1946.

Surplus Property Board—War Assets
Administration Publications

Surplus Property Board. *Aluminum Plants and Facilities: Report of the Surplus Property Board to the Congress, September 21, 1945.*

Surplus Property Administration. *Report to the Congress on Disposal of Government Iron and Steel Plants and Facilities, October 8, 1945.*

———. *Government-Owned Pipe Lines: Report of the Surplus Property Administration to the Congress, January 4, 1946.*

———. *Aircraft Plants and Facilities: Report of the Surplus Property Administration to the Congress, January 14, 1946.*

———. *Aviation-Gasoline Plants and Facilities: Report of the Surplus Property Administration to the Congress, January 14, 1946.*

———. *Interim Report of the Surplus Property Administration to the Congress: Radio and Electrical Equipment, January 31, 1946.*

War Assets Administration. *Quarterly Reports.* 1946–1949.

Federal Reserve Bank Publications

Federal Reserve Bank of Atlanta. *Monthly Review.* 1946–1947.

Federal Reserve Bank of Chicago. *Business Conditions.* 1947, 1950–1951.

Federal Reserve Bank of Cleveland. *Monthly Business Review.* 1945.

Federal Reserve Bank of Dallas. *Monthly Business Review.* 1948.

Federal Reserve Bank of Kansas City. *Monthly Review.* 1947.

Federal Reserve Bank of New York. *Monthly Review of Credit and Business Conditions.* 1945.

Federal Reserve Bank of Philadelphia. *Business Review.* 1945, 1948.

Federal Reserve Bank of Richmond. *Monthly Review.* 1947.

Federal Reserve Bank of St. Louis. *Monthly Review.* 1947.

Federal Reserve Bank of San Francisco. *Monthly Review.* 1947.

Deming, Frederic L. and Stein, Weldon. *Disposal of Southern War Plants.* Washington, 1949.

Miscellaneous

Baruch, Bernard, and Hancock, John. *Report on War and Post-War Adjustment Policies, February 15, 1944*. Washington, 1944.
Bureau of the Budget. *The United States at War*. Washington, 1946.
Executive Office of the President. *The National Energy Plan*. 1977.
Federal Energy Administration. *Project Independence Report*. 1974.
Industrial College of the Armed Forces. *Construction of New Facilities*. Washington, 1947.
United States Government Manual. 1940–1946.
United States Statutes at Large. 1919, 1940–1953.

BOOKS, ARTICLES, AND NEWSPAPERS

Alderfer, E. B., and Michl, H. E. *The Economics of American Industry*. New York, 1957.
American Enterprise Association. *Disposal of Government-Owned Industrial War Properties*. New York, 1944.
Beasley, Norman. *Knudsen*. New York, 1947.
Bradshaw, Thornton. "My Case for National Planning," *Fortune* 95 (February 1977).
Bruner, Jerome. *Mandate from the People*. New York, 1944.
Business Week.
Cantril, Hadley, ed. *Public Opinion, 1935–1946*. Princeton, 1951.
Catton, Bruce. *The War Lords of Washington*. New York, 1948.
Christian Science Monitor.
Connery, Robert H. *The Navy and Industrial Mobilization in World War II*. Princeton, 1951.
Cook, James A. *The Marketing of Surplus War Property*. Washington, 1948.
Cunningham, William G. *The Aircraft Industry: A Study in Industrial Location*. Los Angeles, 1951.
Durr, Clifford J. "The Postwar Relationship between Government and Business." *Papers and Proceedings of the 55th Annual Meeting of the American Economic Association, American Economic Review* 33, supplement (March 1943):45–53.
Etheridge, Fletcher H., and Arbingast, Stanley A. *Disposal of Surplus War Plants in Texas*. Austin, 1950.
Hauck, W. A. *Steel Expansion for War*. Cleveland, 1945.
Howard, Frank A. *Buna Rubber: The Birth of an Industry*. New York, 1947.
Ickes, Harold L. *The Secret Diary of Harold L. Ickes*, vol. 3. New York, 1954.
Janeway, Eliot. *The Struggle for Survival*. New Haven, 1951.
Jones, Jesse H., and Angly, Edward. *Fifty Billion Dollars: Thirteen Years with the RFC, 1932–1945*. New York, 1951.
Kaplan, A. D. H. *The Liquidation of War Production*. New York, 1944.
Ketchum, Marshall D. "Plant Financing in a War Economy." *Journal of Business of the University of Chicago* 16 (January 1943):28–50.
Klagsbrunn, Hans A. "Some Aspects of War Plant Financing." *Papers and Proceedings of the 55th Annual Meeting of the American Economic Association, American Economic Review* 33, supplement (March 1943):119–27.

Lane, Frederick C. *Ships for Victory: A History of Shipbuilding under the U.S. Maritime Commission in World War II.* Baltimore, 1951.

Leuchtenberg, William. "The New Deal and the Analogue of War," in *Change and Continuity in 20th Century America,* eds. John Braeman, Robert Bremner, and Everett Walters. Columbus, 1964.

Los Angeles Times.

"Machine Tool Maker's Dilemma." *Fortune* 26 (October 1942).

McLaughlin, Glen E. "Wartime Expansion in Industrial Capacities." *Papers and Proceedings of the 55th Annual Meeting of the American Economic Association, American Economic Review* 33, supplement (March 1943):108–18.

Mock, James R., and Thurber, Evangeline. *Report on Demobilization.* Norman, Oklahoma, 1944.

Nelson, Donald. *Arsenal of Democracy.* New York, 1946.

New York Times.

Public Affairs Institute. *Big Business Grabs Defense Plants.* Washington, 1951.

Schlaifer, Robert, et al. "Accelerated Amortization." *Harvard Business Review* 29 (May 1951):113–24.

Sheehan, Robert. "Kaiser Aluminum—Henry J's Marvelous Mistake." *Fortune* 54 (July 1956).

Smith, R. Elberton. *The Army and Economic Mobilization.* Washington, 1959.

Stein, Harold, ed. *Public Administration and Policy Development.* New York, 1952.

Sternberg, Roland N. "American Business and the Approach of War, 1935–1941." *Journal of Economic History* 13 (Winter 1953):58–78.

Stone, I. F. *Business as Usual.* New York, 1941.

"Trouble in Synthetic Rubber." *Fortune* 35 (June 1947).

"Two Pipelines for Sale." *Fortune* 31 (January 1945).

Wall Street Journal.

"The War Goes to Mr. Jesse Jones." *Fortune* 24 (December 1941).

Washington Post.

Yoshpe, Harry B. "Economic Mobilization Planning between Two World Wars." *Military Affairs* 15 (Winter 1951):199–204.

———. "Planning between Two World Wars." *Military Affairs* 16 (Summer 1952):71–96.

Index